CW00747337

GONE FISHING

THE UNSOLVED CRIMES OF ANGUS SINCLAIR

Chris Clark and Adam Lloyd

Mango Books

First edition published 2021

Copyright © Chris Clark and Adam Lloyd, 2021

The right of Chris Clark and Adam Lloyd to be identified
as the authors of this work has been asserted in accordance
with the Copyright, Designs & Patents Act 1988.

All rights reserved. No part of this book may be reprinted or reproduced
or utilised in any form or by any electronic, mechanical or other
means, now known or hereafter invented, including photocopying
and recording, or in any information storage or retrieval system,
without the prior permission in writing of the publishers.

ISBN: 978-1-914277-22-1 (softcover)

Published by Mango Books
www.mangobooks.co.uk

18 Soho Square
London W1D 3QL

GONE
FISHING

To all
the victims
of Angus Sinclair

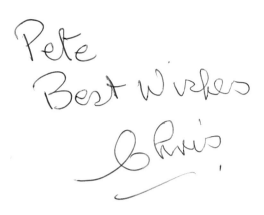

Pete
Best Wishes
Chris

To Jeanne,
whose inspiration and encouragement
continued whilst going through her own
fifteen months of pain.

Chris

To Erica,
thank you for everything.
Always.

Adam

GONE FISHING

Death of Angus Sinclair

It was just before 8.00am on an unremarkable March day in 2019 when the silver Ford Mondeo estate with blacked-out windows pulled up in a covered area outside the main building of Falkirk crematorium. It had opened early for the secret cremation, but there were no mourners, no music and no eulogy.

Wearing black suits, white shirts and black ties, the four undertakers from a local company quickly removed the plain pine-effect brass-handled coffin from the car to a metal trolley and carried it inside to a downstairs room ahead of the cremation.

It took little over ten seconds for the ceremony to be completed, and the ashes were returned to Clackmannanshire Council, where officials later revealed the ashes were 'disposed of at sea' after they went unclaimed.

And so concluded the life of Angus Sinclair, one of the worst killers the UK has ever seen.

*

Angus Sinclair was 73 when he was pronounced dead at 4.20 am on 11 March 2019. It is understood police registered his death after relatives refused. His death certificate listed his occupation as 'painter/decorator', but as Sinclair had been locked up since the late 1980s, work was not something that had been a part of his life for a long time.

Sinclair's death at Gelnochil prison in Alloa was a lonely one. He died alone in his cell, incontinent and bedbound in what is considered one of Scotland's toughest jails. In his final moments, alone and in pain, he cried out for his mother.

Sinclair had suffered from deteriorating health for about a year and a half before his death after a series of strokes. The man who had caused such hurt and misery to so many others was a shadow of the man he had been as the end approached, needing assistance with personal hygiene and dressing, and losing his appetite. He was last seen alive by nursing staff at the prison on 11 March at 01.40 hours, locked in his cell in the jail's Abercrombie wing. When nursing staff checked on him again at 03.50 he was not breathing.

*

Sinclair had been convicted of four murders. His first took place in his home city of Glasgow in 1961, when he raped and murdered his seven-year-old neighbour Catherine Reehill when he was just sixteen. But after spending a mere six years in prison, he was released in his early twenties to kill again.

Teenagers Helen Scott and Christine Eadie were last seen at the World's End pub on Edinburgh's Royal Mile in October 1977. The next morning both were found murdered; not together, but a few miles apart on the East Lothian coast. They had both been raped before they were killed. The largest investigation in Scottish police history didn't find their killer.

Several years later, in 1982, Sinclair was jailed for life after he was charged with and admitted eleven charges of rape and indecent assault. However, twenty years after this, as Sinclair was beginning to be hopeful about being released on parole, a cold case review showed that Sinclair's DNA had been found on the body of 17-year-old Mary Gallagher, a 1978 Glasgow murder that had been previously unsolved.

These discoveries lead detectives to examine the link between Sinclair and several other unsolved cases. Scientific advances put Sinclair and his brother-in law Gordon Hamilton – who died in 1996 – firmly in the frame for the World's End pub murders of Helen Scott and Christine Eadie.

In 2007 Sinclair stood trial for these murders, but a lack of evidence saw the case collapse. But following the change in Scotland's double jeopardy law, Sinclair again faced trial for the World's End murders in 2014, and this time was found guilty. The judge said the words 'evil' and 'monster' were not enough to describe Sinclair, as he sentenced him to a minimum of 37 years in prison for the murders of the two teenagers. This is the longest sentence issued to anyone in a Scottish court, and ensured that Sinclair would die in jail.

You will read over the coming pages how Sinclair's refusal to confess to his crimes has meant that many of the families of his victims have not had a full explanation about the events around their deaths. Yet, following his death in prison, he was then the subject of a fatal accident inquiry at Stirling Sheriff Court, purely because he had died there.

The court heard that Sinclair's next of kin knew about the inquiry but had chosen not to attend or participate. and they made no criticism of his care at the hands of the NHS or the Scottish Prison Service.

Kevin Scott, the brother of one of Sinclair's victims, Helen Scott, said after his death:

> He was a monster. To treat innocent people the way he did was just evil. You would need to be a beast to commit those crimes. I would have wanted him to live longer to serve more of the thirty-seven year sentence, as opposed to getting the easy way out. I do feel for the families of the other victims that he may have had. They'll never be afforded the kind of justice that we received.

In a documentary on Sinclair in 2020, top Scottish investigative journalist Russell Findlay asked whether Angus Sinclair was Scotland's luckiest serial killer. Maybe. But he was helped by very poor policing, with at least two men serving life in prison for crimes he had committed.

Tom Wood, the detective who helped finally bring Sinclair to justice, shares our belief that he killed many more people, and has said Sinclair will go down in history as 'one of the most dangerous men to ever walk the streets of Scotland.' Referring to other possible victims, the former Deputy Chief Constable of Lothian and Borders Police added,

> Let's spare a thought for Anna Kenny, Hilda McAuley and Agnes Cooney, who Sinclair certainly murdered.

Wood said the only regret at Sinclair's death were the secrets that he took to his grave.

There were more victims than Tom Wood mentioned. Many more.

Sinclair was convicted of four murders, but we believe he murdered at least twelve people, maybe fourteen. And in this book, we tell their stories.

Childhood

A month after the conclusion of the Second World War in Europe, on 7 June 1945, Angus Robertson Sinclair was born at Rottenrow, the old maternity hospital in Glasgow. He was the third child of Angus and Maimie Sinclair, joining his fourteen-year-old brother John and eleven-year-old sister Connie. His mum, Maimie, was the daughter of a coal miner from Salsburgh, a small pit town about twenty miles east of Edinburgh. His dad, Angus Sr, was a joiner from Stirling. Since the 1930s the couple had lived in a tenement on St Peter's Street in St George's Cross, within the Maryhill area of Glasgow.

The Glasgow in which Sinclair was born was a very different one to today. Pollution was a real issue, and particularly on winter nights when thick smog meant that pedestrians could often see little more than a few yards in front of them. In 2000, writing on the *Glasgow Story* website, Michael Mair, a Church of Scotland minister, looked back to the Glasgow of fifty years earlier when he went to school in the city centre:

> 'Glasgow in the days when I was a kid was a dirty place. The buildings were all black. I thought stone was black. It was actually dirt. George Square was black. There was this smoky pall hanging over the city.

It was certainly a tough place to live. It was a violent city. Murder rates in the city were the highest in the country, and gangs were rampant. It was a place where the police were avoided, as criminals settled their disputes between themselves. Make no mistake: for Sinclair growing up, he was no stranger to extreme violence – it was a part of everyday life.

There were health concerns, with diseases like polio and tuberculosis still prevalent. It was only in 1957 that Glasgow launched a mass X-ray campaign which pretty much eradicated tuberculosis in the city.

The late 1950s and 1960s was a time of huge change in Glasgow as its traditional shipbuilding industry on the River Clyde began to decline, with ships being built more cheaply elsewhere.

Living conditions were cramped, and this was the time when large sections of homes were condemned as slums and bulldozed, whilst families moved into new high-rise tower blocks and large housing estates known as 'schemes'. Many of these were built outside the city in places like East Kilbride and Cumbernauld. Others saw their houses demolished to make way for the brand new M8 motorway. It was a huge change, as Maryhill, Partick, Govan, Gorbals and Ibrox were places where several generations of the same family had lived in very close, almost self-contained communities. This change in living conditions had a major impact on crime, health and all aspects of life for residents of Glasgow. It also saw changes in religion in the city, as churches adapted to this changing physical and social landscape and the 1950s saw organised religion in the city stronger than ever before. Both the Catholic Church and the Church of Scotland opened new parishes for the new communities that sprang up, and the church halls became the place where many social activities took place in the 1950s.

Another major advance was the introduction of the National Health Service. This meant that even those people from the poorest communities were finally able to access good quality health care.

Some will still argue today that the loss of communities and the spirit which was the very essence of Glasgow was a negative, as it meant that many of the tight communities that made Glasgow such a special place to live were lost. But overall, the changes were much needed and transformed the city very quickly. The end of the 1950s and into the 1960s was a time of hope, when anything seemed possible.

When Angus was aged just two-years-old his dad was diagnosed with chronic lymphatic leukaemia. Until his death at the Glasgow Royal Infirmary two years later – a month before Sinclair entered grade P2 – Sinclair watched his mum look after his dad as his health deteriorated. As he became increasingly unwell Angus Sr wasn't able to work, but he did spend a lot of time looking after a young Angus as his wife brought in some money through working at a nearby tobacconist's shop. A long time later, after Sinclair admitted killing Catherine Reehill, his mum wondered if losing his father early was a factor in his subsequent behaviour, as she believed that growing up Sinclair missed his dad terribly. Although he almost certainly did miss having a father figure in his life, Sinclair's wife Sarah tells a different story of the closeness of the relationship, saying that although Sinclair had told her his dad died when he was young, he never spoke about him or showed any emotion about losing him so early.

In 1950 Sinclair started school at Grove Street Primary, which was a just a few minutes' walk across the road from the family flat. As an adult Sinclair was only 5ft 4in tall, and at school he was the smallest boy in the class, so was bullied from a very early age. He is remembered as an introverted boy who wasn't popular with teachers or pupils. Don Stuart, who lived in St Peter's Street during the late 1940s, said of him:

> Sinclair lived two or three closes down from me. He came from a very strange family. He was a wee smout. His sister Connie seemed okay and was a big girl, but he was very small.

Although the details are unclear, it seems that Sinclair spent some time in care at one stage in his early childhood. It has been widely speculated that maybe this was due to how he behaved after his dad died, when he became very withdrawn and introverted, and was thought to have been suffering from depression. We can never know for certain. Later, when he was locked up at Peterhead prison when he was pushing to be released on parole, other inmates who had been in prison with Sinclair had told how he had been a victim of sexual abuse as a child. But there is no evidence of this happening. Maybe it did, or potentially it was just another example of Sinclair playing what he saw was the game: being cunning and manipulative, trying to gain some sort of advantage.

Academically, Sinclair did ok at junior school. He didn't stand out in any way, but his reports show a boy of average intelligence who did not get into trouble, and was polite with good manners.

After he admitted killing Catherine Reehill in 1961, Sinclair's mum was reported in *Herald Scotland* as saying:

> The Angus I remember is not the boy who did this awful thing. The
> Angus I knew was a good son. He was a wonderful boy at home, but
> something happened to him. He seemed to change three years ago. I
> began to feel a bit frightened and worried about him.

That change described by Maimie was simply puberty. This is when
Sinclair began his obsession with sex and violence that he maintained
for the rest of his life. At the same time, just ahead of his thirteenth
birthday, Sinclair moved up to St George's Road Secondary School.
It was a very unpleasant time for Sinclair, and he was incredibly
unhappy at the school. The girls who interested him all ignored
Sinclair and he continued to be bullied by the boys, this time more
seriously. This school was an incredibly tough environment, with
violence still commonplace – and not just from the children. Corporal
punishment was widely used as a way of maintaining discipline. For
a boy of small stature who was being bullied and had no quick wit or
special talents, school would have been no fun at all for Sinclair.

Sinclair was becoming sexually active, and interestingly, bearing in
mind his later offending, much of his early sexual experience was in
the company of other boys that he knew. In the excellent book *The
World's End Murders* by David Johnston and Tom Wood – which has
been an invaluable source of information for this book – the authors
write that there were two girls who would regularly have sex with
Sinclair in exchange for cigarettes. But Sinclair preferred it when
both he and his friend had sex with the same girl during the same
evening. Later we will hear how, as an adult, many of Sinclair's sexual
attacks were in the company of another man. This period is also
where Sinclair learnt about sexual diseases and he was always wary
about this in later life, almost obsessed by the prospect of catching
something. However, he was not put off by diseases enough to stop
his sexual offending.

This is the time when Sinclair came to the attention of police for
the first time. In 1959 he stole an offertory box from a local Glasgow
church, and was given twelve months' probation. Later the same year
he was on a housebreaking charge. For neither offence did Sinclair
take the punishment seriously, and infringed his probation conditions.

School was getting no better for Sinclair as he got older, and he became increasingly disinterested and disengaged. At the earliest opportunity, in the summer of 1960, Sinclair left school and got a local job as a van boy. Just six months later a seven-year-old girl was indecently assaulted just a few doors away from Sinclair's home in St Peter's Street and Sinclair was questioned about the attack. Although he denied any involvement, in January 1961 he was found guilty of lewd and libidinous behaviour, a law in Scotland which covers an offence that is deemed to fall just short of sexual assault. The reality of this conviction was that Sinclair immediately lost his job, and everyone in the tight-knit community where he lived – still mainly working-class families who had lived in the area for a long time – knew what had happened. Sinclair's conviction for an assault on a young girl would have been shameful for his family.

Before he was sentenced, Sinclair spent time at the Larchgrove Remand Home so that he could be monitored closely before his punishment was decided. The result of this surveillance was that he received three years' probation. If he had been bullied by boys before and shunned by girls, this was only going to make his situation worse.

A report from the Probation Department at the time said the following about this period in Sinclair's life:

Angus Sinclair first came to the notice of the Probation Department in March 1959 when he was charged with theft of an offertory box. The officer then dealing with the boy reported that he seemed very ashamed of himself, and received a severe thrashing from his mother, very sorry for himself.

At the time he was a member of the YMCA where he played badminton from the start of probation supervision. Sinclair was noted to be quiet retiring lad with little to say for himself.

In April 1960 Angus disappeared from home. He had gone off with the lad who was co-accused in the previous offence. Apparently, he broke into a house and stole a Canary, was scared to face his mother and ran away. He was joined by the other lad who had taken £50 belonging to the other lad's Grandfather. They were ultimately traced to Aberdeen and brought home, in the interval a warrant had been issued for breach of probation and the order was extended from one to two years on the housebreaking charge. He was admonished at this time. Sinclair was just under 14 years of age. His co-defendant was

16 years of age during this time. I should say that Mrs Sinclair had been working which meant the boy was left to his own a good deal, but after this very disturbed pattern of events she gave up her job and there was a much closer relationship between mother and son.

In November 1959, when the writer became responsible for supervision, it should be made clear Angus had settled down again. From the first I found him to be quite relaxed but with very little to say, he attended the school woodwork club two evenings a week and I've seen some of his handiwork which was of good order.

In time he was selected to represent his club at the schoolboys and schoolgirls exhibition in Kelvin Hall. Thereafter the case continued uneventually until August 1961 when he was charged at Glasgow Sheriff Court with lewd and libidinous practices [lewd and libidinous practice in Scotland, the crime of an indecent assault towards a victim under the age of puberty – 12 for girls although cases involving older people are not unknown].

To this he pleaded Not Guilty. It was alleged that he had interfered with the girl of seven years. He strongly denied the offence, but admitted that he had given her sixpence, stating he did this in return for the child's mother having handed in books and comics to his house.

But, in a pattern that was to be repeated throughout his life, any punishment he received was not going to be enough to stop Sinclair offending. Just six months later, in 1961, Sinclair found another local victim to attack. But this time it wasn't just sexual assault. It was murder.

Catherine Reehill

On Saturday, 1 July 1961, the future Princess Diana was born in Sandringham, England. She would go on to lead a life that changed that of so many others. This was also the day that Angus Sinclair murdered for the very first time, in a life of crime that caused great misery and which ruined the lives of many of those who had the misfortune to cross his path.

At the time, despite the progress of recent years the centre of Glasgow was still overcrowded with the majority of residents housed in poor quality homes. The air quality was particularly bad in the city due to pollution. Just the day before, on Friday, 30 June, the Queen had visited the city to see an old smoke-blackened tenement being demolished before it was replaced with a modern high-rise block of flats.

Saturday, 1 July dawned clear and hot, and during the day there was no respite as the heat continued to build to unbearable levels in the city. The headline of the *Evening Times* that day was 'Glasgow Sizzles'.

Sinclair's mother Maimie, his brother John and sister Connie were all out that day, leaving Sinclair in the flat on his own. He knew that he had three hours before anyone would be back. When he looked outside Sinclair noticed a girl he had not seen before. She turned out to be seven-year-old Catherine Reehill, happily skipping along the road without a care in the world on that beautiful summer day.

Catherine didn't live in the same tenement. She was there that day as she was staying with her mum's sister Agnes, a neighbour of the Sinclair family, along with her five-year-old brother Jim, whom she affectionately referred to as Jimpy, and her six-year-old disabled sister

Margaret. The siblings were very close, and Jim and Catherine were very protective over their younger sister. Catherine's parents Vera and Patrick were in London that weekend. Patrick, a bricklayer from nearby Hamilton, was looking for a new job, and with Vera he was looking for a house in London. They felt that by moving to London they would be able to provide a better quality of life for their family.

There were no other witnesses to what happened next, so we can't say for certain exactly what took place, but it is widely believed that Sinclair called out to Catherine as she skipped past. She stopped and came over to Sinclair, who gave her some money to run to the shop to buy him a bar of chocolate. Catherine was happy to do so. When she returned from the errand Sinclair suddenly grabbed her, and pulled her into the flat. Immediately understanding the danger she was in, a terrified Catherine called desperately for her dad. But nobody heard her cries for help. Once inside the flat, Sinclair tried to have sex with Catherine, but the young girl put up a real fight, and in the struggle she badly smashed her head. There was blood all over that part of the flat from the wound, but Sinclair wasn't put off and, after overpowering her he raped Catherine, before strangling her with a bike inner-tube.

During the assault Sinclair was disturbed by a knock on the door of the flat. Remaining completely calm, he answered the door to a neighbour he knew well who was about the same age as Sinclair, and the two agreed to meet later that evening. Once he had closed the door, Sinclair returned to his attack on Catherine. This is quite staggering behaviour from a sixteen-year-old — to be so in control and unflustered when carrying out such a dreadful crime. It suggests that the attack on Catherine was pre-meditated, rather than a spur of the moment action, as Sinclair was determined to carry out his plan despite being interrupted. If his victim had not been Catherine that day, it could have been any other young girl.

Once Sinclair was finished with poor Catherine he discarded her, throwing her down the tenement steps. Soon afterwards, two women who lived in the tenement were on their way to bingo when they found Catherine lying at the bottom of the concrete steps. She had a large bruise on her forehead and there was blood on her nose, and it was immediately clear that she was in a serious condition. Although

Catherine was not moving, she was still just about holding onto life, and one of the women detected a very faint pulse. Just moments later Sinclair appeared at the scene, asking what had happened to the girl. When he was told that Catherine must have fallen down the steep stone steps, he said that he would phone an ambulance. When he made the call, he told the operator that 'a wee girl has fallen down the stairs'. Once more, this calmness around the scene displayed by a fifteen-year-old Sinclair is hard to fathom. There was no sense of shock at the act he had committed just moments before.

Tragically, seven-year-old Catherine died of her injuries in the ambulance on the way to the Sick Children's Hospital at nearby Yorkhill.

Her cousin Anne Summers, just a little girl at the time, spoke recently to the *Scottish Sun* about her vivid memories of the police coming to the door of the flat straight after Catherine died:

> It was a horrible, horrible time. All hell broke loose. Nobody slept. I was sick, I was frightened. We had lost Catherine and I didn't know what was going to happen. I remember looking at everyone crying and hugging. I was just angry, really angry that Catherine had been taken. I was just a wee lassie but you know these things.

Meanwhile, in London, the Metropolitan Police were desperately searching hotels in Hammersmith and Fulham, trying to find Vera and Patrick to tell them the heartbreaking news that their eldest daughter was dead.

Quickly after the initial shock of finding Catherine had passed, it was clear to locals that she hadn't died in an accident, but had been murdered. It was also noted that Sinclair, who had been at the scene so quickly after the incident, had disappeared and couldn't be found anywhere. Suspicion immediately fell on him – not just for his appearance at the scene so soon after the attack, but as he had recently been found guilty of the assault on the seven-year-old girl nearby. Sinclair wasn't liked or trusted in the community, and although he had only been convicted of one assault, many people had noticed the way he ogled young girls. This behaviour made them uneasy.

Sinclair had in fact fled soon after calling the ambulance, realising that he needed to get away from the scene. This instinct for self-preservation was a wise move, as Catherine's uncles and other locals hunted for him that night, looking to serve their own form of justice. If he had been found, with emotions running so high there is a very good chance that he would have been seriously injured or even killed in a revenge attack. But, once more, his calmness under extreme pressure was in evidence, as he waited to see his brother John and asked him to provide an alibi for Sinclair. John refused.

As you will read, Sinclair was always very aware of the need to provide an alibi for his crimes, and became adept at manipulating others to lie as cover for him.

The police found Sinclair the next day and he was arrested, charged and brought back to the Glasgow Juvenile Court on Monday morning. Sinclair initially denied being involved, but after speaking to his older brother John, whose opinion he always had time for, Sinclair made an admission to the police. But it wasn't the full story. He told them that he had been overcome by his sexual urges, and there had been a struggle with Catherine which led to her banging her head. Interestingly, on being charged Sinclair realised that there was semen on his underpants and tried to block the police by giving them a different pair from those he was wearing, but he was unsuccessful. This shows that even at that age he was forensically aware.

Sinclair appeared in court in Glasgow that morning at exactly the time that Catherine's distraught parents arrived back in the City. At the back of the court that day was Sinclair's mum Maimie, who sat in silent tears as she heard her much-loved son Angus admit killing Catherine.

During his time in custody the following report was prepared by the Probation Department and submitted to the judge:

> He's a healthy boy of good physique, and keeps himself clean and tidy. His conduct while here has been very good, and he has at all times been cooperative without being in anyway ingratiating. He went about his work in an unobtrusive way, completing any task given to him to the satisfaction of the supervisors and without requiring any close supervision.
>
> He's very reticent boy and it is difficult to assess what lies beneath the surface. His contacts with the staff were kept to a minimum, and he

formed no friendships with the other inmates. I would respectfully suggest to the court that a further period of probation might be sufficient to stabilise this boy's character.

Sinclair was placed on a fresh period probation for three years. Despite the findings of guilt he insisted that he had not committed the offence, indeed this is still his attitude to it. Discussions with the mother revealed no sign by the boy of any abnormality or difficulty in matters of sex, and discreet questioning of the subject by me gave no indication of any problems.

On the night of the offence his mother and sister had gone visiting, and knowing the house was empty he sent the girl for chocolate. In doing so he states it was his intention to invite her into the house with the intention of interfering with her. He also indicates that this is the first occasion he can recall when he felt his sexual desires were out of control.

On the return of the child he took her into the house and began to fondle her. In his own words he then attempted to have sexual intercourse with her, whereupon the child complained of pain and started screaming he put his arm round her neck. He remembers little else until he was on the stair landing outside the house having left her body there. He returned to the house and decided to visit his brother, feeling he had to get away somewhere. He left home but he discovered that neighbours had found the child and it was apparent they thought there had been an accident. He offered to telephone for an ambulance and made the call.

Then when visiting in company with a friend at the time of his court appearance in January there were serious doubts about the earlier sexual advances, but questioning could not shake the boy in his defence of interfering with the other girl and having any unhealthy desires. In sexual matters it is now apparent that he has not revealed the true situation, and that he has been engaging in sexual practises in one form or another for some time.

As you will read in this book, it was most unlike Sinclair to ever admit responsibility for a crime and to confess, however strong the evidence. He was a cold man, who never showed remorse for his actions. But on this occasion he both admitted to killing Catherine and, according to his mum Maimie, he was genuinely remorseful on remand. When asked about that time, she later said:

When I visited him in prison, he kept asking me, "Why did I do it, mother? Why did I do it?" He said he was sorry for the heartache he had brought the little girl's parents, sorry for what he had done to me.

Facing continued hostility in the local community for the actions of her son, it was made very clear to Maimie that the Sinclair family were no longer welcome. She had no choice but to pack her things and move away from the flat in which she had lived for over 30 years.

Ahead of sentencing, a psychiatric report dated 9 August 1961 said the following about the sixteen-year-old Sinclair:

He was not a nervous child and had a happy childhood. His father died when he was six or seven years old and his mother went out to work to keep the family.

He has a brother and a sister older than himself and one younger sister. There is no family history of mental illness. He started school when he was five years old. and appears to have been an average pupil.

He succeeded in passing the qualifying examination. He played truant frequently from school. He mixed well with other boys at school and left in June 1960 when he was 15.

After leaving school he worked as a van boy for six months, leaving this employment because he felt that he was underpaid. He then worked as a message boy for a few months before moving to his last job as a store boy. He had been in this job for 3½ months before his arrest on the present charge. He lived with his mother and two sisters in a room and kitchen tenement flat.

His health has been good, and he has only been in hospital once for tonsillitis when he was about five years old. He is usually a cheerful sort of boy, but he has had spells of depression in the past.

He does not have a worrying nature and mixes well with other people. His interests are swimming, woodwork and cycling, he attended woodwork classes on two evenings a week and went swimming another evening. He also enjoyed skating, went to the cinema and played billiards. He did not read books and held no interest in what was happening locally or nationally. He smokes 15 cigarettes a day, but he did not take alcohol.

When he was aged 13 years he was put on one year's probation for stealing money from a church offertory box, and the following year he was again put on a year's probation for theft by house breaking.

At the beginning of this year he was put on two years' probation on a charge of interfering with a young girl. He first had sexual intercourse when he was 13 years old, and then about every three months, after this he had intercourse every week with a girl of the same age. After this he was promiscuous with girls up to 17 years of age.

He is a small, quiet, rather subdued boy. He showed no abnormality in his appearance, behaviour or conversation. He was able to give a clear account of himself and of the events connected with the offence.

He seems to be of low-average intelligence. He shows no evidence of gross mental illness, and to assess his behaviour will require a period of fairly long observation.

The disadvantage of his going to borstal institution is that he would be amongst those who are only there for relatively short periods, and also that the nature of his crime might cause him to be victimised by the other boys.

Despite this it is felt that Dumfries Borstal is probably the best place to recommend for at least the earlier part of his detention. He would probably respond to the training he would get there, and there would also be a much greater possibility of further psychiatric investigation and treatment than he would get if he went to one of the smaller prisons.

At the High Court in Edinburgh on 10 August 1961, Sinclair pleaded Guilty to the culpable homicide of Catherine. Across the community there was genuine horror at how Catherine had been killed by such a young man barely 16 years old. The way Sinclair had acted, especially directly after the murder, shocked even hardened detectives, and one psychiatrist's report at the time said:

I do not think that any form of psychotherapy is likely to benefit his condition, and he will constitute a danger from now onwards. He is obsessed by sex, and given the minimum of opportunity he will repeat these offences.

Another said:

These circumstances appear to be a progression from the sexual offence committed a few months earlier. The similarities in respect of sexual motivation against young female victims – who Sinclair would have been able to control – and the proximity of the accused, victims and locus is noticeable. It is also possible that Sinclair learned from the earlier offence, and that he attempted to lessen the chance of being linked to the crime by killing the victim, removing her from the locus and attempting to establish an alibi.

It continued:

The similarities between the culpable homicide and the crimes subject of this report may appear tenuous. However, there is sexual motivation against female victims who are brought under some form of control and strangled with ligatures. There is also an attempt made by Sinclair to distance himself from the loci where the victims are last seen alive and where the bodies are deposited.

But as is often the way in court, the experts didn't agree and another psychiatrist said that the way in which Sinclair had acted after the attack was so normal that it showed a degree of abnormality. This finding, combined with his young age, led to the court accepting that there was some diminished responsibility in his actions.

On 25 August, at the High Court in Edinburgh, Sinclair was jailed for ten years for culpable homicide. He was out in just seven.

When Sinclair was convicted of Catherine's murder, his mum was already planning for what her precious son would do when he was released. She really did adore him, and hoped that this was just a blip in his life which he could move on from. To give him every chance of resuming a normal life after prison, Maimie even considered changing his name and emigrating overseas as a family. Over the coming years, she and sister Connie remained close to Sinclair, ensuring they visited him regularly in prison. But his brother John disowned him after he murdered Catherine, and the brothers would never speak again. Speaking in 2009 to the *Herald Scotland* newspaper, John said he wished he had stopped his brother back then:

I would have done time for him. I would have killed him. If I'd known years ago I'd have pushed him in the bloody canal. And all these people, all these girls, would never have had that. I would just have nothing to do with him, nothing do to with him. He can rot in prison.

The actions of his brother had made life a nightmare for John in particular. Although the family had moved home, they were still recognised and pointed at in the street. Then, as now, the family of offenders are often the silent victims of crime, who suffer terribly in so many ways. Sinclair's mum Maimie, as well as being forced to move away from her home, suffered emotionally, as do all families of offenders. While many families are devastated by the imprisonment of a loved one but stay in contact and continue to support them, others react like John and disown the offender. A recent example of this that you may recall was the case of Louise Porton, who killed her daughters Lexi and Scarlett within the space of three weeks. Although in court Porton continued to maintain her innocence, the prosecution argued shockingly that she had killed her young daughters as the children got in the way of her life as a sex worker. After being found guilty and sent to prison for life, Porton's mother Sharon said of her granddaughter Lexi:

> She and her sister had their whole lives ahead of them and Louise took that away for her own evil, selfish reasons. Their own mum. I had no idea what was going on and I feel so guilty that I couldn't do more to protect my granddaughters. She isn't my daughter, she's a monster.

This was so hard for Sharon to live with that just months after her daughter's conviction in August 2019 she tragically took her own life.

With other families there are a confusing mix of feelings which may combine upset, guilt and even sometimes relief that a disruptive or violent person has left the family home. Then there are the difficulties for wider family members and friends, who are uncertain how to react, which often means their support networks suffer.

Sinclair served the first three years of his sentence in Aberdeen, an adult prison, despite only being sixteen years old. He completed his time behind bars in Saughton Prison in Edinburgh. In Aberdeen, through a prison scheme with local businesses, Sinclair received training in joinery and net-making as part of his development, and spent a period working in the cookhouse. Significantly, working for a business that made fishing nets in Aberdeen meant that Sinclair developed an expertise in knot-tying, a highly significant skill we will be discussing in more depth when we talk about the World's End murders.

We have been able to find a number of interesting reports and correspondence from Sinclair's time in prison, and they are produced below.

Report dated 22 September 1966:

> From the age of thirteen years he had frequent intercourse with girls of his own age and with older ones, He has been detained in his current prison since the 11th of December 1964 and has benefited from the training received there and has cooperated well in the training scheme.
>
> In my opinion this youth is making satisfactory progress. He is more mature and he recognises the importance of cooperation with other members of society. If a successful career and happy relationship is to be assured, it is anticipated that the discipline training will prove an effective deterrent to any anti-social behaviour in the future, provided that he is engaged in a satisfactory employment.
>
> Chief officer's remarks: A very good prisoner who cooperates very well and takes part in all recreational activities.
>
> Medical officer's report: He is well mentally and physically.
>
> Chaplain's remarks: This lad seemed to be responding well in voluntary training as a painter and is eager to make the best use of his time in custody. His behaviour is good.
>
> Welfare officer's remarks: Has made no approach to welfare while in Edinburgh.
>
> Governor's remarks and recommendation: This lad has continued to cooperate with staff and makes every attempt to make time serve him, instead of serving time.
>
> Inspector's comments: The failed pale-faced young man who is making good use of his time in prison, he's completed the voluntary training painting course, but is continuing his studies to take his City and Guild examination in May 1967. He likes keeping himself active and appreciates a parole with staff, he's not bitter against society, his move from Aberdeen has been very much in this man's favour. A spell on the works painting programme would help this young man, but this should be looked at after May 1967.

On 2 June 1967, Sinclair's psychiatric report stated:

From the information obtained at the time of my previous examination, it appeared that this youth had not matured normally that there was a diminished sense of responsibility, that his sentence was defective from the age of fourteen years. There were findings of guilt on charges of theft, breach of probation and theft by house breaking and of lewd and libidinous practices.

When in prison in Edinburgh, on 11 August 1967 Sinclair wrote a letter to the Secretary of State for Scotland:

> Since a detention centre sentence qualifies for a 6th remission, surely after six years in a prison I should become eligible for a third instead of the usual 6th. I will have completed six years on the 25th of this month. Surely by now I should be knowing a release date. It would also be of future interest to me to know if I qualify for training per freedom of remission.

A report on Sinclair on 11th September 1967 said:

> In the opinion the progress of this prisoner is satisfactory and encouraging. He is more mature, and will continue with an increasing sense of responsibility his efforts are worth rewarding, and we are of the opinion that he is a suitable candidate for the privilege of home parole and training for freedom prison psychiatrist.

In Edinburgh, Sinclair was put on the Training for Freedom programme. This was a progressive scheme, many years ahead of its time. This programme was aimed to give prisoners a real trade which would lead to a much better chance of not re-offending upon release from prison.

Sinclair trained to be a painter and decorator, gaining his City & Guilds qualifications. Being a part of this programme meant he was released from prison to go to work every morning, returning in the evening after completing a day's work with J&T Harvey, a firm of painter and decorators in Edinburgh.

The prison report described this work experience as follows:

> Sinclair is to commence work on day release with Harvey's on Monday the 13th of November 1967, he has to report on that date. He will be conveyed in the firm's transport to the site. The work is a basic 40-hour, five-day week; Monday to Friday 8.00am to 4.30pm.

Holiday is the first three working days of the year, spring holiday and autumn holiday. Sinclair's travel arrangements from Tuesday the 14th of November 1967 onwards. Sinclair will travel by bus to the top of the Brae and walk to the site at the North End of the Brae. Sinclair was taken to a store in Leith on the 8th of November 1967 and supplied with clothing including a combat jacket and boiler suit coloured white.

His fellow workers at Harvey's liked Sinclair. They were very happy with his performance; he was good at the work, hard-working and reliable, and got on well with the other staff. It was through this period of work experience that Sinclair got to know Edinburgh for the first time. The sheer irony is that his understanding of Edinburgh which helped his later criminal career was all thanks to the Scottish Justice system.

It is easy to mock this unintended consequence. But, in reality, the efforts of the Scottish Justice system should be applauded. With a young prisoner like Sinclair every effort was made to provide him with the opportunity to rehabilitate himself. Despite the pleas of his mum, who, when interviewed about this period in a number of newspapers, always claimed that Angus was sorry for what he had done, he showed no remorse for his actions. He was noted as an accomplished liar, and was still seen as a risk even when he was released from prison.

What other tips and tricks did the young Sinclair pick up from his first stay in prison? It is often said that prison is where some complete their education – was this the case with Sinclair? As a sixteen year old surrounded by adults with a long history of violent offending, he would certainly have had the opportunity to learn. We will, of course, never know for sure.

As well as being let out of prison regularly to gain work experience, Sinclair was also given day release during the final year of his sentence to see his family. He would visit his mum and Connie at his mum's new flat at Bellfield Street, just about two hundred metres from Celtic Park, the home of Celtic Football Club, in the Parkhead east end area of Glasgow.

Angus Sinclair was released on parole from prison on 24 April 1968. In the final prison report it says:

Gus has never looked back since his release. He has experienced two unfortunate romances but has survived OK. He reports to work faithfully and works hard. He has made a good effort. I think the foregoing is also instrumental in supplying a favourable assessment in relation to his future conduct.

Sinclair has proved to be an extremely diligent and satisfactory employee. Such a favourable impression was created and Mr Harvey, a director of the firm, has agreed to retain Sinclair in his employment on his release.

Sinclair has responded to this offer wholeheartedly, and despite the fact that his home is in Glasgow he intends remaining in Edinburgh to continue with this employment. Sinclair has at present accrued earnings from the Training for Freedom of scheme as previously stated on release. Sinclair will remain in the Edinburgh area. Tentative enquiries regarding accommodation have been made, but final arrangements for the accommodation will not be made until just a few days before his release.

In 1968, Sinclair was only in his early twenties when he walked out of prison a free man. He kept his real name and although he did move, it was not abroad, just forty-five miles east to Edinburgh. He chose to live there as he had gladly accepted the offer to continue working for J&T Harvey in a full-time job as a painter and decorator. He took a room in a shared flat at 10a Hill Place, in the Southside area of Edinburgh, which was convenient for his work, and eagerly began the next phase in his life.

Sinclair was under supervision from the authorities for three years after prison, and he seemed to be doing well, holding down his job and living what seemed to be a full, normal life. He had a large number of girlfriends and would boast to his colleagues about his sexual conquests. Despite being under supervision, just weeks after leaving jail he had sex with a girl he knew was only fifteen. Sinclair was well aware this was against the law, but wasn't bothered by the potential consequences. Even then, Sinclair wanted to have total control over the women he was with, which meant that most of those he targeted were vulnerable in some way. If not under-age, they were likely to have suffered sexual abuse or were escaping violent or alcoholic partners. Another ever-present in his life that began at this time was his desire to use the services of sex-workers. Today, Leith to the north of Edinburgh is a trendy part of the city. with fantastic bars, restaurant, hotels and beautiful apartments. Back in 1968 it was very different. Traditionally, Leith Docks became known as the port for Edinburgh, and shipbuilding and repair facilities grew in importance. The presence of ships made it a bustling red light district, which continued right up to the early 2000s. When Sinclair was released from prison there were lots of sex workers working on the streets in and around Leith. He spent a lot of time there using their services.

Sinclair also quickly resumed his criminal activity in Edinburgh, and burgled a number of houses. His job as a painter & decorator was perfect for this, as he travelled around the city, with access to homes that he would closely check out and later target.

Not long after he moved to Edinburgh Sinclair met a student nurse called Sadie Hamilton, who everyone knew as Sarah. She was a student nurse originally from the Townhead area of Glasgow, but was living in nurses' accommodation at Edinburgh's Eastern General Hospital when she met Sinclair. Like most things with Sinclair, this wasn't straightforward. He was dating a friend of Sarah's who introduced him to her, and it was only when that relationship ended that Sinclair and Sarah were able to get together.

In 1970, when Sinclair was aged twenty-five and Sarah twenty, the couple married in the registrar's office in Leith. Sarah would no doubt have not gone through with the wedding if she had known about Sinclair's activity in the red light district just metres from where they took their vows.

Sinclair's mum and Connie were delighted with his choice of wife as they really liked Sarah, who was a nice, straight-forward girl. Maimie was now certain that her Angus had put his troubled past behind him, and told friends and family that she looked forward to better things for her son.

Sinclair's sister Connie and her husband acted as witnesses, and some of both families were there, including Sarah's younger brother Gordon Hamilton, then aged fifteen. Much more about him later. Sinclair's brother John wasn't a guest at the wedding. He was invited, but he had vowed never to see his brother again after he killed Catherine Reehill and stuck to his word. Sinclair didn't tell his wife the real reason for John's no-show, because when they married Sarah was unaware that her husband had murdered Catherine. Although she didn't know the details, she did know that he had been in prison and this was enough for her to deter her parents from attending the ceremony as she was concerned about how her dad, in particular, would react. Later, when Sinclair finally met Sarah's parents, they all got along well.

The wedding was a very pleasant affair, and afterwards the happy couple headed off on honeymoon for two weeks in Campbeltown, on the Kintyre peninsula west of Glasgow. This would become significant some seven years later in the case of Anna Kenny, a woman we believe was killed by Sinclair. There is a chapter on Anna later in this book. On their return from honeymoon the newlyweds lived with one of Sarah's brothers in Glasgow's Gallowgate, not far from Sinclair's mum.

Sarah was a very warm personality and spent a lot of time in the company of Maimie, with the two becoming very close. This bond meant that Maimie was even more thrilled when she heard the news, soon after they returned from the honeymoon, that Sarah was pregnant.

In 1972, after almost two years of marriage, the couple had a son, who they named Gary, and they moved to a home of their own. Sinclair and Sarah were both from Glasgow and they chose to live in Nitshill, to the south-west of the city. Maimie was delighted that her son appeared to have settled down with a very pleasant, hard-working wife, and now had a child too. She saw Angus working hard too, and looked on with pride as her son's family enjoyed a nice lifestyle, and began to make plans for their future together.

But life wasn't easy for Sarah as a new mum. As well as the difficulties faced by being a mother for the first time, Sinclair began to spend increasing amounts of time away from the family home. Often he was away all week with painting work before heading off on a fishing trip all weekend, not arriving back until Monday morning. He was in Edinburgh when his son was born, and didn't even find out about the birth until over twenty-four hours later. Sinclair hadn't lost his desire for a variety of sexual partners, and as well as continuing to visit sex workers he had numerous affairs. At one stage, he even left Sarah and moved in with another woman for a short period of time. It is rumoured that he even had an affair with one of Sarah's sisters. But despite his total obsession with sex and seeming need to have multiple sexual partners, Sinclair always went back to his wife. Sarah would sometimes catch Sinclair out, and became upset that he couldn't remain faithful. But when she did, Sinclair would always promise that this was absolutely the last time, he would never do it again, and he would talk of their plans for the future. Sinclair could be very persuasive, and very charming too. Sarah wanted to believe him, and now they had a son together she also wanted to do what was best for little Gary.

It was during this period of their lives, in the early 1970s, that Sinclair bought an ice cream van to supplement his painting income. Astonishingly, Angus Sinclair was not the only serial killer to operate an ice cream van in Glasgow. Fred West, the English serial killer who committed at least twelve murders between 1967 and 1987 in Gloucestershire, the majority with his second wife Rosemary, also spent some time in Scotland. In the mid 1960s, when Fred West was living in Glasgow, he too owned an ice cream van. West's career in this area came to an abrupt end when he ran over a three-year-old boy called Henry William Feeney in November 1965. The tragedy was widely accepted as an innocent accident.

Thanks to a friend from Glasgow, Eddie Cotogno, Sinclair developed an interest in photography, even setting up his own darkroom. At this stage, Sarah was unaware that Cotogno was an amateur pornographer in Glasgow. The photos that Sinclair developed were all around his main interest. Sex. Sarah was mortified when she stumbled upon a sleazy picture of her husband with another woman in a dingy makeshift studio that had been taken using a timer device. The photo was burnt in a blazing row, but once again Sinclair managed to talk himself out of trouble.

We will go into this much more later in the book with a chapter about the mysterious death of Eddie Cotogno, which is still unsolved. We will show why we believe Angus Sinclair was responsible for Eddie's death.

Significantly in relation to his future offending, this was the period when Sinclair bought a camper van. It was a white Toyota Hiace. Sinclair justified this purchase to Sarah by saying that he wanted a campervan so that he could go on fishing trips, and enjoy the scenery in the beautiful part of Scotland where they lived. He would regularly go on weekend fishing trips alone, or with Sarah's younger brother Gordon Hamilton. But, as his wife Sarah later commented, whenever Sinclair and Hamilton went away fishing they never seemed to catch any fish. The reality was that this campervan gave Sinclair the freedom to travel around Scotland's central belt looking for victims to satisfy his depravity, with nobody else knowing where he was or what he was doing. It was also a perfect vehicle for abducting and restraining victims. Many of the crimes committed by Sinclair that are discussed in the following chapters were only possible due to him owning the campervan.

It was around this time that Sinclair finally confessed to his wife that he had murdered Catherine Reehill. As was standard for Sinclair on the rare occasions that he confessed to any crime, he didn't tell Sarah the full, terrible details of what had happened on that sweltering summer afternoon. But as reported later in the *Herald Scotland* newspaper, understandably Sarah clearly recalled the moment he told her about Catherine, saying:

> It floored me, big time. It was put across to me that he made a mistake and this young child died. That was a horror to me, but I was into my marriage by this time and I thought that I knew him. I looked at my brothers and other people in my life. They had all made mistakes; we all do when we're young. I put it down to him being a kid. I never looked at him as a child killer. I never looked at him suspiciously like he would ever do it again.

As we will hear so many times over the following pages, the devastation caused to the families of those attacked by Sinclair was very real. Few were fortunate enough to gain any closure, as Sinclair wouldn't admit his responsibility to crime. Even though Catherine's family and friends knew exactly who had killed her, it was almost impossible to live any sort of life after what they had been through. Catherine's family moved to London shortly after her death, but her mum never recovered, and died while only in her fifties.

Not wanting any other family to go through their terrible experience, they were appalled and confused by the leniency of the sentence when Sinclair was only sentenced to ten years in prison. They were sure that Sinclair would kill again on his release.

Following Sinclair's death, Catherine's cousin Anne told the *Scottish Sun*:

> I'm glad he's dead. He'll burn in hell now. I hope he suffered, but nothing he felt at the end can even compare to what his victim's felt at the end. He shouldn't have been allowed to pass away peacefully, he should have been made to suffer. I really believe he should've have been hanged after he killed Catherine. If he had, none of these other families would have had to suffer. I just think he was evil, pure evil. I don't think he was human. Who could do that to all these people?

3

Helen Kane

In May 1970 the England football team were preparing to defend their title of World Champions in Mexico. Hopes were high of a second success following their victory in 1966, although it's fair to say that perhaps in Scotland supporters were not so keen. The squad's tournament song, *'Back Home'* was top of the UK charts.

Helen Kane was twenty-five and had been married to her husband Joe, a porter at a local hospital, for seven years. They lived in Greendykes Terrace, Craigmillar in central Edinburgh with their four young children, Joe Jr, then six, Michael, five, Kevin, three, and Raymond, who was ten months old at the time.

Life was tough with four young children under the age of six, but the family were happy. On the night of 24 May 1970 Helen and Joe were in very good spirits. That night was their wedding anniversary, and as a treat Helen's sister Janet had agreed to babysit their children so they could go out for the evening and enjoy themselves. Helen and Joe arranged to celebrate with another couple at the popular Dockers Club in Academy Street in Leith, Edinburgh. It was an enjoyable night in the packed venue.

As closing time approached, Helen left on her own. It is unclear quite why she didn't stay with the group, and it was a four mile taxi trip home to Greendykes Terrace. Helen rarely went out, so possibly she was keen to get home to check on the children, or maybe she got separated from the group at the end of the night. There were, of course, no mobile phones back then. Did Helen decide to call it a night and make her own way home? What is for certain is that Joe and the other couple stayed at the club a little longer to enjoy some final drinks before heading home themselves. In the club with her husband was the last positive sighting of Helen alive.

A witness later came forward to say they saw a woman fitting Helen's description getting into a cab on Duke Street, just a two-minute walk from the club, with a man who was never identified. Was this Helen? A taxi driver later confirmed that he had picked a woman up he believed to be Helen from near the club, and he had dropped her off in Royal Terrace, one of the most exclusive streets in the centre of Edinburgh.

At about this time, a couple were walking along at Royal Terrace and recall seeing a woman fitting Helen's description talking to a short, stocky man — the description of Angus Sinclair. This was the final potential sighting of Helen Kane.

The next morning, 25 May, was a beautiful, warm, early summer's day. Christopher Holmes, a computer programmer who lived in Edinburgh, was out walking his dog on their usual route, enjoying the weather. Near Royal Terrace, on a building site where new homes were being built between the Pleasance and the Dumbiedykes council estate overlooking Holyrood Park, he thought he saw something strange. Looking more closely, to his horror he realised that he was looking at a human body in the building site.

On Helen's death certificate it shows the exact location as Development Site, Arthur Street. Officers were quickly at the scene, where they found the terrible sight of Helen's partially clothed body. She had suffered a number blows to her head, inflicted with a rock or large slab or stone that had presumably been taken from the building site where she was found. Helen lived just half a mile from where her body was discovered.

There are many questions unanswered about Helen's final movements. If she had been the person in the taxi outside the club, why was she with another man? Had they agreed to share the cost of a taxi, or was there another reason? If Helen was the person dropped at Royal Terrace – as would seem likely as her body was found close by – why had she got out of the taxi there rather than being taken the extra half-mile to her home? Helen was known as a loving and caring mum who rarely went out, and would have been keen to get home to her children. Had she been short of the full fare and chosen to walk the extra short distance home? What about the sighting of Helen talking with a stocky man near Royal Terrace? If this was Helen, who was this man and what were they discussing? Maybe the more likely explanation is that Helen wasn't in the taxi at all – it was someone of a similar build and appearance – and she chose to walk home. It was on this walk that she met her killer.

Despite many appeals for information over the years, nobody has even been charged with the murder of Helen Kane, but there have been people of interest to detectives. At the time, the main suspect was a man who lived close to where Helen's body was found and who had only been released from prison a few days before she was killed. On the night of the murder he didn't return home, telling his flatmate that he had been visiting friends out of the city. Police later checked this story and found it to be inaccurate; the suspect had actually checked into an Edinburgh hotel that evening. A police report was sent to the procurator fiscal, but on this occasion there was not enough evidence to launch a prosecution.

Serial killer Peter Tobin was looked at as a suspect at one time. Tobin, who is currently serving life in Edinburgh prison for the murders of Vicky Hamilton, Dinah McNicol and Angelika Kluk, was discounted when it was realised that he was jailed for four months on 15 May 1970, just over a week before the murder.

We would argue that Helen was another victim of Angus Sinclair. At this time Sinclair was twenty-four, and living in Edinburgh with his wife in Hill Place, just two hundred metres or so from where Helen's body was found, and matched the description of the man seen with Helen. As an ex-offender living in the local area, he was interviewed by detectives following the murder, but he had his usual alibi in place, which this time came from his brother-in-law, Gordon Hamilton.

The description of the stocky man seen talking to Helen in Royal Terrace certainly matches the description of Sinclair. If she had walked home, the route could have taken her past Royal Terrace. It is absolutely feasible that Helen walked home from the club and then met Sinclair, who persuaded her to go with him to a quiet area, perhaps telling her he was looking for someone and needed assistance. Once there, he sexually assaulted and murdered her.

Just a few weeks later Sinclair and Sarah left Edinburgh to live in Glasgow.

Former Detective Superintendent Allan Jones, who knows Sinclair as well as anybody, agrees with us, and he is convinced that Sinclair was responsible for Helen's murder, later being quoted in the *Edinburgh News*:

> He was actually questioned about it. Helen was a mother intercepted as she walked home and taken to a construction site at the base of Arthur's Seat. She was disrobed, we think sexually assaulted, then she was killed by being struck over the head with a stone or a rock. There were no ligatures involved with that one, but again there was no clothing. And it was close proximity to where Sinclair stayed.
>
> There are enough common factors to persuade me he was the most likely culprit in Helen Kane's death. Her body was left in much the same way as his other victims, with her lower clothing and underwear removed, leaving her exposed. The degree of violence was extreme, another one of his hallmarks. Also, she was targeted after a night out drinking. That was always the way he operated.

This view is also shared by Helen's family. Her son Michael, who was just five years old when his mum was killed, later told the *Scottish Sun*:

> Because some of the police officers who worked on the case seemed sure that Sinclair was the man, I became more convinced he killed my mum as the years passed. I always hoped he'd find his conscience when he knew he was close to death and maybe say something about the murders he denied.

A frustration shared by investigators close to the case is that in the original investigation so much evidence was destroyed that could have solved the case today following advances in technology. This included a clump of hair that was found in Helen's fist, which was almost certainly from her killer. If it could be examined today, it would almost certainly have solved the crime by concluding that Sinclair was the killer. Or, of course, it could have proved him innocent. Either way, the family would have been spared all these years of not knowing just who killed Helen.

Also lost were a number of statements and documents relating to the investigation, including the post-mortem report. Unfortunately, this is not the only time in this book that you will read of items going missing that could have been vital to solving the crime. It is tempting to give police officers the benefit of the doubt on forensic evidence, as back then it was impossible to appreciate just how important forensic evidence would later become. But as for losing documents such at the post-mortem report, unfortunately, it is hard to argue this is anything but sloppy police work.

In this book we will hear again and again about families destroyed by not just the murder of someone they love dearly, but by the killing remaining unsolved. Dr Stephanie Fohring, a specialist in criminology and victimology at Edinburgh Napier University, commented in the *Sunday Post*:

> The type of extreme crime is so shocking and so traumatic because it messes up how we see the world. It can be quite common in families who have lost a loved one to murder that the stress of it all can lead to disintegration and conflict. There is all this anger and tension, and often there is no perpetrator caught, then we don't have a proper target for that anger so it can be turned towards loved ones or family members. It can destroy a family.

Helen's family were torn apart by her murder. Her husband Joe, who has since died, moved away to Manchester to start a new life. Helen's sister Janet, who babysat the children on the night Helen was killed, looked after her nephews. But Janet too is now dead, passing away almost twenty years ago. Janet died just three weeks after Helen's son Raymond was tragically found dead after taking methadone. He was just thirty-two. His brother Joe died in 2015 at a flat he had shared with his brother Michael. These tragedies caused Michael, the surviving son, to ponder how things might be different for the family if Helen hadn't been murdered, telling the *Scottish Sun*:

> I was five and I have very few clear memories of my mum. But I remember she was quiet and kind. I wonder how things would have been different if we'd had a mum. I would just like to know for certain what happened to her after all this time. When it happened we were all so young, but as the years went on and we got older it was a case of always wondering. It's not just us. There are other families who have had a loved one murdered and it might have been him. It's really difficult to think that if it wasn't him then someone else has got away with it.

Anne Marie Davy, Mrs Kane's niece and goddaughter, concisely sums up the view of the family when she spoke to the *Scottish Mail on Sunday*, saying:

> When no one is brought to trial, there is never any justice so there can be no end to it. I don't want her just to be a statistic, or a footnote in Sinclair's story. I want people to remember her and to know that she lived, she loved and was loved.

4

Gordon Hamilton

It was in 1970, when he was fifteen years old, that Gordon Hamilton first met Angus Sinclair, who was ten years older, when the latter married his sister Sarah, and Gordon was a witness at the wedding in Edinburgh. On that initial innocent meeting, neither man could have guessed how entwined their futures would become.

It was the start of a devastatingly unhealthy relationship which saw Sinclair dominate Hamilton. Although the two of them together committed the most terrible acts, including most notably the awful murders of Christine Eadie and Helen Scott, there was never any doubt about who was the driving force in their relationship. It was always Sinclair.

The DNA of Sinclair and Hamilton was recovered from the bodies of the girls and from each of the five ligatures used to restrain and strangle them. Lord Advocate Frank Mulholland admitted in court while summing up the evidence at the first trial for the World's End murders that his only regret was that Hamilton had died and was not sitting in the dock beside Sinclair.

Anna Kenny, 20, Hilda McAuley, 36, and Agnes Cooney, 23, had all been bound and gagged in similar fashion to Helen and Christine, and Anna and Hilda had also been strangled by ligatures.

Hilda was bound with a type of industrial string sold to tradesmen, which from descriptions in statements from the time matched string found in the back of a car Sinclair had bought after trading in the camper van he had used for so many of his crimes. When he was finished with the car he had dumped it in a quarry but, later, a tip-off from an informant revealed to police where it was. Although it had been underwater for almost thirty years by now, police divers recovered it during the investigation into who murdered Hilda McAuley – a murder that is still unsolved, but in a later chapter, we suggest that the man who murdered Hilda was Sinclair.

Bundles of string that were found in the car were identified, and one of Hamilton's former employers confirmed his company had used it at the relevant time.

There were also numerous murders of other young women in Strathclyde following Sinclair's incarceration in 1982 – we will cover this much more fully in later chapters – up to Hamilton's death from heart failure in 1996. Many victims were sex workers, and a number of the cases remain unsolved. Were these crimes the responsibility of another serial killer, or were they all killed by different people? Or was Gordon Hamilton responsible? Did he continue to attack and even potentially kill without his partner Sinclair? So far, where there was DNA taken none have matched with Hamilton's DNA profile.

This point about just what else he may have done is typical of the reaction to Gordon Hamilton. Whereas we know a lot about Sinclair, Hamilton is much more of a mystery. So just who was Gordon Hamilton?

Gordon Hamilton was born on 1st March 1955 in Stirling Road, Glasgow to parents Sarah McCulloch Hamilton (née Kerr) and Thomas Hamilton, a boiler de-scaler. Gordon grew up in Glasgow with three sisters and six brothers. Life was tough for many families in Glasgow who struggled at this time, but Gordon's upbringing was a particularly difficult one. He and the rest of the family were subjected to violence from his alcoholic dad, and he witnessed regular criminal behaviour from other members of his extended family. The Hamilton family was blighted by alcoholism and violence, with Gordon's brother Joe later being sentenced to life in prison for murder.

Gordon had an especially problematic relationship with the rest of his family, who found him overbearing and a little pompous. After he had left home the family had little contact with him, and knew little of his life. They knew he had married, but no further details. It is tempting to reach the conclusion that Sinclair would later fill that void in his life left by his family.

Gordon was a practical man who was very useful with his hands. He used to help friends with a variety of jobs around the home such as small electrical repairs and painting and decorating. He was also a man who many women were attracted to physically, at 5ft 7in tall, a medium build, heavy stubble and a handsome face. He was also charming, and could be very good company.

There was something about Sinclair that Gordon found intriguing and mesmerising, and from very early on in their relationship he was prepared to do anything in order to assist and protect his brother-in-law. Even in late 1970, very early in their relationship, we have heard that Gordon lied to the police as he provided the alibi for Sinclair as detectives investigated the murder of Helen Kane.

But although Sarah's parents and Gordon liked Sinclair, not all the Hamiltons felt the same way. Their brother, Thomas, really couldn't tolerate his company. More than that, he didn't trust him at all, referring to him as a 'nonce' after learning that he had spent time inside for killing Catherine Reehill. Thomas wasn't particularly close to his sister, but his wife became very close to her. Despite this growing friendship, Thomas remained very wary and wouldn't even let his wife get in the same car as Sinclair, warning her to stay well away from him.

At the other extreme in the Hamilton family was another close relative who found Sinclair utterly charming, and was rumoured to have had an affair with him.

It transpired later that Gordon had carried out a number of crimes with Sinclair very soon after they first met in 1970. He had been living with Sinclair and Sarah at the time, and Sinclair managed to get him a job with a painting company. In addition, he began to carry out a number of criminal jobs with Sinclair.

When years later detectives strongly suspected that Sinclair was responsible for other crimes and wanted to talk to Gordon Hamilton about potential crimes the pair had carried out in the 1970s, life hadn't treated him well. They located him in a London bedsit and he was in a pitiful state, wrecked by a lifetime of booze and crime. He told detectives about a number of crimes that he and Sinclair had committed together. He confirmed that they would often return to offices where they had been painting during the day, then steal from the same businesses. Other times they would steal from shops, usually with a very basic process of storming the shop and demanding money. More often than not Sinclair would accompany this with his trademark violence, before giving the cashier time to react.

Often Sinclair took advantage of information he had overheard in pubs, in the street and at his work. He was always listening for any pieces of information. He would have no qualms about burgling a property where he was working if he found out that the residents were going to be away for any period of time. He was devious, and always on the lookout for snippets that he could use to his advantage.

For Sinclair, it seemed to be as much about the pleasure of the violence as the money. On one occasion, when he was with the youngest Hamilton brother rather than Gordon, he randomly attacked a man with a hammer who had left a Glasgow pub as he happened to be walking past the premises. The young Hamilton told detectives that actually stealing money from the man was almost an afterthought for Sinclair.

Among all the petty crime and burglaries that Sinclair carried out throughout his life, the youngest Hamilton brother spoke of his involvement in a vicious attack in April 1976, in Moodiesburn, a town north-east of Glasgow. He explained how he was working with Sinclair on a painting job when, as was so often the case in his robberies, Sinclair heard information that he could use to his advantage. He heard that the rent collector in nearby homes always arrived at the same time, and that one man who lived nearby would give the money to his young daughter as he slept after a night shift.

As the rent was collected on a Friday morning, the following rent day this worker lay asleep in bed after a late shift at work. His wife had already headed out to start her job, so before retiring he gave the rent money to his seven year old daughter with instructions to pass it to the rent man when he knocked on the door at the usual time that morning. At about 10.00am the young girl was disturbed by a knock as she watched television. When she opened the door, rather than the rent man she was confronted by Sinclair and the youngest Hamilton brother with stockings over their heads, carrying weapons. She was terrified. Hamilton grabbed the young girl, holding the knife very close to her throat as he dragged her through the house shouting loudly. Meanwhile Sinclair, armed with a hammer, stormed into her dad's bedroom. Both father and daughter were dragged downstairs and made to lie face down in the living room, where they were bound with Sellotape at the arms and feet and gagged, with the dad wondering if they were going to survive this attack. When the rent man duly arrived, he was relieved of the keys for his safe by Hamilton and Sinclair, before also being bound in the kitchen.

As they left with their money Hamilton came back to the father, who was still on the floor, to give him some cash which he said was to cover the inconvenience before the two men fled. As we hear regularly with Sinclair, he enjoyed the violence and almost always the level used was higher than necessary, and so it was in this incident. Here the rent man, who was no threat, had suffered a terrible beating in the head with a hammer and there was blood everywhere. Luckily, he survived. The younger Hamilton described again how Sinclair didn't seem to be troubled in any way by carrying out extreme violence. Just ten minutes after the attack at Moodiesburn, Sinclair was back on the painting job just around the corner as if nothing had happened.

Interestingly, in light of what follows in this book, another man was arrested for this brutal attack and then picked at identification parade. Luckily for him, he had a very strong alibi and at his trial the jury found him Not Guilty. If he had been found guilty, Sinclair wouldn't have given a second thought to another man spending time in prison for his crime.

During the period covered by this book, when Sinclair was attacking, sexually assaulting and murdering women, Sarah didn't suspect for a moment that was what he was doing. It is hard to comprehend how this had no effect on Sinclair. Unlike many other criminals, he didn't ever feel the need to unburden himself by telling others what he had done.

Following the murder of Helen Kane, Sinclair and his wife Sarah left Edinburgh, moving to Glasgow. Gordon Hamilton had meanwhile become fairly settled, in 1970 securing a job working for a manufacturer of buttons. According to his colleagues, he was a pleasant, likeable, reliable and valued member of staff.

It was not until the summer of 1977 that Sinclair and Gordon spent more time together and their relationship became much closer as a result. It was at this time that Sinclair bought the Toyota campervan which he used for going fishing at weekends, and sometimes for longer periods, with Gordon usually joining him. It comes as no surprise that, due to the time spent with Sinclair and the crimes they were committing together, Gordon became a changed man towards his friends and family from around this time. It was the same at his workplace. Gordon had always seen as a good worker at the button manufacturer, right up until 1978 when he appeared to lose his capacity for hard work, and according to his employer changed from 'a really strong worker' to someone who was unreliable. Although it can't be said for certain, this was almost certainly down to the crimes Hamilton was committing with Sinclair. Was it the excitement of what he was doing with Sinclair which meant he was unable to concentrate on the more mundane parts of his life? Or maybe he was struggling to deal psychologically with his new life of crime.

This deterioration in Hamilton again emphasises the difference between him and Sinclair, who was able to remain cool and unflappable, giving nothing away, no hint to anyone of the crimes he was carrying out. This isn't normal. Almost every criminal who has ever carried out a serious crime has been affected by their actions and it has changed how they behave in normal life, even if it just feeling the need to tell someone what they have done. Sinclair's coolness is another trait that marks him apart from others. His wife Sarah had no idea that her husband was committing such terrible crimes. There was nothing she saw in his behaviour that provided any clues.

As we will discuss later in the book in more detail, in 2004 three Scottish police forces came together in an initiative known as Operation Trinity, which was a review of unsolved murders where Sinclair was a potential suspect. In 2007 Mark Safarik, the FBI profiler consulted by police in 2004 as part of Operation Trinity, explained to the BBC just how, in his view, Sinclair was able to live a seemingly normal life despite carrying the most dreadful crimes:

> People like this are psychopaths, which allows them to kill someone and, half an hour later, be eating a ham sandwich as if nothing had happened. It's what allows them to go back to the people they know – family, friends and co-workers – and act normal.
>
> They don't have empathy for their victims. There's no remorse. It's all about "What's good for me is to get this person, sexually assault them and then, when I'm done with them, discard them like they're

garbage and just move on with my life." It's their ability to blend in that makes these guys successful.

Although Hamilton's behaviour had experienced marked changes noticeable to all who knew him, it was in 1978 that another major event occurred. Something happened between Sinclair and Hamilton which resulted in a major argument. We can only speculate on the cause of this disagreement – was it about the crimes they had committed together? It seems likely, but what is clear is that whatever the cause, their disagreement was so significant that the two men went from being very close to never speaking again.

After the argument, perhaps in an effort to return to some sort of normality, Gordon met his future wife Wilma Sutherland just before Christmas 1977 and the couple married in October 1978. Wilma had been the last person to see twenty-year-old Anna Kenny alive in August 1977. Wilma was Anna's best friend, and had been out with her on the night she disappeared at the Hurdy Gurdy pub. It was in the very same pub that Gordon met Wilma a year after she had spent her last night with Anna there. Coincidence? Or was there more to it? Sarah Sinclair, Gordon's sister, later told detectives that she didn't think that Gordon was directly involved, although she admitted that it was too much of a coincidence for there to be nothing in it. We cover Anna's murder in a separate chapter later in the book.

Was this apparent coincidence actually a startling indication of a combination of twisted minds? Or was this perhaps the cause of the argument between the two men?

Whatever had initially attracted Wilma to Gordon, and persuaded her to marry him, soon changed. It was a short and very unhappy marriage for Wilma, who saw Gordon descend into alcoholism. This was accompanied by him physically abusing her, and having a number of affairs. They soon separated, after which Gordon accelerated his bid to self-destruct.

Tracking his movements from this point is difficult as there is so little information available about his life; however, we do know that by 1994 he was living in Robertson House, a hostel in the then run-down Mile End, in the east of Glasgow. It was a tough place, surrounded by individuals like Gordon down on their luck and usually suffering from social issues such as drug abuse or alcoholism. Hamilton moved from there to Broad Street Glasgow, but the alcohol abuse was now really taking its toll on his mental and physical health. The good looks of his youth had long gone, and he looked at least ten years older than his real age.

Gordon Hamilton died on 7 December 1996 at just forty-one, suffering a heart attack at Glasgow Royal Infirmary. The death certificate stated the cause of death as myocardial infarction and ischaemic heart disease, with his occupation listed as a Paint Match Colour Blender. He was noted as single at the time of death. According to records Gordon's sister, listed as J. Hamilton of 32 Silverfir Street, Glasgow, was the informant to the Registrar.

Gordon Hamilton died a free man. His victims and their families would never see him face any form of justice.

Speaking to the *Herald Scotland* in 2007 after Sinclair's conviction for the World's End murders, when it was shown that Gordon Hamilton had been present and raped both victims, his sister finally accepted that that he had been involved, but felt that responsibility lay firmly with Sinclair. She said:

> Angus could never have got those girls on his own. Only Gordon could have. Gordon was a handsome, lovely-looking man. I had no idea Gordon was involved, but he never murdered either of those girls. He was an accomplice but was manipulated by this creature Angus Sinclair. I know in my heart he corrupted Gordon. It wrecked Gordon's life. He proved to be key to the investigation because he raped, or had sex with, both girls and left that crucial evidence. But in no way do I believe he was the instigator.

It was true to form for Sinclair that at the 2007 trial for the World's End murders, despite all the help Gordon had given Sinclair over the years of their friendship, Sinclair didn't hesitate to put the blame for the killings firmly at his door. Following the conclusion of the trial Lord Advocate Frank Mulholland stated that his only regret was that Hamilton had died, and was not sitting in the dock to be tried for his crimes alongside Sinclair.

Gordon is often obscured in discussions about Sinclair even though he played such a prominent part in his crimes. This is partly due to his early death, and also due to the lack of information about him that can be found. In fact only two photographs of him survive, as his family destroyed all his possessions upon his death. It is almost as if his existence has been wiped from those who knew him.

As Gordon was cremated following his death, it made it very difficult for detectives investigating the World End murders to even obtain his DNA to prove any links to the murder scenes. There were no cups, clothes and or any keepsakes to remember him by. It was as if he had been deleted from family history. Detectives eventually visited a house where Gordon had carried out some electrical work and managed to obtain a tiny segment of his DNA from coving strips he had laid.

This lack of information about Gordon's life made it difficult for detectives to carry our further investigations following Sinclair's conviction for the World's End murders. As they began to look more closely into Gordon's links to other women who had gone missing, or whose murders remained unsolved, this lack of information hindered them greatly. These difficulties were enhanced by Gordon's lack of contact with friends or family, and that he never had any police convictions in his lifetime. He had not been seen as a potential sexual predator or what people would describe as 'creepy' in any way by those who knew him. Former girlfriends later told how he could be violent in their relationships, but police said there was no evidence that he was 'overtly sexualised'.

Many find it inconceivable that he only committed one serious crime, however dominated he was by Sinclair. Tom Wood, who was Deputy Chief Constable of Lothian and Borders Police at the time he led Operation Trinity, told the *Edinburgh News*:

> It was such a brutal and devastating crime. It's virtually inconceivable that an offender's first crime is a double rape and murder, or that he commits such a crime, gets away with it and never reoffends. Sinclair was ten years older and I have no doubt he was the dominant partner, but there is no doubt Hamilton participated fully and, considering the general nature of such offenders, it's hard to believe there was never any build-up, or any repeat later in his life.

Labour's former Justice spokesman at Holyrood, Graeme Pearson, former Assistant Chief Constable at Strathclyde and later the Head of the Scottish Crime and Drug Enforcement Agency, agreed with these sentiments being reported in the *Edinburgh News* as saying:

> I would hope that Police Scotland will evaluate Gordon Hamilton's life and all his background to ascertain whether he could be linked to the unsolved murders of young women at that time.

After Sinclair's conviction in 2014 for the World's End murders there were calls for cold case reviews into Gordon's activities in the 1970s, '80s and '90s. Was he responsible for any of the numerous murders of other young women in the Glasgow area when Sinclair was in prison? A Police Scotland spokesman replied to these calls, saying dryly:

> During the Operation Trinity period, the investigation looked at all homicides in Scotland up until the period of Gordon Hamilton's death to consider if he would be potentially relevant to any investigation. Clearly, we will seek to retain this sample [of DNA] in order that any future unresolved case work will have forensic data to compare if new information or advances in forensic science becomes available.

So Gordon Hamilton has been allowed to stay hidden in the shadows. A strange and mysterious figure, protected by his early death and the destruction of his possessions. Despite this, and the natural focus on Sinclair in this book, Hamilton at the very least gave Sinclair an alibi when Helen Kane was murdered. We will never know for sure what other crimes he may have been responsible for, but we can be certain that Hamilton raped both Helen Scott and Christine Eadie after meeting them at the World's End in Edinburgh in October 1977. He was there when they were murdered, even if it can't be said for certain that he actually killed one or both. Although he is the quiet man for many, his part in the World's End murders will never be forgotten.

5

Patricia Black and Sandy Davidson

22-year-old factory worker Patricia Black was last seen at 5.00pm on 9 October 1976 at a bus stop in Irvine, a town around 35 miles south-west of Glasgow. She had been waiting to catch a bus back to her home in Saltcoats, just six miles away.

Tricia, as she liked to be known, was one of five children, and she had left her home on Friday 8 October to go dancing with an old friend named Carol at hotels in Irvine.

In this book there are lots of references to dancing, and the dancing venues, especially in Glasgow, feature heavily. Let's pause briefly to set some context for the importance of dance venues in and around Glasgow at the time.

As with all Scots, Glaswegians have always been known for their love of dancing. The city's first dance hall opened in 1905. Named the Albert Ballroom after Queen Victoria's husband, it was opened in the city centre on Bath Street. The hall was stunning, and was so popular that it was soon hosting dance nights six nights a week. During the 1920s it became even more popular, as more modern dances like the Charleston attracted a young crowd. Of course, it was not all about the dancing. It felt special with a live band playing, and for many this was an opportunity to dress up; a real contrast to the drudgery of many lives, and something to really look forward to. For many Glaswegians, this is where they first found romance.

A fire ravaged the Albert in 1953, but when it re-opened the band all wore firemen helmets to celebrate. Later the building became Joanna's disco but fire again struck, which this time destroyed the building.

Opening in 1920s was the Locarno Ballroom on Sauchiehall

Street, which quickly became another popular hall. In time it became a disco named Tiffany's. Over on the other side of town, the original Dennistoun Palais opened in 1922. The resident bandleader Lauri Blandford and his Orchestra often stood aside for famous big bands such as the Joe Loss Orchestra. 'Denny Pally', as it was known, remained popular until 1962, when the building was converted into a supermarket.

All the dance halls shut for the Second World War, but as a mark of their popularity they were re-opened just two weeks after the end of hostilities in 1945. This was the boom time, where soldiers and civilians finally could relax and have fun after the horrors of war.

The Plaza Ballroom, at Eglinton Toll/St Andrew's Cross, also opened in 1922. It had a fountain in the middle of the dance hall and was well known for the ice-cream delights sold, including Knickerbocker Glories. In 1981 it was the venue for one of New Order's first live shows, and was still open in the 1990s. But as the popularity of dancing declined this lovely old building was demolished in September 2006 to make way for new flats.

The most famous dance hall in Glasgow was the Barrowland Ballroom, which opened in 1934 in the mercantile district to the east of the city centre. The Barrowland had street-level halls where weekend markets were held, with the large dance hall above. This iconic building, with its famous neon sign, is still going strong, although it is now used as a concert venue for top pop and rock bands.

With the popularity of dance halls, smaller venues could be found at most decent-sized towns in Scotland. Often they were just in halls and hotels. Irvine had a thriving scene, which is where Patricia Black and her friend Carol were heading to go dancing on Friday, 8 October 1976. As expected, they had a great time dancing and enjoyed lots of laughs, returning to Carol's house that night, looking forward to more of the same the following day.

The next day, Carol's husband dropped the two women into Irvine again for more dancing and shopping. At about 5.00pm Tricia phoned her mum to say she was going to catch the bus home that evening. She asked her mum to put the immersion heating on so that she could have a bath when she got home. But her mum didn't know that this was the last time she would ever speak to her daughter, as

Tricia didn't ever come home. This wasn't like Tricia at all, and her parents reported her to the police.

Detectives traced Tricia's movement on the day she went missing. She and Carol had stopped for a lunchtime drink in a hotel in Irvine, before Tricia headed to the bus stop to catch her bus to Saltcoats. On the way to the bus stop, at around 4.00pm, Carol and Tricia met four men in the walkway beneath the new shopping centre. They all chatted for a while before Carol headed home and three of the men headed off to the High Street. The fourth man, local 21-year-old labourer John Hepburn, told detectives that he walked with Tricia the five hundred or so yards to her bus stop in Eglinton Street, a continuation of High Street.

John Hepburn was the last person to see Tricia alive. He and the other men in his group, along with Carol and everyone who had seen Tricia that day, were tracked down and interviewed. There was lots of publicity locally as detectives looked for the key breakthrough, but still there was no sign of Tricia. The bus stop where Tricia disappeared wasn't in a quiet, rural area, but in a built-up part of town just outside the busy Turf Hotel. Detectives struggled to understand how Tricia could disappear seemingly without trace from such a busy area in the early evening.

Just what happened to her? Clearly suspicion fell on the last man to see her alive, but he maintained his innocence and was never charged. Detectives received information about a courting couple who were seen in the moor area of the town – around half a mile north-west of the town centre – from about 5.00-6.30pm. The woman matched the description of Tricia, and detectives appealed for witnesses. But this couple were never found and eliminated, and no man came forward saying he had been with Tricia, so the lead never progressed.

Detectives quickly feared the worst for Tricia and one part of the police investigation, headed by Detective Superintendent Derrick McAllister, involved frogmen dragging the River Irvine to search for a body. A week after her disappearance, in the weir area just five minutes from where Tricia was last seen, her handbag was found with the purse missing. It had been weighed down by stones, so it was clear that whoever dumped it did not want it to be found.

When she disappeared Tricia was wearing a cream dress and brown fur jacket lined with leather, but none of her clothing or any other clue to her disappearance was ever found. Detectives believed that if Tricia had been dumped in the river the strong tides in the area were likely to have swept her body out to sea.

Almost six months later, when neither Tricia or her body still hadn't been found, John Hepburn explained more fully to the local newspaper what had happened that day:

> I only spent ten minutes with her, and she explained that she was going home. The only reason I walked with her to the bus stop was because I was going shopping for a Christmas present for my wife at the jewellers near the bus stop. I left her there and I walked back down the street. I have had an awful lot of sleepless nights. I have racked my brains to try to think of some little clue which might help find her. She was in a cheerful mood and didn't seem distressed at all. I just wish she would turn up safe and alive. It is causing endless worry for me and my wife.

We believe that Patricia Black was killed by Angus Sinclair. As you will read, Sinclair at this time targeted young, pretty women who had been out on a weekend. He was living locally, and the seemingly professional swift abduction and getaway certainly doesn't point to an amateur. With his fondness for fishing, Sinclair had every reason to be in the Irvine area. The River Irvine flows through south-west Scotland and around the area fishing is a very popular pursuit, with many angling clubs maintaining the banks and rivers. There are plenty of salmon, brown trout and sea trout, just the sort of fishing to attract Angus Sinclair. As Tricia's body has yet to be found, it isn't possible to see how she was murdered and whether the modus operandi matched Sinclair's usual methods of sexual assault, followed by strangulation with the victim's own clothing.

Tricia's family recently talked in the *Scottish Sun* of a suspect who interested the police at the time but is now dead. His girlfriend had provided an alibi for the day in question which was accepted, so this line of enquiry didn't go any further. But perhaps a girlfriend of the sort of man capable of murdering Tricia would be scared of him, and give him the alibi he needed? As we hear on numerous occasions in this book, Sinclair certainly relied on false alibis to keep him out of jail.

Tricia's parents never recovered from the grief of losing their daughter. In an interview in 2012 with the *Scottish Sun*, Tricia's brother Alan told how he was just a week short of his 18th birthday when his sister disappeared, and he told how his dad died in 1979 at just 65, followed by his mum Janet in 1990 at 76. He said:

> My parents were quiet people and they didn't show their emotions, but the one thing I know they longed for was that Tricia would be found so they could give her a decent burial. My mother kept her room just the way it was when she went missing for years afterwards. I can't imagine what she was going through. My father used to sit every day at the window and wait for her coming round the corner – it was so sad to see. He died three years after she disappeared and I personally think it was of a broken heart. We were all devastated.

Alan was tormented by questions of whether he should have done things differently after dropping his sister off the day before to meet Carol. He recalled:

> She asked me to give her a lift and she planned to stay overnight with a friend. She was just her normal self, looking forward to a night out. I dropped her off at a place called The Turf and she asked if I wanted to come in for a drink but I said no, and that was the last time I saw her. I often wonder if I'd gone in for that drink, would things have been different, would she still be here. You can't help thinking about it and I still feel guilty.

Was the murder of Patricia Black connected to another unsolved murder in Irvine in April of the same year?

Philip and Margaret Davidson were overjoyed when they moved into a new house in St Kilda Bank in the Bourtreehill area of Irvine. It was a lovely home in a nice area, and as an added bonus it was just four doors away from Margaret's mum's home, which would be really handy. It was great news too for Margaret's mum, Mary Bonce. She loved her grandchildren – Sandy, who was four, and two-year-old Donna – and spent time with them whenever she could. The family moving so close would mean she could see even more of them.

The Davidsons moved into their new home in March and, keen to earn money to give their children the best possible life, Philip and Margaret often dropped their children at Mary's to babysit. This is what happened on 23 April 1976. It was a lovely sunny day, and soon Donna and Sandy were playing in the enclosed garden with Kissie, the family's Afghan hound. Mary stayed in the house whilst the children played, checking on them occasionally and listening to them playing.

It seems that Kissie managed to get out of the garden and Sandy naturally followed him, but whereas the dog returned shortly afterwards, Sandy didn't. When Mary came out of the house a few minutes later to see Donna, Kissie and an open gate and no sign of Sandy, it was her worst nightmare. But these things happen, and she was sure they would quickly find him nearby. They didn't. He was reported to the police, who searched the local area along with the family and local residents. At the time, there were lots of houses being built in the area and the building sites would be interesting to a curious boy, but there was no sign of Sandy. The young boy loved cars and had once climbed into a friend's van, and it was only some miles later that the friend realised he was there and brought him home. Had this happened again, and there was an innocent explanation?

But as the hours turned into days and weeks, and there was still no sign of Sandy, it was clear that something terrible had happened. The police felt he had wandered out of the garden and then got lost, potentially drowning in a nearby burn. But Sandy's parents didn't agree with this explanation at all. They thought somebody had taken their precious son. In time, many detectives involved with the case agreed with them, and wondered if the outcome may have been different if the case had initially been treated as an abduction.

There are many theories about what happened to Sandy, and there were some likely sightings of him in a car with a man. If this was the man who took the boy, was this serial killer Robert Black, who was active at the time and lived nearby in Greenock for a while? For us, although it is impossible to totally rule out a man like Black, his timeline in London during the early part of 1976 would suggest it would be prohibitive for him to travel the four hundred and twenty miles to Irvine on a whim.

If Sandy had been abducted, it could have been a random one-off crime, or perhaps someone who had taken other children. The perpetrator may have then been in prison for another crime, moved away or died, and so never been caught. Or was it Angus Sinclair?

During 1976 Sinclair was living in Glasgow, just thirty miles north-east of Irvine, which would be attractive to this avid fisherman, and a hot sunny day during the Easter holidays would present numerous targets of teenagers and children in light clothing.

Sinclair sexually assaulted many children, and although he denied it, when he was arrested in 1982 for sexual assault he was thought to have sexually assaulted boys as well as girls. A charge of assault against a nine-year-old boy was left to lie on his file. There is also the possibility that with his curly blonde hair, Sinclair may have mistaken Sandy for a little girl. Had he been in the area that day and taken the chance to abduct Sandy? He often used fishing trips as cover for his crimes, so he and his brother-in-law Gordon Hamilton may have been at the nearby Annick Water or the River Irvine, its weir an ideal salmon leap. Alternatively, as a painter and decorator Sinclair could have been working on the large housing estate, where there was lots of construction going on at the time.

Sandy's family believe that there is a strong possibility that Sinclair could have been responsible, and whilst he was still alive they urged Police Scotland to make Sinclair take a lie detector test to prove his innocence. Sinclair refused.

Neither Patricia Black or Sandy Davidson have ever been found.

6

Frances Barker
and Thomas Ross Young

Frances Barker was born on 3 March 1940 to Annie Barker, née Reilly, and Francis Barker, an Ordnance worker. In June 1977 37-year-old Frances was unmarried and living on her own at 289 Maryhill Road, Glasgow, working at the city bakery nearby. The company owned her flat.

On Saturday, 11 June, a taxi driver dropped Frances outside her home after she had been visiting family in nearby Parkhead. Frances had drunk a fair amount of alcohol that afternoon, so much so that she had to be helped into the taxi by her sister and other family members. When he dropped her outside her home, the taxi driver kept an eye of Frances in his wing mirror as she was a little uncertain on her feet, but before he could confirm she had gone into her house he picked up another fare and pulled away, thinking no more of it. But that was the last time she was seen alive.

It wasn't until the Friday, almost a week later, that her colleagues at the bakery grew so concerned that they contacted Frances's parents. They hadn't seen their daughter either, and were now very worried. Her brother Thomas met some of her work colleagues at her house that afternoon. There was no sign of Frances, but also no indication that there had been any sort of disturbance.

Sixteen days later Frances' semi-clothed body was found by a farm worker in a quiet lane near Inchneuk Farm, Glenboig in Lanarkshire, which is just off the M73 Motorway and around eleven miles north-east of Glasgow city centre.

She had been bound at her hands and feet, her arms tied with the scarf she had been wearing and her tights had been used to tie her legs together. Her pants had been forced into her mouth as a gag, and she had been strangled with a ligature tied around her neck. An attempt to hide the body had been made by covering it with leaves and branches from nearby trees. Frances had been raped.

Police initially believed that the man who had taken Frances was likely to be a kerb crawler, so they focussed on men who frequented Glasgow's red light district. This thinking appeared to pay off, as they heard of a lorry driver who would regularly cruise around the area before picking up sex workers. Fortunately for detectives, one had noted his registration number in a Mills & Boon novel she used for recording the details of suspicious clients.

Detectives traced this lorry to a haulage firm in Bishopbriggs, near Glasgow and arrested the driver, 44-year-old Thomas Ross Young. Forensic analysis of his cab revealed hairs belonging to Frances Barker, and her green make-up compact was found under the floorboards at his house. This had been given to Frances by someone she knew who worked in the make-up business, and the product was distinctive. It was not commonly available, and detectives were certain that it belonged to Frances. This evidence was very strong, and detectives were certain they had their man. Unfortunately, attacks on sex workers were even more common in the 1970s, and another sex worker had recently been raped nearby. This woman picked out Young in an identity parade and he was arrested and charged.

Retired Detective Chief Inspector Alex Cowie, who was involved with the investigation into Frances' murder, later told the *Daily Record* how Young refused to cooperate with police interviews:

> We gave up after about ten minutes as he refused to answer any questions. He was physically intimidating. His lorry firm colleagues said he was so strong he could lift a trailer and put it on the lorry himself.

He added:

> He was the most frightening, dangerous and evil man I've met. God knows how many other victims he had.

In court, Young faced a number of charges including the murder of

Frances Barker. He was convicted of eight charges on an indictment, and all but one of the offences involved violence towards women, with many involving a significant sexual element. The most serious charge was in relation to the murder of Frances Baker.

Although Young protested his innocence throughout his trial at the High Court in Glasgow, the jury didn't believe him and it took them only an hour to return a Guilty verdict on 26 October 1977. He was jailed for a minimum of at least thirty years, which at the time was the longest sentence ever to have been imposed by a Scottish judge.

Thomas Young was a physically imposing man with a short-temper, who had displayed a propensity for sexual violence from a young age. At just thirteen, he was sent to what was then called Borstal for indecent assault. Like Sinclair, Young was obsessed by sex, and had as many sexual partners as possible. Although he later married, he wasn't happy in his marriage and took a job driving a lorry which gave him an excuse to pick up women for sex. In fact, he later boasted about having sex with over two hundred women just in the cab of his lorry.

In January 1967 he faced a charge of raping a nineteen-year-old woman he had given a lift to near Ross-on-Wye, Herefordshire. Then, just a month later, he was questioned about what is now one of Scotland's oldest missing person cases, the disappearance of seventeen-year-old Patricia (Pat) McAdam. Young was always looking for women on his journeys, and Pat and a friend were picked up by Young. Pat and Young kissed and cuddled in the cab for a while, and then later Pat's friend was dropped off in a layby near her home, before Young planned to drop off Pat. But Pat was never seen again. When he was interviewed, Young admitted being with Pat, but told detectives that she had agreed to consensual sex in his cab. After this, he had dropped her back to the outskirts of Dumfries, near her home. Although this story seemed unlikely, detectives had no body and no evidence against Young, so they felt they had no option but to let him go without charge.

Meanwhile, Young was found guilty of the earlier rape in Ross-on-Wye and was sent to prison for eighteen months. Shortly after his release he was given an eight year prison sentence after being found guilty of another rape. This time his victim was a fifteen-year-old girl in Lanarkshire.

With this history of committing sexual crimes, and the solid evidence found by detectives, it seems the jury were absolutely correct in convicting Young. But not everyone agreed, arguing that the evidence all seemed too convenient, and that Young was someone who, because of his track record, could be fitted up to take the blame for the murder of Frances Barker. Make no mistake that detectives were under intense pressure to solve this high-profile and well-publicised crime.

Young always denied being involved, and he was still protesting his innocence when he died in prison in 2014 aged seventy-three. Following his death, his lawyers were allowed to continue in their attempts to quash his conviction at the appeal court. His legal team argued that he had been the victim of a miscarriage of justice, after the Scottish Criminal Cases Review Commission sent the case to the Court of Criminal Appeal in Edinburgh. But Appeal court judges rejected the claim that there hadn't been enough evidence to convict Young.

In the court judgement, judges Lord Eassie, Lord Menzies and Lord Bracadale ruled that there was enough evidence to allow the conviction to stand. They pointed to the fact that bleached hairs similar to those of the Frances Barker were recovered from the cab of the lorry driven by Young.

Lord Eassie wrote in the judgement report:

> The appellant accepted in an interview with the police that he might well have committed this murder during one of what he described as his 'blackouts'. Particular personal items belonging to Frances Barker were recovered from the appellant's daughter, having been given to her by the appellant. Other such items were found by the police underneath the floorboards of a room in the dwelling in which the appellant was residing at the time of his arrest.

He continued:

> Having regard to all of the foregoing matters, we have come to the view that we cannot uphold any of the grounds of appeal advanced by the appellant. The appeal therefore fails.

But was this the correct judgement? Young's legal team certainly didn't think so. His lawyer, John McLeod, was certain of his client's innocence, speaking to the *Guardian* in 2007:

> I first learnt there were doubts about Young's involvement in Barker's murder in 2005, when police asked if they could re-interview my client. 'They asked him if he had really killed her. Yet that was supposed to have been established in the High Court in 1977. So why ask now? As for my client, he vehemently denied killing Barker.

McLeod was also confused by the timing of the decision to charge Young in 2007 with the murder of Patricia McAdam:

> They have no body, no new evidence and no DNA to link Young with this case, yet they have decided to charge him. It is curious, given this lack of new evidence, that the allegation is being made now.

Young never faced trial for this murder, as shortly before he was charged the Scottish Criminal Cases Review Commission lodged an appeal doubting the safety of Young's conviction for the murder of Frances Barker. This was due to Operation Trinity, the police initiative launched in 2004. Essentially, this operation commissioned reports by Glasgow University forensic pathologists and an FBI profiler, which examined more than 1,000 murders of women in Scotland between 1968 and 2004. After a thorough analysis of the evidence, they concluded that six crimes bore a 'unique signature' and that 'Angus Sinclair and Gordon Hamilton were responsible for all the linked crimes.' Each of the women identified were found in the countryside, bound and gagged. They had all had gone missing after a night out at a dance hall or pub, or had at least been out drinking, and all had died extremely violently. One of these six murders was Frances Barker. We cover all these murders in the coming chapters.

Operation Trinity clearly pointed the finger at Angus Sinclair. Did Sinclair kill Frances Barker? We believe so.

Let's examine the evidence. Frances Barker was last seen outside 289 Maryhill Road; Sinclair's mum lived at number 375, just a short two minute walk away. At the time of her disappearance Sinclair was likely to have been staying at his mum's house, as at the time he and Sarah were going through one of their temporary separations.

And Frances' body was found close to Garnqueen Loch, a popular carp and perch fishing spot which Sinclair knew well. The site where the body was found is close to where Sinclair used to take his cars to be repaired. It was also an area where he had recently spoken of buying and renovating a run-down cottage, so he had been in the area very recently.

Frances had been killed in the same way as other women we believe were killed by Sinclair: abducted from the street and taken to a quiet, rural spot well off the beaten track, where they were bound with items of their clothing and raped, before being strangled.

Following Operation Trinity, Scottish police planned to charge Sinclair with the six murders investigated. But there were two issues: firstly, Strathclyde police had lost all the evidence from the unsolved Glasgow murders, including post-mortem reports and key forensic evidence. This was bad enough, but even more difficult was the fact that Thomas Young was already in prison for the murder of Frances Barker, and had been there for almost 30 years. If Thomas Young was shown to be innocent, this would lead to a whole host of other difficulties about the actions – or lack of action – taken by Scottish police forces in the preceding years.

The Crown decided to not charge Sinclair for the Glasgow murders, focussing their energy on gaining a conviction for the high-profile World's End murders.

We strongly believe that Frances Barker was killed by Angus Sinclair, not Thomas Young. Many former detectives close to the investigation at the time agree with us, and struggle to see why Sinclair wasn't charged with this murder. One of these is retired superintendent Eddie McCusker, who led the Strathclyde Police team on Operation Trinity. He said:

> Frances Barker lived on Maryhill Road, a short distance from the home of Sinclair's mother. When Sinclair bought a caravanette before he murdered Frances, he registered it at his mother's address. We found string, similar to string used in the murders, made in the form of a ligature. More women were murdered by Angus Robertson Sinclair. I have no doubt. I include Frances Barker.

He also cast doubt on the evidence that convicted Thomas Young saying, 'Given I believe that Thomas Young was innocent, then how the items got where they were found is a matter for speculation.' Uncomfortable as it is to read, what he seems to be suggesting is that the evidence used to convict Young was planted by detectives.

But there is another possible explanation for the evidence found, and that is that Young and Sinclair were working together. Sinclair certainly worked with his brother-in-law Gordon Hamilton in a number of crimes.

Although this sounds unlikely, there are a number of people who support the theory, including Mark Williams-Thomas, who in his recent television programme *The Investigator: A British Crime Story* claimed that Sinclair and Young knew each other well, and suggests they even once shared a house together in Glasgow:

> We've spoken to two people who told us Sinclair and Young lived together close to where Frances was. It's the first time a direct link's been made between them. And it supports my theory that Young didn't kill Frances alone – his accomplice was Sinclair.

We aren't convinced by this theory, and believe that Sinclair killed Frances Barker alone. Also holding this view is former detective Allan Jones, who was involved with the successful prosecution of Sinclair. He is very clear in his belief that Sinclair should have been prosecuted for all six murders identified by Operation Trinity, including the killing of Frances Barker:

> Knowing the evidence that exists, and having the ability to have my own opinion, I still believe there's very strong evidence to support the case against Angus Sinclair.

7

Lesley Perrie

The death of nineteen-year-old Lesley Perrie is a mysterious one, and is often overlooked.

Lesley was a receptionist and she disappeared in July 1977 whilst on her way to work at a taxi firm in Cambuslang, just to the south-east of Glasgow city centre.

Two weeks after Lesley disappeared her partially buried body was found in a wooded ravine on the outskirts of Hamilton, two miles south-east of where she was last seen. Lesley was in a shallow grave, with grass and barbed wire placed over her head. She was buried in a relative close area, ten miles south of where Frances Barker had recently been found.

Despite suspicion that she had been killed, the case has never officially been treated as murder by the police. Unfortunately, it is another case from Strathclyde where almost all material related to Lesley's death has been lost. Again, it is both incredibly frustrating and annoying that so much key material about many cases has been lost by Strathclyde police. We must give the benefit of the doubt to the police force in those days of manual records and assume it was just poor record and evidence keeping rather than anything more sinister, however hard that is for us to comprehend.

A Fatal Accident Inquiry into Lesley's death recorded an open verdict. This doesn't tally with officers involved in the investigation at the time, who felt that Lesley's death was highly suspicious. A number of items had been taken from her body which have never been found, including a shoe and house keys. A distinctive canvas bag she often carried, and had with her on the day she disappeared, was not found for several months.

Lesley's body was so badly decomposed that medical experts were unable to say for sure what exactly had caused her death, and they were not able to prove that criminality or violence had taken place. Interestingly, the Fatal Accident Inquiry into her death said there were signs of 'minor strangulation'. Does this suggest that somebody tried to strangle Lesley but then stopped? In lieu of a pathologist report, let's examine what physical evidence of strangulation in a badly-decomposed body there would be available to the pathologist.

Throughout the investigation of a death by suffocation or smothering, the pathologist will look for the tell-tale signs: the bloodshot eyes, the high levels of carbon dioxide in the blood, and bruising around the nose and mouth. They may even collect trace evidence such as hairs and fibres from around the nose and mouth of the deceased.

In a recently deceased body signs of suffocation-related asphyxiation such as strangulation can include bruises and fingernails scratches on the neck, and bleeding around the throat. There are non-specific physical signs used to attribute death to asphyxia. These include visceral congestion via dilation of the venous blood vessels and blood stasis, petechiae, cyanosis and fluidity of the blood. Petechiae are tiny haemorrhages.

However, in the case of a badly-decomposed body, these indicators disappear and, in some cases, all that is evident is the fracture of the U-shaped hyoid bone at the base of the tongue. Observation of hyoid fracture in skeletonized remains offers potentially valuable information on the history of the skeleton or evidence of foul play, or both. Perimortem hyoid fracture frequently indicates manual strangulation, although ligature strangulation, hanging and other forms of trauma to the neck cannot be ruled out without additional evidence. Both ante-mortem and post-mortem origins of the fractures must also be considered.

Lesley's daughter Laura was only two when her mum died and has only very vague memories of her, but she is desperate for answers. Recently she spoke to the *Herald Scotland* about her fears that her mum was another victim of Sinclair, saying:

> My mum died in suspicious circumstances right at the height of what murder experts now believe was Angus Sinclair's killing spree. I asked Strathclyde Police whether there were any links between Mum's death

and Angus Sinclair, and was devastated to be told all the files and evidence had now been lost. There were so many suspicious aspects, although the exact cause of death was never established.

My family were promised the file would always remain open in case there was ever a breakthrough. My grandmother attended the FAI every day, and evidence showed someone else was at the scene because my mother's body was deliberately covered up. Mum was terrified of insects and the family don't believe she would have gone into the woods. She was also wearing wedge espadrilles, which would have made walking in woodland very difficult.

Laura, who now has two daughters of her own, continued:

I had to grow up without my mum. Now my daughters are growing up without knowing their gran. We deserve to know the truth.

This is one murder where is it hard to suggest for certain that Sinclair killed Lesley. Circumstantial evidence suggests that Sinclair could potentially be responsible. He knew very well the area where Lesley was taken and deposited. Trophies were taken, which fits with Sinclair who often took belongings of the victim, but the method of murder is substantially different. But that doesn't necessarily mean he didn't kill Lesley; there are any number of reasons why he may have changed how he killed her.

Forensic psychologist Ian Stephen provided an explanation to the *Herald Scotland*, when he said:

Men like Angus Sinclair enjoy a ritualistic method of killing. But if the ritual is broken, perhaps because a victim dies of fright, the thrill of the kill is no longer there and that may be why a case like this may not appear to be consistent with his usual MO. If Sinclair was involved in this case, he could have panicked and simply concealed the body. The police shouldn't discard any suggestion of a link because the usual MO didn't appear to be present.

Once again, as you will read so often in this book, due to poor policing the documents relating to Lesley and any forensic evidence have been lost. This means that Sinclair, and other potential suspects, can't be positively eliminated from the investigation. When Richard Baker was Labour's Shadow Justice Secretary in Scotland he demanded an inquiry into how many other cases against serial killers such as Sinclair remain undetected because of lost files.

He told *The Times*:

> There are suspicions Angus Sinclair is one of our worst serial killers. It's unacceptable for Laura to be told files and evidence that may show whether he was involved in her mother's death have been lost. We know police reviewed the deaths of more than 1,000 females from 1968 while they were looking at Sinclair. I want to know just how many other files and evidence from those cases have been lost. Men like Angus Sinclair should be prosecuted for every crime they commit, no matter how much time has passed.

Laura added:

> Growing up without Mum was very sad. However, I was lucky to have a dad and two sets of grandparents who did everything they could for me. I owe everything to them. I was just two when Mum died but I remember her being very pretty and always happy. And I remember the terrible sadness when she died, a sadness that never left my family.

8

Anna Kenny

Just weeks after Frances Barker and Lesley Perrie were killed there was another murder of a woman in Glasgow.

Twenty-year-old Anna Kenny left the Hurdy Gurdy pub in Lister Street, in the Townhead district of Glasgow, on 6 August 1977 and was never seen alive again. Lister Street is just a short stroll from Stirling Road in Glasgow, where Sarah Sinclair's family lived. In fact, Gordon Hamilton was born in the Stirling Road flat and had left home only three years previously, when he was nineteen.

Anna had been out with her friend and work colleague Wilma Sutherland the night she disappeared. The two were enjoying a drink celebrating their first wages from their new jobs at a nearby bottling plant in Port Dundas Road. It was a normal night for the two women, and they arranged to meet on Glasgow's High Street, near the Royal Infirmary.

At the busy bar they drunk vodka and beer and chatted to a number of their friends who were in the bar at certain points of the evening. Towards the end of the night they met two young men and they enjoyed each other's company. At the end of the night, all four left together.

Whilst Wilma stopped in a doorway to kiss the man she had met, Anna and her man walked ahead. They had been kissing for a while too, but Anna made it very clear to the man that she needed to get home, so they walked together to George Square in the centre of Glasgow, where she planned to catch a bus home.

Anna never made it back to the house where she lived alone that night, and when Wilma popped round the next morning to chat about the night before, there was no sign of Anna. Wilma was incredibly worried that her friend wasn't there and called Anna's parents. They hadn't seen their daughter either, and alerted the police.

Detectives were quickly able to trace the man that Anna had left the bar with that night. It turned out that he was married with a young child, and for that reason initially denied being with Anna. Detectives were certain he wasn't telling them the whole truth and they initially considered him as a suspect. Later, when he realised he was getting into a world of trouble, he came clean about what had happened that night, despite the obvious domestic problems doing so would cause.

He explained how at 11.45pm Anna had left him to hail a taxi at the corner of Lister Street and Baird Street. Just after she had turned a corner and was no longer in view, he had heard the sound of a car braking. Naturally, he had assumed that Anna had found a taxi, or she had been picked up by someone she knew and offered a lift home. He had thought no more of it until he was contacted by the police.

Detectives could find nothing suspicious that happened on the night Anna went missing at the time she was last seen. There were no reports of anyone acting suspiciously, and there were no assaults in the area. They were determined to find out who what had happened to Anna, and one member of Strathclyde Police in particular, WPC Karen Findlay, covered a tremendous amount of ground for the investigation. She interviewed Anna's family, friends, employees at the brewery and people from the Hurdy Gurdy and other nearby venues. The WPC had no success. She even travelled south to Filey on the Yorkshire coast to talk to staff at the holiday camp where Anna and Wilma had worked for a month in June that year. She discovered that Anna had enjoyed a brief romance in Yorkshire, but there were no concrete leads from this trip. In early September WPC Findlay dressed in a black wig and reconstructed Anna's last moments to try to jog any memories for those in the area. On the same day, forty officers searched a disused railway tunnel and other buildings in the Townhead area of Glasgow. The Forth and Clyde Canal was searched too. Despite these efforts there was no sign of Anna, and frustratingly not a hint of the breakthrough in the case that was desperately needed.

It was some twenty-one months later that Anna's remains were found. Her body was found buried in two feet of soil by two shepherds in Skipness, a village on the Kintyre peninsula and a 115 mile drive from Glasgow. Detectives believed it was likely Anna had been taken by motor vehicle via the Western Isles Ferry from Glasgow, rather than the long drive around Argyll.

Two distinctive gold earrings helped detectives identify the body, as there was not much left of Anna – just her skeleton and some material which was later found to be the shirt she was wearing the night she disappeared. This shirt had been used to bind Anna's neck and ankles. The post-mortem examination showed that she had been sexually assaulted and strangled, and detectives believed she had been tortured. It was apparent that Anna's last hours must have been utterly terrifying.

Anna's family never recovered from the shock and the terrible manner of her death. Her dad Francis died in 1994, and her devastated mum Mary committed suicide two years later. Anna's brother Frank also died early, from a fatal heart attack in 2004 aged just forty-six, leaving behind two sons aged just eleven and thirteen.

Nobody has ever been convicted of the murder of Anna Kenny. Was she murdered by Angus Sinclair? We believe so. Anna was another of the murder victims that Operation Trinity indicated has been murdered by the same person. But before moving on to the evidence to support this, let's briefly examine another potential suspect in the frame – Peter Sutcliffe, the so-called 'Yorkshire Ripper'.

Sutcliffe, who lived near Bradford in Yorkshire, was a long-distance lorry driver who made regular deliveries to the General Motors plant at Newhouse, near the M8 motorway east of Glasgow, and to oil-based companies in Aberdeen. James Hobson, head of the Ripper investigations, was sent files on all the unsolved murders of women in Glasgow in 1977 by the Strathclyde Police, but he didn't see a connection. Despite this, in July 1982 two Scottish detectives travelled south to Parkhurst prison on the Isle of Wight to personally talk with Sutcliffe.

The similarities between the murders of Anna Kenny and the other victims identified by Operation Trinity suggests they were killed by the same person. Anna Kenny was strangled, which fits Sutcliffe as it was a method he used twice in 1980. Other evidence doesn't support Sutcliffe being the killer. Anna Kenny had her feet tied and bound with material from her clothing, which doesn't match the 'blitz' style normally used by Sutcliffe. Assuming Operation Trinity was correct, and all were killed by the same person, Sutcliffe can be ruled out as a suspect, because on the same day that future victim Hilda McAuley was being murdered – covered in a later chapter – Sutcliffe was killing Jean Jordan in Manchester. For these reasons, it is widely agreed that Sutcliffe didn't kill Anna Kenny.

So what is the evidence for Anna Kenny being murdered by Angus Sinclair?

Sinclair was living close to the area where Anna was taken, and the method of abducting young women who had been out for the night at the weekend fits how he targeted his victims. Like his other victims, Anna had been bound. Anna's remains were found in a very quiet area, off the beaten track that it would have been hard just to stumble upon. Sinclair was very familiar with the area where Anna's body was buried. She was found at Skipness, which is a village on the Kintyre peninsula on the road to Campbeltown. This is where Sinclair spent his honeymoon for two weeks and it is another popular fishing resort.

Mark Williams-Thomas looked at Anna's murder for his TV series *The Investigator: A British Crime Story*. He focussed on Sinclair's white caravanette, which he had purchased to travel around Scotland as a decorator, and for his fishing trips which seemed to lack any fish.

Williams-Thomas tracked down a shepherd in Skipness called Alex McCluish who believed that he had seen a van similar to Sinclair's' close to where Anna's body was found shortly after she disappeared. McCluish told him:

> Well, it was sitting with the curtains drawn and doors closed. And it was a lovely warm afternoon. And I thought, that's a bit strange. Usually folk would be out enjoying the sunshine but there was nobody to be seen at all... I remember it quite clearly. We'd been competing at a sheep dog trial on the Saturday.

Was this Sinclair?

Anna's last living relative, her 81-year-old aunt Agnes Byrne, was quoted in the *Sunday Post* before Sinclair died saying that she held him responsible:

> He killed the whole family when he killed Anna. I had two girls myself,

and I always worry about them because of what happened to Anna. You never stop worrying about them. It's still affecting people. I hope he dies roaring for what he put them through.

As an aside to Anna's disappearance – well, maybe an aside, but then again it could be central to what happened – one year later her friend Wilma, who had been with her on the night she disappeared, married Gordon Hamilton. She met him at the Hurdy Gurdy bar from where Anna had gone missing. Even stranger, if that is the right word, is that Wilma had only been to the Hurdy Gurdy twice after Anna disappeared, and it was on one of those occasions she met Hamilton sometime just before Christmas 1977. Was it just coincidence?

When it was later discovered that Hamilton had been responsible for the World's End killings, Wilma was interviewed by the police about why she had married him. She could only suggest her vulnerability and confusion after losing her friend, and she told detectives of a very unhappy and violent marriage.

Interestingly, Sinclair and Hamilton had a huge row the night before Hamilton married Wilma. Whilst it is not known what this argument was about, it was a serious disagreement, so much so that neither Sinclair nor Sarah went to the wedding the next day. Was it about the murder of Anna Kenny? Was this another murder where Hamilton played a part?

Even if Hamilton had not been directly involved with Anna's murder, he had been with Wilma when she had visited Anna's parents when her friend was still missing and after her body had been found. Hamilton had been at Anna's parent's house with Wilma on the very day that the police arrived to tell them the news that her body had been found.

Could Hamilton have supported Wilma through all of the above if he had been involved with the murder of Anna Kenny?

9

Hilda McAuley aka Miller

Matilda McAuley, or Hilda as she was normally called, was thirty-six, divorced and lived with her mum Martha and her two children – thirteen-year-old George and nine-year-old Mark – in the Maryhill district of Glasgow.

Hilda worked really hard to make ends meet. She had two cleaning jobs, one at a local engineering company and another at a hairdressers in the centre of Glasgow. As a single woman with two young children life was tough for Hilda in many ways, but she was reliable and did what it took to get by, and ensure her children had what they needed. It wasn't all about work. Hilda had very strong relationships with her mum and children, and their house was filled with fun and laughter.

But like all parents, however much she adored her children she also needed a break from routine and some time to enjoy herself as a grown-up. For Hilda, this was dancing. She loved and looked forward to Saturday nights when her mum would babysit the children so she could go out dancing with her friends.

The night of Saturday, 1 October 1977 was the same as any Saturday night for Hilda and her family. Hilda was heading out to Glasgow, to the Plaza ballroom. George and Mark shared their mum's excitement as they helped her get ready as she told them stories about the Plaza. When Hilda left the house that evening she gave them both big kisses as she wished them goodnight, and told them to behave for their Grandma. Hilda met up with her three best friends early in the evening, and as usual they stopped for a drink at two pubs on their way to the Plaza. This was almost better than the dancing, as the three caught up on all the latest gossip as well as chatting about the latest music and fashion at the time.

Hilda didn't come home that night. By the next morning, when she still hadn't arrived home Martha was frantic with worry, and when Hilda still hadn't returned on Monday she knew something was seriously wrong. This was completely out of character for Hilda, who would always let her mum know if she was running late for any reason. In those days before mobile phones and the internet, Martha phoned Hilda's friends, but they hadn't seen her either.

Martha hoped desperately that the nagging feeling in the back of her mind was incorrect and that nothing had happened to her daughter. She was very well aware that other young women in the Glasgow area had disappeared and been found murdered after a night out in the city. When the evening paper was published later that Monday her worst fears were confirmed. Shortly afterwards, a sobbing and totally distraught Martha walked into nearby Maryhill Police Station carrying a copy of that day's *Daily Record* newspaper. She had recognised her missing daughter from a detailed description of a murder victim who had been found the previous day. Detectives were appealing for help in identifying the young woman. Martha tearfully told the officers at the police station that the woman they had found was her daughter, Hilda.

Hilda's body had been found on the Sunday morning by a father and son who had been shooting rabbits in long grass, on a verge close to what is now the M8. In 1977, the spot where Hilda was found was just off the main road from Glasgow to Greenock, near a decent-sized caravan park, some twenty-five miles from where she had been abducted from outside The Plaza.

It was a quiet spot that was popular with couples dating, where they knew they wouldn't be disturbed, as the spot was set back from the busy road. It was a part of the city where a car or van could sit for days and not attract any suspicion. It wasn't a thoroughfare or a location that could just be stumbled on, so whoever had chosen this spot and dumped Hilda's body there must have known the area well. For this reason, detectives suspected that her killer was a local man who had met Hilda either just as she was leaving the Plaza or just outside the venue.

Hilda's body was semi-naked, and her hands had been tied behind her back. She had been sexually assaulted before being strangled, and had suffered dreadful head injuries. Her attacker had taken her handbag, platform shoes, coat and a hairpiece. Were these taken as a trophy to remember the murder? It would seem so, as despite detectives making a number of large public appeals for information about the items they were never recovered.

The first task for detectives was to establish Hilda's movements on the night she disappeared. After stopping at pubs on the way to the venue, Hilda and her friends had arrived at the Plaza just after 10.00pm. This was about the time they always arrived, when they knew that the dancing would be in full swing and the hall packed. After leaving their coats in the cloakroom, they headed downstairs to the dancefloor where, as usual, they headed off in their different directions to chat to people they knew and to dance. This was perfectly normal for them and many of the other groups who came together to the Plaza. In the time Hilda was there that night, it seemed from witnesses who had seen her that she had spent most of the time alone. But nobody had seen anything of concern happen in the Plaza that evening, and there had been no reports of anyone suspicious present that night. In fact, all of those interviewed said it was just another busy, but standard Saturday night, just like any other.

Hilda was last definitely seen alive in the early hours of Sunday morning as she headed upstairs to the main foyer from the dance floor at 12.35am. She picked up her jacket from the cloakroom, but from there the trail went cold. Nobody saw her leave the venue, and there was no positive sighting of her outside the Plaza. Detectives did discover that, with money being tight, Hilda often tried to get a lift home from one of the men she had met at the Plaza, and on many occasions she had accepted lifts from total strangers. But detectives couldn't find anyone who recalled seeing Hilda with a man outside the venue on this particular evening. This isn't surprising, as 12.35am was the time when most of the revellers were leaving the venue to catch the last buses so it would have been busy outside, and there was nothing distinctive about Hilda that evening that it would have stood out and be easily remembered.

There had been close to a thousand people at the Plaza that evening, but despite repeated appeals and detectives visiting the ballroom to quiz dancers on many occasions, still over three hundred of the men present that evening failed to come forward. And of those people they did talk to, many denied being there on the night that Hilda disappeared as they didn't want their wives or husbands to know they had been there.

It was tricky for detectives. Of the thousand or so people who were at the Plaza that night, between two hundred and fifty and three hundred failed to answer police appeals. All of these were men. Three female detectives from Paisley Police HQ were even sent undercover to dance venues in Glasgow to try a different avenue to get people to talk who wouldn't feel confident sharing details in a formal interview. Detective Constables Sandra Harris, Nancy Robertson and Caroline Sneddon spent evenings dancing with a number of men, asking if they were regulars and trying to find out any snippets of information which could lead them to the person who killed Hilda.

Although the murder wasn't officially being linked publicly with the other sexually-motivated murders in Glasgow, internally detectives were very aware of the pressure to solve this crime quickly. The investigation into Hilda's murder was a massive undertaking, with over 1,200 people interviewed. But, despite all this work, the only other substantial lead that was uncovered was a black taxi had been seen twice in the Langbank area, close to where Hilda was found. The driver was never identified to be eliminated from the investigation.

So who killed Hilda? One person who was secretly quizzed again was Peter Sutcliffe, although he was cleared of any involvement after DNA samples ruled him out as a suspect.

We believe that Hilda McAuley was another victim of Angus Sinclair.

Unfortunately, as we have already heard with other murders at the time, all the forensic evidence retrieved from the scene has been lost or destroyed, including the material used to bind Hilda and the gag. Also lost are most of the documents relating to the investigation, including the official post-mortem report.

When Hilda's murder was looked at again as part of Operation Trinity, detectives searched everywhere where this material may have been stored, even in the back of dusty filing cabinets that hadn't been used for years, without success.

An interesting aside here is that the investigation in 2004 did reveal that Sinclair sold his caravanette in a private deal shortly after the World's End murders, which we discuss in the next chapter. He replaced the caravanette with a Toyota Carina. He only kept this a matter of months, but rather than scrap or sell the car he dumped the car in a water-filled quarry in Glenboig. This quarry is very close to where the body of Frances Barker was found.

When this car was recovered by detectives thirty years later, it produced some interesting results. The car contained five pairs of handcuffs and some children's coats. Had the car been used to abduct someone, and the coats trophies kept by Sinclair? Or had he dumped the car before he had been given the chance to use the items kept in the car? Unfortunately, after being underwater for thirty years it was impossible to obtain any samples of DNA so the evidence couldn't be put in front of a jury, but children's coats and handcuffs are certainly not what you would expect to find in family cars.

Another item found in the car relevant to Hilda's murder was string. Although the string used to bind Hilda had been lost, some of the remaining documents related to it, including a report from the University of Strathclyde, survived. In a piece of good old-fashioned detective work, the original investigation had tracked down the unique sting used to a company in the south of Ireland. A Glasgow company, Henry Winning & Co., sold this string in Scotland from their business based in Caroline Street, to the west of Glasgow, in an area both Sinclair and Hamilton knew well. But although a promising line of enquiry, when detectives found out just how much string was sold by Winnings, it was impossible to trace where all the balls of string sold had ended up. But in the later investigation, when detectives were clearer that they were looking for links to Sinclair and Hamilton, neither of whom were a suspect in the original investigation, the boss of the company Hamilton worked for, A.M. Robb Ltd, was approached. Now it started to get interesting. He confirmed that his company bought this string from Winnings. Unfortunately this line of investigation couldn't progress any further, but it just increases the frustration at the original forensic material being lost. If this wasn't the case we could say for certain whether or not Sinclair was the man who killed Hilda. Even without this, we suggest that this killing has all the hallmarks of Sinclair. Although he was never a suspect in the original investigation, looking at the murder with the information we know now he has to be a very strong suspect.

Let's review some of the evidence. Hilda's body was found near to the West Ferry caravan park in Langbank. This was a popular fishing location just sixteen miles from Glasgow – exactly the sort of place Sinclair would have visited in his caravanette at a time when he was regularly going away for long weekends fishing or painting & decorating. Like other murders carried out by him, the spot where Hilda's body was dumped was a quiet, secluded area.

Even without the fishing, Sinclair knew this part of Glasgow incredibly well. His sister Connie didn't live very far away, and an ex-girlfriend would later tell police that Sinclair would often drive her to this part of the city on dates. At the time of Hilda's death, Sinclair had been splitting his time between his mum's house in Maryhill and another flat in nearby Govanhill, which was just six hundred yards from where Hilda had last been seen that evening.

Sinclair knew the general location at Langbank very well, as an acquaintance later told detectives how he and Sinclair used to go to that area to test firearms they planned to use in future crimes. When later interviewed by detectives, although this criminal acquaintance of Sinclair's couldn't provide the specific details of where they used to test the guns, he did recall that it was a bit of a dumping ground for burnt-out stolen cars. The area adjacent to where Hilda was found had a number of dumped cars, strongly suggesting that it is exactly the place being referred to.

In addition, Hilda was taken at the weekend close to midnight and was expertly bound, gagged, sexually assaulted and then strangled.

A recent investigation by ex-detective Mark Williams-Thomas for *The Investigator: A British Crime Story* covered the murder of Hilda McAuley. This involved the presenter visiting the Channel Islands to interview a witness who had claimed to see a man near the site where Hilda was found on the day she was found. This witness told him: 'It was in a lay-by. I was in a car. I happen to see a man walk up by the lane past me.' When shown a picture of Angus Sinclair as he looked at the time, this witness – who said they had never heard of Angus Sinclair before – responded by saying, 'Yes, that's him.' Asked if there was anything in particular that stood out about the man, she said simply: 'His eyes.'

Hilda's mum Martha died in the summer of 2004. At the time, she knew that her daughter's death was being re-investigated as part of Operation Trinity. But she died not knowing for sure who had killed her daughter – another victim of Sinclair who was never able to gain closure due to his refusal to confess to his crimes.

Although this death caused fear and outrage across Glasgow and nationwide, these feelings were amplified just two weeks later when 17-year-old friends Helen Scott and Christine Eadie were found strangled on the east coast of Scotland, having last been seen leaving the World's End pub in Edinburgh the night before.

10

Christine Eadie and Helen Scott: The World's End Murders

October 1977 was the month when undertakers took strike action in London. The papers were full of the news that missing 26-year-old sex worker Jean Jordan had been found dead in Chorlton, Manchester, nine days after she was last seen alive. Police suspected that the 'Yorkshire Ripper' may have killed her in his first suspected crime outside Yorkshire. On 15 October actor David Soul, of *Starsky and Hutch* fame, was top of the UK music charts with 'Silver Lady', and music charts were dominated by Elvis songs following his death two months earlier.

Two young women who were into all the latest music were Helen Scott and Christine Eadie, and they would spend hours together listening to all sorts of music, in particular Donny Osmond and David Cassidy. They were both aged seventeen in October 1977, and lived in Edinburgh. They had known each other since their first days at Edinburgh's Firrhill High School in the Oxgangs area of the city. This 1960s building housed around a thousand pupils from the local area, and both Helen and Christine studied at this school until they left at fifteen.

Five months younger than Helen, Christine was brought up by her Grandma. It was a loving and secure childhood, and Christine was a bright, popular and inquisitive child. After starting work, she moved out of her Grandma's home to a flat which she shared with another friend, Toni Wale. Christine was fiercely independent, outgoing and great company. She kept a regular diary recording all the things that had happened to her so far in her life and wrote about her hopes and dreams for the future, just like so many other teenagers.

After school, Christine spent some time in a junior position for the Education Department at Edinburgh council before moving to a company of surveyors, where she worked as a typist. Christine was worldly-wise beyond her years. At school, one of her best friends was the shyer and quieter Helen Scott. Now away from school, the young women continued to enjoy each other's company and along with others in their friendship group, mainly from school, they enjoyed exploring all the nightlife offered by a city like Edinburgh. Although by law they were too young to drink and shouldn't have been allowed into licensed premises, like so many other teenagers before them and since they managed to do so regularly.

Helen Scott lived with her mum Margaret, dad Morain, two older half-sisters and a younger brother. As a little girl Margaret had moved the fifty or so miles south from Edinburgh to Coldstream and enjoyed an idyllic childhood in the rural community by the River Tweed.

Margaret met and married Morain Scott, and they welcomed their daughter Helen a year later, followed by her brother Kevin. By now the family had moved to Penicuik, south of Edinburgh in the commuter zone, before a further move for the family to Swan Spring Avenue in the Comiston district of Edinburgh, when Morain started a job as an engineer for British Telecom.

Helen's family were very close, and she enjoyed a happy and secure childhood. At school, she was initially a quiet pupil, but her confidence grew as she got older and by the time she left at fifteen she was popular, with a wide circle of friends. Like most young women in Edinburgh at the time, when Helen left school she was into her music, clothes and films. As well as Christine Eadie, Helen had made other close friends at school, and as a group they tended to socialise at the same pubs and cinemas in the city. Even if they went out in smaller groups, they would tend to bump into each other at the same places.

In October 1977 Helen had just started a new job at a kilt shop in Edinburgh's busiest and most famous thoroughfare, Princes Street. Although she enjoyed being in a busy, bustling environment at the centre of the city, and loved meeting and helping customers, she didn't think that retail was the long-term career she wished to pursue, instead being increasingly certain that she wanted to spend her working life in childcare. Helen had babysat for her sister's two children and really enjoyed it. Helen was so good with them that her sister always went to her sister first when she needed help with the children. To help pursue a career in childcare, Helen had looked into what she needed to do and had just begun night classes in Higher English and Maths.

Saturday night was always an exciting time for Helen, Christine and their friends. The local bar they favoured was on Morrison Street in the city centre, The Spider's Web, but the group tended to move from pub to pub during the evening, which is easy to do in a city such as Edinburgh which has a compact city centre and no shortage of pubs and bars.

On the night of 15 October 1977, a fortnight after the murder of Hilda McAuley, Helen was looking forward to a night out. She went straight from work where she met a friend from school, Jacqueline Inglis, at Jenners, the large department store on Princes Street. From there they walked to the Mount Royal Hotel a bit further down the street, between Edinburgh old and new towns. After one drink there they crossed Waverley Bridge and carried on up to the Royal Mile to the Wee Windaes pub. It was here that they had arranged to meet Christine and her flatmate Toni at 8.00pm. Toni was slightly older than the others, but she was always good fun and as a group all got on well. The four made their way along the Royal Mile, stopping for drinks at several pubs, where they saw a number of people that they knew.

As the evening wore on there were a couple of incidents. Helen suffered a small nosebleed in the toilets of one of the pubs, which freaked out Toni as she was very squeamish, and a few seconds later she raced out of the pub saying she couldn't tolerate the sight of blood. A little later Helen and Christine had a minor disagreement, with Helen possibly a little tipsy and in a particularly light-hearted mood. Christine got a little annoyed and told her to stop acting in that way. These minor events were all standard stuff for young people on a night out, especially with alcohol involved, and there was nothing about this evening that was exceptional in any way.

At 10.00pm the group arrived at what they planned to be the last stop on their Saturday night out, the World's End pub.

The pub is still a popular one in Edinburgh, and while the name might seem an unusual one there is a very good explanation. At the conclusion of the 1513 Battle of Flodden between England and Scotland, during which James IV of Scotland was killed, the residents of Edinburgh's Old Town built a wall for protection. The exterior wall of the pub is part of the ancient Flodden wall. The gates to the city were situated just outside the bar, and brass cobbles in the road show exactly where they were. Outside the walls, the inhabitants of the Old Town considered they weren't in their world any longer and had reached the world's end, hence the name of the pub.

The World's End was always a busy pub, and when Helen, Christine and their friends got there it was packed. Just like you might find it today late on a Saturday night, the traditional bar packed with more than two hundred and fifty people; locals, students, tourists and football fans alike all crammed in under the wooden rafters.

Helen and Christine ordered a whisky each and found a small space just near the payphone. They had another minor disagreement soon after when Helen spoke on the payphone to a boy she knew in Coldstream, from where she knew a lot of people due to her mum's association with the area. After the call, Helen didn't like it when Christine made a throwaway comment about it being strange that the boy had to take a call in a public phone box, and not in his home. For a few moments Helen walked out of the pub, but was persuaded to return and all was well again. Just a normal night for friends.

Soon after this a group left and Helen and Christine managed to take their table. They were joined by others and the friends found themselves sitting as part a large group of young men and women, who all knew each other to varying degrees, and met up most weekends. Like good friends always do, Helen and Christine had minor squabbles but made up almost instantly, and the group were having a fun time.

At one stage Jacquie and Toni went to the toilet together, and when they came back to the bar two young men had joined Helen and Christine. One was sitting at the table with another standing, and they seemed to be in a deep, intense conversation. This was once again standard for a Saturday night as the group often got chatting to new people, especially later on in the evening after a few drinks, and there was nothing about the two men which stood out.

Jacquie and Toni headed off to chat with other friends and the group were invited to a house party. Jacquie headed back to Christine and Helen to see if they and the two men they were with wanted to join them. Helen was deep in conversation and didn't respond, but Christine indicated to her friend that she was happy where she was and didn't fancy a party. Jacquie and Toni got ready to go, but just before she left Jacquie glanced at her two friends and later recalled seeing one of the men buying Helen and Christine a drink. With that, they were out the door of the pub and into the cold, foggy Edinburgh evening on their way to the party. How could they ever have suspected that they would never see their friends again?

Helen's parents were instantly worried when she didn't come home soon after closing time at the pub – back then 11.00pm. Between 11.30pm and midnight the phone rang at their home, but it stopped ringing before they could reach it. They wondered if this had been Helen – was there something wrong? Morain and Margaret couldn't sleep and sat up all night, waiting for Helen to come through the front door.

It was at 10.30am the next morning that Morian called Jacquie's house to see if Helen had stayed there the night before. Jacquie confirmed that she hadn't and was immediately concerned, as Helen and Christine hadn't been at the party with the rest of the group. She headed over to Christine's flat, hoping that the pair of friends would be there, but Christine's flatmate Toni said that they weren't there. Jacquie called Morian to tell him that she didn't know where Helen was, and now very worried she called a number of their other friends to see if anyone had seen Helen and Christine, but with no success. The group agreed to meet at a pub on the High Street shortly, where they were joined by Helen's parents, who were trying to reassure themselves that there must be a simple explanation. As the minutes passed and there was still no news, they reported Helen missing at Edinburgh's south side police station.

After the cold foggy evening before, it was a lovely, sunny day on the east coast of Scotland. Edinburgh couple Derek and Ruth Taylor decided to take a drive east to the East Lothian coast for a picnic and walk. It is a beautiful part of southern Scotland, popular with walkers, bird watchers and kite-flyers, with a backdrop of forest and cliffs.

The tide recedes a long way, leaving a beautiful expanse of sand and shingle. On a day like this the views were stunning, looking towards the waterfront of Edinburgh ten miles to the west. The couple enjoyed a picnic lunch at the small village of Longniddry before taking a walk on the beach, south towards the Georgian mansion Gosford House, home to the 13th Earl of Wemyss and March. It was about 2.00pm as they approached the grounds of the house, and looking seaward, Derek thought he saw a dummy lying on the beach.

Walking closer to get a better look, to his horror he realised he was in fact looking at the body of a young woman. He had discovered the body of Christine Eadie. She was lying at the high water mark, on her back, and she was completely naked. Christine's legs were outstretched and slightly apart. There was a gag in her mouth, which was later confirmed to be underwear, which was held in place by a bra tied round her head. Part of a pair of tights formed a ligature round her neck, and her hands were tied behind her back, also by part of a pair of tights.

Shocked to his core, Derek raced to the lodge at Gosford House where he called the police. Christine hadn't been reported missing yet, so detectives desperately began trying to find out the identity of the dead woman. Shortly afterwards, Helen was reported missing in Edinburgh, and having found one body already, local detectives had a sense of dread about what was going to happen next.

About four miles inland from Gosford, on a pretty country road leading towards the small town of Haddington, off the beaten track, is Coates Farm. That evening, local gardener John Mackenzie followed his normal routine of taking his dog for a walk in the area around the farmland. It was around 6.00pm when he saw it. Like Derek Taylor, when he first spotted the object John thought it was a dummy. As he looked more closely, he too realised that what he was looking at was the lifeless body of a young woman. He had found the body of Helen Scott. She was lying face down with her hands tied behind her back. She was naked from the waist down and her pants were lying, rolled up, to the left of her head. A pair of tights and a belt had been used to create a ligature around her neck. Helen wasn't wearing any footwear. She was still wearing her new black coat, which she had only bought that week.

John ran to his house, jumped in the car and headed to Haddington Police Station to report the body. The two bodies were approximately four miles apart, and fourteen miles from the World's End pub.

The news that two bodies had been found was released to the media and the newsflash about the discovery interrupted TV and radio programmes.

Later that afternoon, back home after reporting Helen and Christine missing, Jacquie Inglis's heart sunk when she heard the newsflash on the radio, reporting how the bodies of two young women had been found near the coast at East Lothian. Jacquie didn't want to believe what she was hearing, but deep down she knew the identities of the two bodies. She took a deep breath and made the call to the police to tell them her fears, and a detective was at her house shortly afterwards taking a statement about the events of the night before. The detective was able to tell Jacquie the news she had been dreading: although the identity of the bodies was subject to formal identification, the two women found were indeed her friends, Helen Scott and Christine Eadie.

At the post-mortem Christine was found to have congestion and haemorrhages in her eyes, which was indicative of strangulation, and she had an area of pallor consistent with a strap or use of a gag of some sort across her mouth. There was bruising on her chin consistent with being struck with a blunt instrument, or striking something blunt. There were a number of marks and abrasions on her neck which were consistent with strangulation with a ligature, while the abrasions were likely to be from fingernails. It was suggested that this could indicate an attempt to prevent the strangulation taking place, and an external injury found on Christine's lip could be from trying to stop the ligature. There were internal mouth injuries, considered likely to have been caused by something being forced into her mouth. Well-defined ligature marks were present on both of her wrists, which were consistent with her hands being tied together. There was a recent bruise over the front of both upper thighs and an abrasion over the lower front of the right knee which were consistent with fingers or a thumb being used to push her thighs apart.

The cause of Christine Eadie's death was certified as asphyxia, due to strangulation with a ligature and by the gagging of her mouth.

When Helen was examined she was found to have a recent black eye on the left side and a bruise to the outer side of that eye. It was thought this was caused by a blunt object, such as a fist. There were injuries to both the front of her ear and behind it, which was thought likely have been made by the sole and heel of a shoe. In her last moments alive Helen had been stamped on by her killer. There were force marks on Helen's neck which were consistent with manual strangulation. An injury to the left of her chin was consistent with ligature strangulation.

There were a number of abrasions on Helen's arms, which indicated general violence towards her. There was bleeding in the vaginal area, with a tear and bruising to the left part of the hymen. This indicated penetration of some sort, which could have been penile.

The cause of Helen Scott's death was certified as asphyxia consequential upon strangulation.

Crucially, although the DNA science we take for granted today to solve so much crime wasn't available at the time, the forensic scientists, led by Lester Knibb, were incredibly careful with all the potential forensic evidence taken from the scene. They hoped that one day advances in forensic technology would help solve the crime. Where the bodies were found, they carefully removed samples from the sites, along with the clothing worn by Christine and Helen and the ligatures that were used to bind them, with all the knots in place. They also retained the swabs from the post-mortem, desperately hoping all this carefully preserved material would be significant at some stage in the future.

Edinburgh was a city in shock at news of the murders. Parents wouldn't let their children go out, and the number of people – especially women – visiting pubs in the city plummeted. The innocent faces of Helen and Christie were on the front pages of every newspaper and on each news bulletin. Emotions were running very high. Detectives now had the task of working out just who killed these two young women who had everything to live for.

The investigation was run by Detective Superintendent Macpherson, with Detective Chief Inspector Bert Darling responsible for the investigation in East Lothian and Detective Chief Inspector Andrew Suddon taking responsibility for the investigation in Edinburgh.

In East Lothian, of particular interest was the caravan site at Port Seton just up the coast from where the bodies were found towards Edinburgh. This was a popular spot, and although closed at the time of the murders holidaymakers there were likely to have a good understanding of the area where the bodies were found. Hundreds of holiday chalets and caravans had to be checked out. The names of several well-known gangsters were considered by this team as potential killers. One who immediately sparked interest was Arthur Thompson junior, the son of Arthur 'The Godfather' Thompson, a major gangland figure in Glasgow, who had recently been to Seton where one of his cousins had a caravan at the time. Christine's body was found on the nearby beach, and Thompson was known to haunt Edinburgh pubs to pick up young women from city centre pubs. But officers questioning Thompson found he had a rock-solid alibi, and he was eliminated from the investigation.

The other key focus was to see if anybody had witnessed the bodies being dumped, but detectives drew a blank with this line of enquiry. It seemed that there were no witnesses as the killer had chosen the deposit sites carefully. Helen's body was left in a very quiet spot where, late on an October evening, it would be very unlikely that there were other vehicles in the area. Although Christine's body was left close to the main coast road, it was placed at the mid-point of the road between two villages, with very good lines of sight in both directions. In the dark, the headlights of an approaching car would have given the killer plenty of warning to retreat into the shadows.

In Edinburgh, attention focused on the group of friends who had been out with Christine and Helen that night, but they were all quickly discounted as suspects. Locals with a criminal record, particularly with a conviction for rape and sexual assault, were interviewed, but all appeared to have a strong alibi clearing them of the killings. Information was flooding into the incident rooms about potential suspects, and each piece of information had to be fully investigated and the person eliminated. Over thirty anonymous letters suggesting possible suspects had to be investigated. The investigation was a huge undertaking, and required a large number of officers.

One of the first tasks in the investigation was establishing who was in the World's End that evening and whether they had seen anything.

In a busy central pub in a large city, this is much easier today with CCTV, phone records and credit card information from the till. Today, there is every chance that the vehicle used to take Helen and Christine away would also be traced via surveillance cameras. But in 1977 this was tricky to say the very least; a real challenge involving cross-referencing the large number of witness statements from people who had been in the pub at various stages of the evening. It was remarkable that 150 of those who had been in the pub that evening were actually traced.

At the time, policing was a little different in the centre of Edinburgh to today, and beat constables were assigned to certain areas. In the High Street that night were Police Constables George Owenson and John Rafferty. As usual on a busy weekend evening, they were on hand to keep an eye on the people spilling out of the pubs at around 11.20pm – remember, back then all pubs called last orders at 11:00pm and there was no staggered release of people from venues like today.

PC Rafferty thought nothing of the two young women he had seen emerge from the World's End pub talking about how they were going to get home. He vaguely recalled seeing them being offered a lift by a young man, whilst another man hovered nearby. Was this Helen and Christine? Although it cannot be said for certain, it certainly seems likely. One of the two women were happy to accept the lift, and her seemingly more reluctant friend joined her. The two women were last seen with the two men as they headed down St Mary's Street, where the vehicle belonging to one of the men was presumably parked. Later, despite looking at numerous photos, PC Rafferty still couldn't confirm for certain that the two women he had seen were Helen and Christine, as what they were doing was so unremarkable for a busy Saturday night, he had not made a mental image of them. Likewise, PC Rafferty remembered nothing distinguishing about the two men, except maybe that one of them had more of a country accent.

Although the focus was on the two men who had been speaking to Christine and Helen and suspected to be the same two men offering them a lift at closing time, it wasn't necessarily the case that they were responsible for the murders. They had been seen by a lot of people in the busy pub, and although many differing descriptions were given, a common theme is that they had short hair and looked smart. In the

1970s moustaches and long hair were more common, so the initial thinking was that these two men with their clean-cut looks could have been connected to the military garrison at Edinburgh Castle. At the time it was an operational army base, and many of those based there would head out to the city centre pubs at the weekend. Suspicion also fell on soldiers from Redford Barracks and Dreghorn Camp. Every one of Scotland's ten thousand military personnel was interviewed. But this was a blind alley, as the men they were looking for were not employed by the armed forces.

Another line of inquiry at the time focussed on the clothes one of the men was wearing. He had been sporting unusual high-waisted trousers with a row of buttons. Despite a number of detectives gaining a crash course in the fashion of the day in Scotland and beyond, this line of inquiry did not produce any positive results.

Speculation that the killings had been the work of two men and not just one was heightened when it was revealed that the type of knots used to tie the young women's hands behind their backs were of different types. But there were still no concrete leads as to who these men were. Once again, Angus Sinclair was not a suspect in the investigation and he wasn't interviewed.

In May 1978 Lothian and Borders Police announced that they were scaling down the investigation. The inquiry had no solid leads despite their most talented officers working on the case, but this a time when paper, pen and filing cabinet were the tools of the trade. Close to 150,000 interviews took place, which resulted in over 13,000 statements on over 24,000 sheets of paper, producing a shortlist of 500 potential suspects.

Morale among detectives in the inquiry was flagging, as frustration became the dominant feeling. Was there something they had missed? Or worse, was one of the many suspects they had interviewed and eliminated in reality the killer. The decision was taken by senior officers at the Lothian and Borders Force to stop the investigation until that time that any new evidence came to light. This meant that huge amounts of material were stored in cardboard boxes on the top floor of the Fettes HQ. Among this material were the forensic samples so carefully taken by Lester Knibb and his team.

Police responsibility for the investigation moved to the East and

Midlothian Division, as this is where the two bodies had been found. Although the case was no longer active, there were occasionally new leads that reached detectives which needed to be investigated.

The next major development was in 1988. A prisoner at Edinburgh's Saughton prison contacted detectives to say that a fellow inmate had one night confessed to the murders and, moreover, he was able to demonstrate very specific knowledge of how the bodies were left. This felt highly important, as this information hadn't been released to the general public. By this time significant strides had been made with DNA technology and, much to their frustration, detectives were able to categorically rule out this new suspect as the murderer.

In 1992 there was another lead. This time a man claimed that on the night of the killings he had been joyriding in a stolen car when he picked up a convicted rapist, John McGranaghan. Detectives were a little sceptical as fifteen years had passed, and queried why this hadn't been reported earlier. But as is often seen in appeals for information on cold cases things change, including loyalties. Maybe there had been a falling out. As detectives investigated the lead, they discovered that the brother of McGranaghan, Charlie, had been murdered and the rumour was that he was killed to silence him. This sounded promising. Could this have been because he knew too much about the World's End killings? It was an intriguing possibility. But once more hopes were soon deflated. DNA showed that John McGranaghan was definitely not the killer of Helen and Christine. As an aside, in 1991, after spending a long eleven years in prison, McGranaghan's convictions for three separate counts of rape were quashed.

In 1997, with further advances in DNA, forensic scientists were able to gain a much better, more complete DNA profile from Helen Scott's coat. With this, detectives were now ready to go through all the files. This information was transferred to the HOLMES database, which had finally made the management of all this data significantly easier. All the suspects could now be tested and categorically eliminated if their DNA wasn't a match. Detectives were on the one hand hopeful that one of their suspects was responsible, but also, like all detectives, another part of them hoped that the killer had not been missed the first time around.

The first set of people tested were those who had been in the

World's End pub after 10.00pm on the night that Christine and Helen went missing, and with no matches they were quickly eliminated as suspects. Other potential suspects who were potentially of interest were also eliminated. Detectives felt that they were getting close to finding the killers of Christine and Helen, but they still needed a crucial breakthrough. They were hopeful that the rapid advances being made in DNA technology would provide it.

Coincidentally, the World's End murders were committed the weekend before Thomas Ross Young was due to face court on the Monday for the murder of Frances Barker. It has been suggested that Sinclair was angry that another man was facing trial for a murder that he himself had committed as he wanted to be seen as a criminal genius who had got away with murder – again. Surely this wasn't really the reason why Helen and Christine were targeted on this specific weekend?

11

Agnes Cooney

Agnes Cooney was born on 5 May 1954 to mum Catherine (née Plunkett) and dad Francis, a Security Officer in Glasgow.

When in 1971 tragedy hit the family with Agnes's mum and Grandma both dying, Agnes immediately took over the care of her five younger sisters and brothers. This is the sort of person that Agnes was: caring, responsible and incredibly mature for someone so young, with a real sense of responsibility.

It is perhaps not surprising from what we know of her personality that Agnes had always dreamed of working as a nurse, but with her extra family responsibilities she knew this wouldn't be possible until her brothers and sisters were older and more self-sufficient. Instead, knowing it wasn't for the long-term, Agnes took a job at a Glasgow department store, Bremner's, to bring in more money to the family. When the time came that she felt her siblings could be left without her full-time care, Agnes enrolled in nursing training at a hospital in Mauchline in Ayrshire. Agnes stayed in nursing accommodation nearby and she thrived in this environment. As well as thoroughly enjoying the nursing training, Agnes loved spending time with the other nurses, and although she was naturally shy and reserved, this period of her life saw her really develop socially. She was even more certain that caring for others through nursing was how she wanted to spend her life.

By December 1977, 23-year-old Agnes was single and lived in Coatbridge, about nine miles east of Glasgow city centre. She was a qualified children's nurse who had taken a responsible job as a house parent at a children's home in Bellshill, Lanarkshire.

On 2 December Agnes wasn't at work, but staying at an aunt's home who was old and needed support. It was typical of Agnes to live-in at her aunt's house to be able to provide the comprehensive support that she needed.

With work, and the extra caring responsibilities around her aunt, Agnes hadn't been out for weeks, and so on Friday, 2 December 1977 she was really looking forward to going to watch an Irish band play with her friend and fellow nurse Gina Barclay. The two had met during nursing training and become really good friends, and enjoyed spending time together. They had lots in common, and as well as chatting about nursing, shared an interest in music. They were such good friends by this time that they were planning to rent a flat together. During the day of Friday, 2 December, the two women viewed a prospective flat together.

Gina's partner played in an Irish band, and the two women planned to see them play later that evening at Glasgow's Clada Social Club, in Westmoreland Street, Govanhill on the south side of the City, not too far from the Plaza Ballroom where Hilda McAuley had spent her last evening. Gina's partner joined her and Agnes for dinner in the centre of Glasgow, before the three headed off to the club where the band was due to play.

Once they arrived at the Clada Club Agnes and Gina waited outside for the band to arrive, and then helped them unload their equipment into the hall. Once the band were all set up and ready to play, excitedly the two women headed into the audience to watch the show. It was a fun night with great music, and once the band had finished playing at just after eleven o'clock Agnes and Gina again headed backstage to help the band take their equipment apart and load it back into their van. This job usually took just under an hour. Once they were done, Gina and the band noticed that Agnes wasn't around, and they were a little concerned that she was on her own in a part of Glasgow with which she wasn't familiar. They looked around the club for her, but staff working at the venue told them that Agnes had said goodnight to them as she was leaving. They reassured them that she seemed perfectly happy as she headed outside. Gina and some of the band members looked around outside to see if they could see her, but she didn't seem to be there. Gina headed down the road a little to see if Agnes was at a nearby bus stop, but once again there was no sign of her. After a little more searching, they assumed that she must have got a lift and they returned to their van and headed home.

Agnes didn't make it to her aunt's house that night. When she didn't arrive at work the next day her colleagues were immediately concerned, as the ultra-reliable Agnes would never just not turn up to work. It was totally out of character for Agnes. Her work colleagues phoned her family, who in turn called other family members and friends to see if anyone knew where Agnes was. But nobody had seen her. It had been seven weeks since the World's End murders which had rocked Scotland and Agnes' family remained hopeful, but even at this very early stage they feared the worst. They reported her as missing on the afternoon of Saturday, 3 December.

It was the next day, at 9.00am, that the terribly mutilated body of Agnes was found by a farmer at Shields Farm, near Caldercruix, a small village in Lanarkshire, around fifteen miles east of the Clada Social Club where she was last seen.

Caldercruix is a semi-rural village in North Lanarkshire, Scotland. The nearest major town is Airdrie, four miles to the west, with Glasgow some twenty miles east. The village is situated by the North Calder Water, which was dammed in the late eighteenth century to create Hillend Loch, used recreationally by angler and sailors. Another ideal fishing spot for Angus Sinclair.

A farmer was out on his tractor that morning on a quiet, relatively unused road that ran past his fields, when out of the corner of his eye he thought he saw something just inside one of the fields. At first he thought it was just rags, but on closer inspection he saw what appeared to be a human body laying lifeless in front of him. The farmer immediately drove to his neighbour's home to report what he had just seen, and the two returned to the scene. This time they walked right up to the object, and this time they could clearly see that they had found the body of a young woman and they called the police.

When detectives arrived at the scene they found that Agnes was fully-clothed, with her hands tied behind her back. Her right sock had been used as a gag, held in place by a length of electrical flex. The cause of death was established as a stab wound to the neck, and

Agnes had been stabbed in total twenty-six times. Detectives believed that she may have been held against her will for up to twenty-four hours or more, possibly in a van or empty house, before she was taken to the farm where she was killed on either the Saturday night or early on the Sunday morning. If she had been there any earlier, the farmer would have either seen the vehicle taking her to the site, or found her body. Although there was no evidence at the time that Agnes had been sexually assaulted, she was a powerful woman and detectives later suspected that Sinclair was surprised at just how much she had fought back and so had killed her sooner than planned to end the struggle.

Detectives urgently had to find just what had happened to Agnes after she had left the club. Had she left with someone she met inside, or got a lift or hailed a cab outside the venue? At this time taxis were expensive and not easy to find, so it was common for some young people to hitch a lift home following a night out. Is this what Agnes had chosen to do that evening?

Detectives appealed for information, describing the clothing she was wearing when last seen: a blue cagoule, blue cords and fawn boots. They were particularly interested in information they had been given about two men who were seen in separate vehicles outside the Clada Social Club at about the time Agnes left the club. One man had been in a Ford Cortina and the other in a white van. Neither were ever traced. Could the white van have been Sinclair's white Toyota campervan? In the dark it would pass as a van, before closer inspection. It looks like a vital clue in not identifying the van was missed.

There were a number of sightings of someone who looked like Agnes walking alone to the city centre at about the time she left the club. The descriptions of the clothing worn matched what Agnes was wearing that evening, so this had to be her. It seemed that she had left the club on her own and was walking to the city centre alone as she made her plans to head back to her aunt's house.

The next sightings of Agnes were near the motorway, close to the Castle Street slip road to the M8, where she had been seen trying to hitch a lift. A number of people came forward to say they had seen someone who appeared to be Agnes up to 2.00am, but it is unclear just how many sightings were actually of her.

If you are familiar with Glasgow, you will know it is quite unusual for a big city in that the M8 motorway passes straight through the centre. Either side of the busy road there are patches of wasteland, and a number of underpasses before houses are reached. If Agnes had been here late on that cold December night, with traffic thundering past, it would have been a frightening place for her to be on her own. Sensible as she was, Agnes would still have imagined all sorts of horrors in the shadows. A friendly man with a local accent in a white van stopping to offer a lift home at the time probably felt like a relief. Sadly, it probably turned into her worst nightmare very soon afterwards.

Immediately after details of the murder were released to the press, journalists were understandably speculating about links between the recent unsolved murders in Glasgow, especially Hilda McAuley, Anna Kenny and Helen Kane, and of course, the World's End killings, which still dominated the news. But detectives at this time, again, without the knowledge we now have about Sinclair, believed it was more likely that Agnes was taken or abducted by the driver of either a car or lorry that had spotted her near the M8. A passing lorry driver would naturally be the leading line of enquiry for a police force investigating the murder of a young woman who was last seen hitching a life home by the side of the motorway.

Police immediately suspected that the murders of Hilda McAuley and Agnes Cooney were linked, and publicly talked of the connection within two weeks of Agnes being murdered. Detective Chief Inspector John McDougall, who was leading the investigation, confirmed that both women had their hands tied behind their backs, and both had disappeared as they had left venues. They believed that there was a sexual motive behind both crimes, even though Agnes did not appear to have been sexually assaulted. He said in a police press conference:

> We are bearing in mind the girls murdered in Edinburgh as well as Hilda McAuley's murder and the disappearance Anna Kenny. There are certain similarities – the victims disappeared at midnight from places of entertainment and were found in the country.

He warned that the 'weekend killer' could strike again, and appealed to young women not to leave dance halls and clubs unescorted.

Sinclair was not a suspect in the original investigation into the murders of Agnes. But we believe that she was murdered by Angus Sinclair.

At the time that Agnes was killed, Sinclair was spending his time either living at his mum's house in Maryhill or a flat at Daisy Street in Govanhill. Agnes was last seen less than four hundred yards from the Daisy Street flat. When interviewed by detectives, a member of the band said that once they had packed up their equipment he noticed a vehicle parked across the road, which looked like a white transit van. Was this actually Sinclair's Toyota caravanette, and had he subsequently trailed Agnes from the club to the motorway slip road, just waiting for his opportunity to abduct her when the time was right? Another witness who came forward spoke of a white van driving towards the site where Agnes's body was found.

Mark Williams-Thomas, in *The Investigator: A British Crime Story*, which covered Agnes's murder, also talked to a witness who was in the area that December, who recalled that he had seen a white van in the area where Agnes's body was found the night after she disappeared.

The witness said,

> Looked like a Volkswagen caravanette. And I noticed that the registration number was RGG and finished with R. And that was similar to a registration, my father's at that time, his current car.

When shown a picture of Sinclair's caravanette, he said:

> That was the vehicle! I can be sure of that… I'm so sure that's the vehicle.

Was this white van driven by Sinclair? It seems highly likely. To be fair to detectives working on the original investigation, with the information we now know about Sinclair, the presence of a white van outside the club is highly significant and points to his involvement. At the time, this would have been just one piece of information that flooded into the investigation and at the time would have had no special significance.

Sinclair was familiar with the area where the body was discovered. It is bounded by North Calder Water Reservoir and Hillend Loch/

Reservoir, a popular trout fishing spot where Sinclair had fished in the past. Once more, it was on a quiet road that would have been known to someone locally.

Like other victims of Sinclair, Agnes was taken around midnight after an evening out in the centre of Glasgow. When found, she had been bound and gagged with her own clothing.

Sinclair's wife Sarah was very helpful to detectives as they later built a case against her husband for the World's End murders. She is convinced that Sinclair killed both Hilda McAuley and Agnes Cooney, being reported in the *Herald Scotland* before her husband's death as saying:

> The case against him will never close until they have put him with those girls in Glasgow. They know he did it. He did it, I'm convinced. I've been to the sites, I've been everywhere with the police. They are all places where he could have been.

Some detectives working on the case also believe that Sinclair killed Agnes, and even privately apologised to her family for the errors in destroying vital evidence. Unfortunately, Agnes's dad was another of the relatives who died not knowing for sure who had killed his daughter, and the torment for Agnes's brothers and sisters continues. After the World's End trial saw Sinclair convicted of two murders, Agnes's sister Mary said:

> Everyone has let us down. We tried to get a case to get justice for Agnes, but we can't because there is nothing. God is the only one now who can do anything.

Agnes's cousin Michael Connarty, a retired Labour MP, said in 2019 that Agnes will never be forgotten:

> People are not forgotten, people are never forgotten. It's how people deal with these matters in the long term. It's still there but the family don't get involved in it as a way of not reopening that wound again.

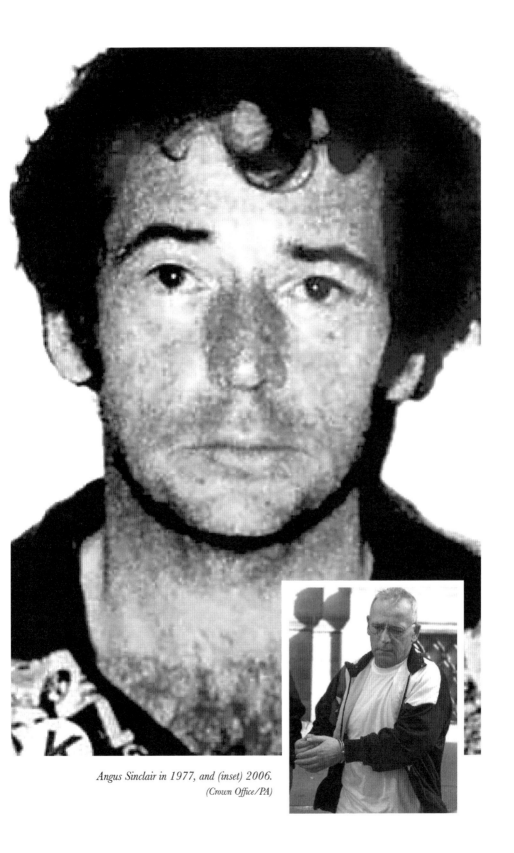

Angus Sinclair in 1977, and (inset) 2006.
(Crown Office/PA)

'Evil and Depraved' – Sinclair on the cover of the Daily Record of 31st August 1982 during his trial at Edinburgh's High Court for the rape of young girls (Mirrorpix)

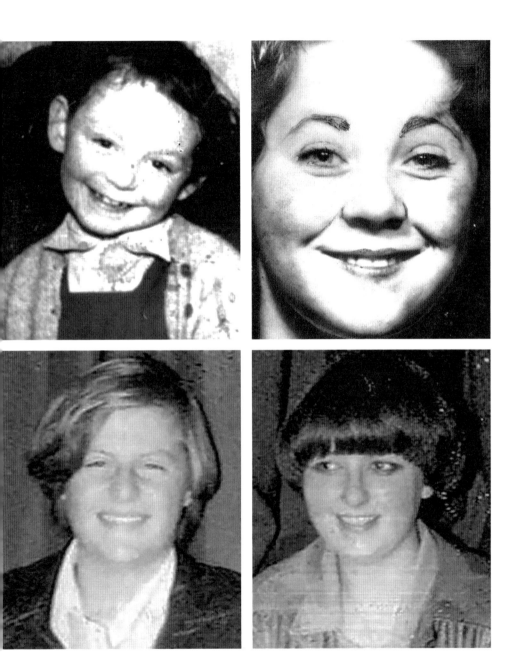

His four confirmed victims.
Top: (left) Catherine Reehill; (right) Mary Gallagher
Bottom: (left) Helen Scott; (right) Christine Eadie

(Crown Office/PA/Authors' collection)

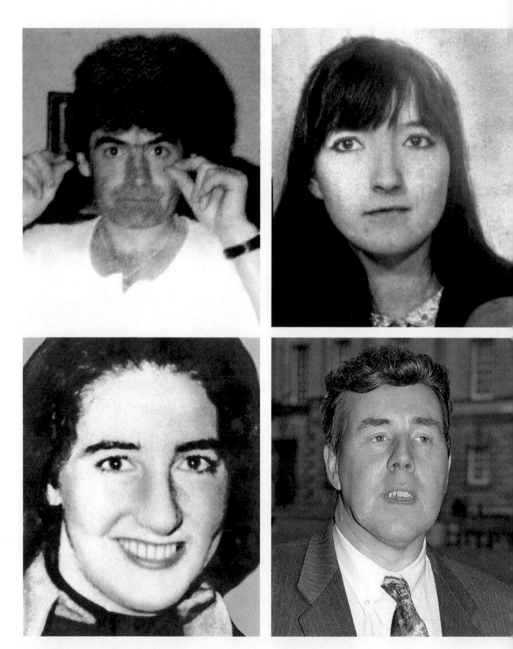

Top: (left) Gordon Hamilton, Sinclair's brother-in-law and accomplice; (right) Helen Kane, murdered in 1970
Bottom: (left) Margaret McLaughlin was stabbed 19 times while walking to Carluke railway station in 1973;
(right) George Beattie, convicted of Margaret's murder
(Crown Office/PA)

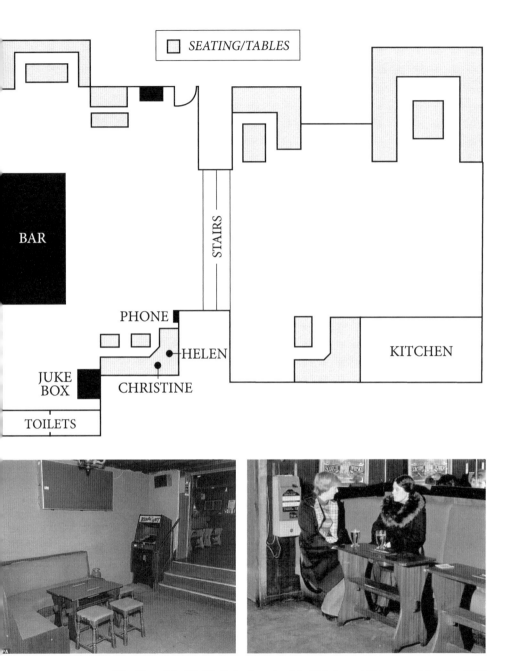

Top: Plan of the World's End pub on the night Christine and Helen were abducted in 1977
Bottom: (left) The corner table where Christine and Helen sat;
(right) A reconstruction was staged in an appeal for witnesses
(Crown Office/PA)

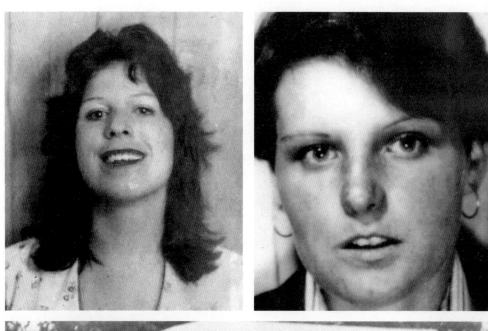

Top: (left) Patricia Black, murdered in 1976; (right) Anna Kenny, found murdered in August 1977
Bottom: Once lured into Siunclair's campervan, the assaults began

(Crown Office/PA/Authors' collection)

Top: (left) Frances Barker, murdered in July 1977; (right) Thomas Ross Young, who was convicted of her murder
Bottom: (left) Hilda McAuley, murdered in October 1977; (right) Agnes Cooney, found murdered in December 1977

(Authors' collection/Crown Office/PA)

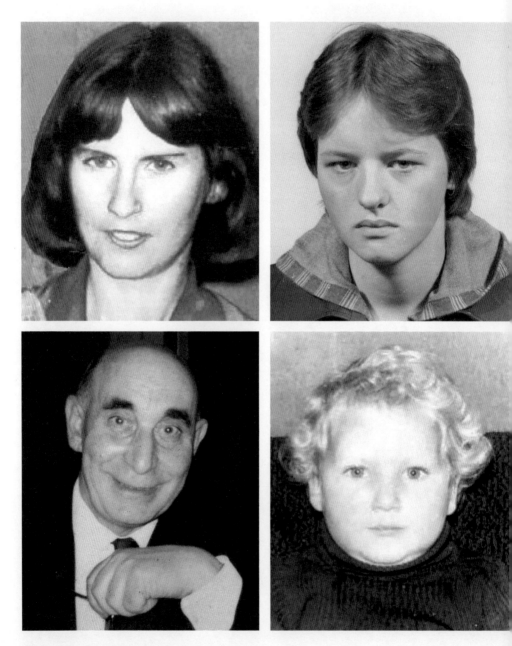

Top: (left) Elizabeth McCabe; (right) Carol Lannen
Bottom: (left) Eddie Cotogno; (right) Sandy Davidson – more victims of Angus Sinclair?
(Crown Office/PA Authors' collection)

12

Mary Gallagher

In the summer of 1978 the film *Grease* had been released, and by the autumn soundtrack songs *'Hopelessly Devoted To You'* and *'Summer Nights'* were still in the Top Ten of the UK music charts. Later that year, on 18 November, the world was rocked when in Jonestown, Guyana, 918 members of the Peoples Temple were murdered or committed suicide under the leadership of cult leader Jim Jones.

The very next day, 17-year-old Mary Gallagher was murdered by Angus Sinclair on the outskirts of Glasgow. Mary's family would not get justice for her murder until 2001.

Mary Gallagher was petite, at just four feet eleven inches tall. She was the eldest of six children who lived with their parents in Springburn, four miles north of Glasgow city centre. On 19 November 1978 Mary had planned to meet two of her friends near her house and then the three of them were going to get a lift to the Firhill Social Club, just by the Partick Thistle Football Club stadium, in Glasgow's Maryhill district.

As normal, Mary said goodbye to her mum, then left the family home at 16 Endrick Street, Keppochill at about 6.30pm. She was going to meet friends who lived on the other side of the railway track in Avonspark Street, just a few minutes away. Mary took the familiar route down Endrick Street, onto Keppochhill Road, and then on to Flemington Street where there was a well-used shortcut across a railway bridge onto the pathway. Mary never made it to meet her friends.

On the quiet pathway that made up the shortcut, between 6.45pm and 7.30pm Mary was brutally attacked, raped and murdered. It was not until the next morning that her body was found, stripped to her waist with the lower part of her body exposed, on waste ground near a footbridge at Barnhill railway station, less than half a mile from her home. Mary's killer had taken off her clothing and used the leg of her trousers to strangle her before raping Mary and slitting her throat.

Mary's murder caused feelings of horror and deep fear in the small town. Detectives were immediately under pressure to make an arrest, and this was intensified when it was discovered that another seventeen year old woman had been attacked on the same pathway the previous evening. On this occasion the woman was fortunate, and had managed to escape her attacker. Was it the same person who had attacked both young women?

Detectives had an immediate lead, as there had been a witness to Mary's abduction. This witness was an eleven year old boy who had been walking close to Mary, going the same way across the waste ground which was a common shortcut used by many. But when they had both noticed a man by the side of the road staring at them, the boy had got frightened and run away. It is hard to comprehend just how much that boy must have thought of what happened that evening in later years and wished he could turn back the clock.

Frustratingly, the description provided by the witness wasn't enough for detectives to get the quick breakthrough they desperately needed. The investigation stalled and they were unable to make further progress, despite interviewing more than two thousand people in door-to-door inquires and taking hundreds of statements. Police knew that the killer would be bloodstained after the attack, and thought it was likely that someone locally had shielded him directly afterwards.

As detectives continued to appeal for any information about the murder, Mary's handbag was discovered in a tenement building in Edgefauld Road, about ten minutes' walk from where her body was found. Detectives believed that it had been placed there deliberately by someone who wanted them to find it. Why the murderer would do that remained unclear. Was the killer playing games with them?

With no progress made over the following days, weeks and months, the investigation inevitably wound down as the police force faced new priorities. But just like the specialists who had worked on the World's End murders, this forensic team took great care when removing items from the scene. They too were hopeful that even if the murderer wasn't caught quickly, the forensic evidence would one day play a part in securing justice for Mary.

All the forensic evidence, and all the accumulated paperwork related to the killing of Mary Gallagher, was carefully stored in dozens of cardboard boxes. Detectives wanted to ensure that, one day, all the information they had gathered would be available to future colleagues.

Angus Sinclair was later convicted of killing Mary Gallagher. We will fully cover in another chapter how Sinclair, who once again wasn't a suspect in the initial investigation, came to be charged and convicted of her murder.

13

Conviction for
the 1978-1982 Rapes of Children

From 1978 to 1982 a large number of rapes and sexual attacks on very young girls were committed across Glasgow. Sinclair was responsible, and he had a very simple method of attack. He would spot victims on estates or around blocks of flats and tell them to knock on a door with news that a neighbour had given birth. As the child headed off to deliver the message, Sinclair would follow them and attack them in quiet alleyways or the landings of flats. This method appears very similar to how he had managed to lure seven-year-old Catherine Reehill to his flat back in 1961.

Why had Sinclair suddenly changed from raping and murdering young women to sexually assaulting children? He knew he had been close to being caught for the murder of Mary Gallagher. The young boy who had been a witness ahead of the attack had seen him, and it is likely this spooked him. Was this the reason he shifted his attention to children? Perhaps he had changed his choice of victim because, if he had indeed killed Agnes Cooney, he would have been shocked at how much Agnes fought back, and he switched from attacking adult women to the easier target of sexual assaults on children?

But sometimes it is easy to read too much into certain decisions people make, and over-complicate things. There may have been other, more simple reasons why Sinclair turned his focus to sexually abusing children, connected to what was happening in his personal life at the time.

Soon after Agnes Cooney was murdered Sinclair sold his caravanette, the vehicle he and his brother-in-law Hamilton had used as cover for their violent attacks, probably because he was concerned that it had been spotted at too many of his crimes. Even though the Scottish police forces had so far resisted linking the recent spate of murders, he must have figured that they would have done so soon, and he didn't want to take the risk of still owning the vehicle he had used to commit the crimes.

This feeling would have been enhanced as increasing numbers of journalists had speculated about a white van being used to take Agnes, so it is probable Sinclair felt he needed to sell it. Even though forensics was only in its relative infancy, he could still have been worried about the fingerprints which would have been found in the caravanette, along with other potentially damning evidence. Although brazen with no regard for his victims, he certainly didn't want to get caught and spend more time in jail.

We know from the murder of Catherine Reehill and the attack on the seven-year-old girl at that time for which Sinclair was convicted that he was at one point earlier in his life interested sexually in children. Without his trusty van any longer, the form of transport which was so perfect for abduction of adult women, Sinclair needed to look at other ways to satisfy his urges which could be done without a vehicle. Another potential explanation is that following his conviction in 1980 for possession of a gun, Sinclair knew that he needed to lie low, but he still couldn't control these urges.

Although at this time not yet convicted of any further murders except the killing of Catherine Reehill in 1961, Sinclair was well known to the police. He had stopped paying his taxes and National Insurance contributions in 1974, and was supplementing his income from painting and decorating with other criminal activities. Sinclair never seemed short of cash and he was often upgrading his car. To keep the cash flowing, he was carrying out a number of burglaries and violent muggings. Sometimes with brother-in-law Gordon Hamilton and sometimes with Hamilton's younger brother, such as the terrifying 1976 attack in Moodiesburn, which was covered earlier.

Although there is no specific evidence to indicate that Sinclair used guns in any attacks or robberies, we do know from informants who later helped with police enquiries leading up to the World's End murder trial that he was testing firearms with an acquaintance, so he was certainly planning to do so. With Sinclair, anything is possible.

He was on remand at Barlinnie Prison from 30 January 1979 to 14 June 1979 (offence unknown), when he was bailed. Then, in 1980, Sinclair was caught by police in possession of a handgun, a .22 revolver, and spent six months in prison for this offence. His wife Sarah took the chance to leave Sinclair whilst he was inside, but when he was released at the end of his sentence the couple reconciled.

Sinclair was still close to his mum and the couple moved in with Maimie, who was now seventy-four, and his sister Connie's daughter Heather. They all lived in a semi-detached house on Wyndford Drive in the Maryhill district of Glasgow. This wasn't a long-term move, and Sinclair and Sarah put down a £3,000 deposit on a £27,250 new-build Barratt home on a new estate in South Nitshill, to the south-east of Glasgow. This was particularly exciting for Sarah, as it was the first home they would own as a family.

In June 1982, whilst many were focussed on the ongoing war in the Falkland Islands, the attacks carried out by Sinclair on children escalated. In Govanhill, Glasgow, one young girl was tricked into a quiet alleyway but began to scream loudly when she realised that she was going to be attacked and managed to escape. Sinclair managed to get away from the scene without being seen, and, not put off by the narrow escape, later that day, in a quiet alleyway in nearby Partick, he sexually assaulted a seven-year-old girl wearing a swimsuit.

As the attacks continued, more of the victims were able to give details about what they had been through and describe the man who had assaulted them. Later in June, a girl of six was raped in the Woodlands area of Glasgow and when she was interviewed, she clearly recalled green paint splattered on the shoes of her attacker. Another girl said that the man who attacked her had a very distinctive smell of turpentine. This clearly suggested someone who was in the painting and decorating trade. Police already suspected Sinclair as a serious suspect, due to his history of sexually assaulting children, the presence of paint/turpentine which he used in his job as a painter & decorator, and also as so many of the attacks took place in a part of Glasgow which he knew so well.

With so many attacks taking place in Glasgow detectives were able to study the incidents, and slowly a pattern began to emerge. Detective Superintendent Joe Jackson later told the *Herald Scotland* how his team looked at the details of the attacks and noticed that the attacker usually operated at the weekend, especially on a Saturday afternoon. He altered his manpower to ensure the maximum number of his officers were out and about at these key times.

Detective Superintendent Jackson explained how a seven-year-old victim was able to identify Sinclair, saying:

> She spoke about a guy with green hair and green on his ears, as well as dirty shoes but not normal dirty shoes. We wondered if she was fantasising because of her very young age.

But when the young girl looked at Sinclair's picture and pointed him out as the man who had attacked her, detectives were certain they had their man. This was enough for the officers, and on 7 June 1982 they turned up at Sinclair's new house, at Craigflower Avenue, South Nitshill. Although Sinclair denied any wrongdoing, he was taken into custody and charged with three rapes and nine sexual assaults. His victims were all girls aged between six and fourteen. As Sinclair was taken into custody on that day, at just thirty-seven years old he could never have believed the possibility that his days of being a free man were over and that he would spend every single day of the rest of his life in prison.

Detective Superintendent Joe Jackson later said of Sinclair in the *Daily Record*:

> He was just a nothing. A wee, horrible nothing. He looked pathetic, but he was clearly far from pathetic. This guy was obsessed with sex − he was just so dangerous. When you consider his crimes, he was more than odious. There had been attacks on children, so this was a very, very high priority for the force. The children were being taken up closes and raped or sexually assaulted. I was told that yet another little girl had been raped. We could not interview her at the time as she was in a traumatised emotional state. Her family was completely devastated. It seemed that no one could get anywhere near this man- but I was determined to get near him.

At first, Sinclair was very quiet and didn't confess to being responsible. Being certain that he had his man, Jackson took a big chance to try to get a confession from Sinclair, and that was by speaking to him whilst his wife was also present. He brought Sarah, a psychiatric nurse, into the interview room.

Jackson explained to the *Daily Record* what happened next:

> I pointed out, very brutally, what had happened to these kids. I knew she could handle it because of her nursing background. It was quite a chance I was taking, but these were horrible crimes and they had to stop.

Sarah instantly had a strong feeling that her husband was guilty, and she made it very clear to Sinclair that neither she, nor their young son Gary, who wasn't quite ten years old, could face going through a high-profile trial. She told Sinclair in no uncertain terms that he if he was guilty he should admit right there and then exactly what he had done. After a pause, Detective Superintendent Jackson started to read out the charges one by one to Sinclair. To his surprise and delight, Sinclair admitted he was guilty of them all. The only charge he didn't accept was abusing a young boy. It isn't clear whether he was innocent of this crime, or because he knew he was facing a long stretch in prison and he knew that prisoners who had sexually assaulted young boys attracted a real stigma among other prisoners.

Sinclair turned to his wife and told her that he had attacked so many young girls over such a long period that he had lost count of how many attacks he had carried out. When pushed by detectives on just how many there were, he said:

> I have done so many I can't remember all I have done. I honestly can't. It might be fifty, it might be five hundred. If you can find out where and when, I'll tell you whether I did them or not.

He didn't expand on this, but it poses the question of whether Sinclair had abused young girls all his life, alongside the attacks on mature women, although there is no evidence to suggest that he actually murdered any young girl.

Reflecting on the case later in an interview with the *Daily Record*, Detective Superintendent Jackson said:

> I think I got to him because his wife was there. I think she knew a lot about him, but didn't realise the lengths he was prepared to go to.

As well as all the girls he attacked and their family and friends, the other victims here were Sinclair's own family. Just as his mum had to leave her home of over thirty years in Glasgow after he killed Catherine Reehill, on this occasion his wife Sarah had to leave the first house she had ever owned. She moved to the south of England to make a clean break, feeling that she and Gary needed a new start due to the inevitable publicity surrounding the case. It wouldn't have been fair to Gary at school where he would suffer for the crimes of his father.

Following Sinclair's admission of guilt for the attacks on children, Gary had no further contact with his father. But he undoubtedly suffered from Sinclair no longer being around. Having no father in his life and moving home and school, as well as being old enough to appreciate the upset his mum had gone through, affected Gary's behaviour in a negative way. At his new school he could be violent and aggressive, struggling to control his temper, which resulted in him getting into a lot of trouble and performing poorly academically. We will return to Gary in the final chapter of this book to look in more detail at the path his life took.

Sinclair faced court for the sexual assaults on children. At the time, rape was not a crime that tended to be punished with a life sentence in Scottish courts. But when Sinclair faced the court in Edinburgh, having pleaded guilty to the sexual assault and rape of eleven children aged six to fourteen, the Judge, Lord Cameron, was very clear that this was the only sentence he could pass, telling Sinclair,

> The penalty for rape is entirely discretionary and without limit. I have considered very carefully whether a limit should be placed on the extent of the penalty, and I have decided there is only one limit — namely your life.

The judge recommended that Sinclair serve a minimum tariff of thirty years, and on 30 August 1982 he arrived in Barlinnie jail in Glasgow.

*

We should talk a little about Angus Sinclair in jail, as it was a major part of his life. The prison where Sinclair spent most of his time was at Peterhead, on the north-east coast of Scotland, where he was held in the specialist unit for the detention and treatment of sex offenders. Peterhead is not a popular jail among the prison community, as it was a bleak, desolate granite building before closing in 2013 to be replaced by the new HMP Grampian, the first prison in Scotland to jointly house youths, men and women, with the first inmates arriving in March 2014. But it wasn't just the look of Peterhead; the location was tricky to access from other parts of Scotland, with public transport particularly challenging. Once a visitor had made it to Aberdeen, there was still an hour-long bus journey to the prison.

But Sinclair liked it there, and was an absolute model prisoner. The advantage for a prisoner like Sinclair being housed in Peterhead was that with all the inmates coming from similar offending backgrounds, there was much less change that he would be attacked by his fellow prisoners.

In the very early days of his time there he was given trusted inmate status, which allowed him to take a job in the kitchen, where he was a revelation. Sinclair had to order all the food and other supplies needed for the kitchen and he managed this very well, naturally taking the leadership role among his fellow inmates working in the area. It was said that if members of his kitchen team didn't meet his high standards he was happy to give them a serious telling off. He showed a real pride in his work and, of course, the prison authorities were delighted to have Sinclair running such a tight ship in their kitchen.

But more than this, Sinclair was a liked and trusted senior member of the prison company, who acted almost as a mentor for other prisoners. He would give them advice about their situation and his insight on any appeals, as well as situations in their private lives. It is hard to imagine that Sinclair was the sort of person that anyone would turn to, but in prison he was seen by younger inmates as a man of experience who was able to provide strong advice.

Unlike Peterhead prison, Barlinnie prison was not a specialist unit for sex offenders like Sinclair. It was an adult prison, and he was a paedophile who was arriving from a court case that had been covered extensively on television and in the newspapers. Talking to those in the prison service – who aren't prepared to go on the record – Sinclair was very wary about prison. He knew it was going to be difficult for him, and he was frightened about being attacked. At every possible opportunity he worked on his physical condition to build his strength and fitness. But Sinclair was a small man, an easy target due to his high profile and the nature of his offending, and within weeks of arriving he was beaten up on a number of occasions.

Despite being happy in his position at Peterhead later in his prison career, he had never forgotten these torrid first few weeks in Barlinnie. He was always anxious about being attacked by other prisoners, and genuinely scared about being moved into the general prison population again.

14

Eddie Cotogno

You may recall the name Eddie Cotogno, who was mentioned in an earlier chapter. He was the man who helped Sinclair develop his interest in photography, including showing him how to develop his own pictures.

63-year-old Eddie Cotogno was found battered to death in the workshop attic of the top floor flat where he lived alone in Valeview Terrace, Dumbarton, north-west of Glasgow in July 1979. He suffered a terribly violent death, with his head being caved in by blunt force trauma from a murder weapon likely to have been a hammer – a particularly brutal and frightening death. His body was found on a blood-soaked mattress, and all around him were scattered nude and pornographic photos of local women, photographs that had been taken by Eddie in his attic studio. In an effort to destroy the evidence, Eddie's killer had set light to his flat before making their escape. Nobody has ever been convicted of his murder.

We believe Angus Sinclair killed Eddie Cotogno. To explain why Sinclair would have changed his modus operandi from murdering young women and sexually assaulting children to killing a man in late middle-age, let's first take a step back and find out a little more about Eddie – the man better known locally as 'Wee Eddie', supposedly because this was an easier pronunciation than Cotogno.

All his life, Eddie had kept himself occupied with a number of day jobs including being an optical technician and a security guard. He often kept odd hours, which was understandable due to shift work that was part of his job. He was known as a quiet, understated man, but despite this he had a large number of female visitors visiting his flat at various times of day and night. In this part of Glasgow, neighbours were busy enough getting on with their own lives rather than worrying about what Eddie or anyone else was doing. They did notice, however, that there was one man who was often with Eddie, a man that they had heard referred to as 'Gus' – the name used by a number of his associates. Eddie didn't ever introduce his friend Gus to people. When locals saw him he would never speak, but occasionally would nod in recognition. Eddie's friend Gus was Angus Sinclair.

Being a security guard wasn't where Eddie's passion lay. He had a weekend job which was a cover for a secret life which he really enjoyed. Every weekend would see him running a stall at the Barras Market, a long-established outdoor weekend market in the centre of Glasgow, selling all sorts of items from antiques to tat. Eddie sold a variety of – well, let's kindly call it bric-a-brac. That was his cover. Where he really made his money, and why he was there, was for the goods he kept under the counter; home-made pornography. These were the days when it wasn't possible to turn on a computer, or phone, and access any sort of pornography desired at the touch of a button. Back then pornography had to be bought from expensive dealers, who often had high-quality items from Amsterdam and other parts of Europe.

The UK had a very different approach to pornography regulation from that found in most other western countries, who had legalised hardcore pornography during the 1960s and 1970s. It was completely illegal to sell pornography until the end of the last century. This created a strong black market for such material.

The expensive pornography from Europe wasn't Eddie's scene at all. He wasn't into professional porn. His photographs – and sometimes videos – all featured local women, and he took and developed all the pictures himself.

Photography had always been of interest to Eddie, and he had made some money over the years taking wedding photos and family portraits. He had his own dark room and processing facilities in the attic of his flat, which was where the stream of visiting women were photographed, and then he developed all the material at his home. The advantage of this for Eddie is that it meant he didn't have to send any of his work to be developed in the traditional shops who offered this service, so everything he did was shielded from prying eyes.

Eddie encouraged women to join him for shoots, suggesting this could be the first step in a professional career as a model. He sometimes showed those who seemed reluctant some pictures of Marilyn Monroe before she was famous, and describing what she and other women had done to break into the modelling industry. For Eddie, as well as enjoying the photography this side-line generated some good money. Local businessmen paid very well to join him and take photos of women posing. If those men then went on to have sex with the women in Eddie's dingy attic, or watched as another man did, the price that Eddie could charge would double. Many of the men who bought his material would hang around Eddie's stall at the markets at the weekends before heading off for a drink or two, and then maybe going on to the Barrowland Ballroom nearby, where they might meet a woman who could be persuaded to go to Eddie's the next day to pose for photos.

Eddie's mate Gus found plenty of willing subjects for him. Sinclair started off by bringing sex workers from the streets of Glasgow, who often welcomed the extra cash. This wasn't cheap and the fees they charged were too high, so Sinclair would go to the pubs on Glasgow's East End and find women of all ages, from teenagers to grandmothers, who were interested in posing for Eddie. Sinclair always had a knack for sensing when someone was vulnerable and could be exploited for his own gratification, and this is yet another example. Usually there was no fee for the women as it was sold as an opportunity, but they were sometimes paid a small amount for their time. Sinclair brought a steady stream of women to Eddie's makeshift studio, at least two or three women a week.

What was in it for Sinclair? As we know, from an early age Sinclair was obsessed with sex, so he thoroughly enjoyed seeing naked women posing for provocative shots. He and Eddie shared the same taste in porn so it would have been for fun, and he was likely to have been paid for the women he introduced to Eddie. No doubt there were also times when he and/or Eddie were able to have sex with the model, which would always have been welcome to Sinclair.

He also dabbled in porn himself, using an interest and knowledge of photography and his frequent contact with sex workers to build up a collection of hardcore pictures for his own collection. After the disagreement with Sarah when she found him developing photos of himself with another woman, Sinclair would develop his own pictures in a darkroom at his mum's house in Maryhill Road, using the skills and techniques taught to him by Eddie.

With Sinclair's ability to procure models for Eddie, and both making money and enjoying the work, the relationship seemed to be a match made in heaven. Then, on 30 July 1979, Eddie was murdered.

Who killed Eddie Cotogno? Was it an angry husband who had found out that Eddie had been taking explicit photos of his wife and distributing them locally? It could well have been a woman who had modelled for Eddie, and later felt she had been pushed into posing – or more – and told an angry boyfriend or father what had happened. This would certainly explain why some of Eddie's pictures were scattered around his body. It was a risk that Eddie knew, and he had confided in friends that he had been threatened in the past.

Our view is the Eddie's friend Angus Sinclair killed him. Sinclair felt that he could learn things from Eddie, who had taught him how to develop his own black and white films, but the pair fell out when Eddie wouldn't show him the knack of developing in colour. Did this disagreement lead to Sinclair killing Eddie? It is possible; Sinclair didn't react well when he didn't get his own way and, as we have read, he was always happy to use extreme violence.

The murder was only months after Sinclair had killed Mary Gallagher. Sinclair and Eddie maintained regular contact, so one possibility is that Eddie had found out and had used this information to blackmail Sinclair. Or, with Sinclair's sexual interest in underage girls, perhaps there was some sort of dispute around child pornography. There are many possibilities as to why Sinclair want Eddie dead.

Our view is that Sinclair murdered Eddie for the following compelling reason. As we have heard, Sinclair enjoyed a large number of affairs following his marriage to Sarah. Two of his ex-girlfriends from the mid-1970s, who Sinclair later referred to in prison as 'K' and 'M', had agreed to pose naked for a series of photos at Eddie's flat. At the arranged time, the two women stripped off in front of him and his brother-in-law Gordon Hamilton, who was there too that day. Sources claim that Sinclair was livid when he discovered that the photos of his two ex-girlfriends were for sale to anyone in the local community at Eddie's market stall; other wives and girlfriends were fine, but not anybody that Sinclair cared about. He always liked to be in control, so for Eddie to do this without his knowledge or permission would have angered him greatly. It was shortly afterwards that Eddie was killed.

After his murder, police discovered that Eddie had told family members that he had arranged a meeting with an acquaintance for just before he was killed. It is fair to assume that whoever this acquaintance was is likely to know who murdered Eddie, and the man he spent most time with was Sinclair. Is this who he was meeting with on that day?

As is the case in many investigations, detectives kept small details of Eddie's murder back from the public — key details that only the killer could know. In this case, detectives didn't publicly reveal the murder weapon, which they believed to be a hammer of some description. This was Sinclair's weapon of choice for his robberies and other violent attacks that weren't sexually motivated. As he was only five foot four inches tall, he needed a deadly weapon in order to quickly gain control, with men particularly. If Sinclair has murdered Eddie, he would have chosen a hammer to carry out the attack.

Many reports you will read about Eddie's death say Sinclair wasn't quizzed about the murder. These are inaccurate. He was interviewed as either a witness or a suspect, which isn't clear. Strange as it may seem, back then detectives would sometimes phone ahead of their visit. This way of operating, as so often in his criminal career, gave Sinclair time to brief his wife Sarah, who told detectives that the two were together when Eddie was killed, having a meal at his mum's home. Sarah had once again provided Sinclair with an alibi — one of many she knew was totally untrue and later regretted. It was only much later that Sarah admitted she had lied on numerous occasions to provide Sinclair with the alibi he demanded. On each occasion he had told her exactly what she must say to the police. This was one of those times. The events surrounding the police interview with Sinclair about Eddie's death are enlightening. At the time, the police were constantly at his house speaking with him about his suspected involvement in some robbery or other. After Sinclair took the call from detectives to make an appointment to interview him about

Eddie, although they didn't tell him that was what it was about, he instantly turned to Sarah to tell her that it would be about the death of a man he knew. He also tape-recorded the whole interview, which doesn't sound like a man not concerned about what might happen next. Again, it was all about Sinclair trying to take control of the situation.

The two former girlfriends mentioned earlier were also interviewed by detectives about Eddie's murder, along with many of the women photographed who came forward after Eddie's death. They claimed that they were not in the area at the time of the killing and this was accepted by detectives. 'M' later married and lived in Lanarkshire. For understandable reasons she never felt the need to tell her husband about her relationship with Sinclair. 'K' lived in Glasgow's East End but died some years ago. Sinclair wasn't aware that she had died, and later told a fellow prisoner that of all the women he had known in his life, she was absolutely the one for him, the real love of his life. He boasted how she would have done anything at all for him, whatever and whenever he asked. He told another inmate that he was actually still in love with both of these women, claiming that they adored him too and the only reason that he didn't hear from them was as police had intercepted their letters. Had Sinclair convinced himself that this was the situation, or was it just idle bragging?

In addition to 'K' and 'M', there was one other significant woman in Sinclair's life who he saw whilst married to Sarah, a lady who afterwards moved to England before Sinclair carried out most of his killings. Interestingly, when interviewed all three women told detectives that Sinclair had been very kind to them, and they could not believe he was a murderer. Sarah always said the same: although he wasn't a perfect husband, he was always kind to her. This perhaps isn't what would be expected from a man like Sinclair, who was capable of carrying out such terrible acts of sexual violence against women. In a way, it is similar to the contrast of the Sinclair in prison who was an exemplary prisoner, who took great pride in his kitchen and was seen as a mentor to other inmates. This is a completely different person to the Sinclair on the outside – a clear indicator of a psychopath.

Although hairs, clothes and other forensic evidence were taken from the scene of Eddie's murder, the identity of the killer is still unknown. The 2004 joint police initiative Operation Trinity later looked for evidence of Sinclair's involvement in Eddie's murder but could find none. But taking a cynical view of the police approach to Sinclair's crimes, it wasn't necessarily in their interest to go beyond the six unique murders identified as being carried out by the same person. The inclusion of the murder of an older man could have diluted the strength of their proposals.

Eddie Cotogno was a 63-year-old single man. Some would see him as a seedy photographer and the stereotypical dirty old man; perhaps the effort made to solve the murder of a man like Eddie was less than that of other crimes. This is something we still hear today, when you consider the press attention given to the story of Madeleine McCann compared to that of Shannon Matthews, and numerous other missing children. It seems this is more the media's attitude to the victim's family and social background. There is certainly something in this.

But whatever the merits of the investigation, and the efforts made to find Eddie's murderer, we would strongly suggest that the man who killed 'Wee Eddie' went to his grave in 2019. This was another of the many secrets Sinclair took with him.

15

Carol Lannen and Elizabeth McCabe

Carol Lannen was just eighteen-years-old when she was murdered in March 1979.

The youngest of five children, Carol had experienced a difficult childhood which had led to her being placed in care. Before she was ten years old her dad Norman, who had previously been in the RAF, was sent to prison for a long stretch after being convicted of fraud. Whilst he was in jail Carol's mum met someone else, but that second relationship didn't last. Norman had no further contact with his daughter following his release from prison and moved back to Bradford in 1970, where he was originally from, and he was unaware of his daughter's death until contacted by detectives in 2005.

Carol attended a good quality Roman Catholic secondary school in Dundee, but found it a difficult experience. She struggled to make friends and left school at sixteen. One classmate later spoke to the *Courier* about her memories of Carol at school, saying:

> We used to feel sorry for her. She didn't have a circle of friends. Not even one close friend. People would try to get her involved but it wouldn't work. It was difficult to talk to her one-to-one. I don't think she had a happy home life; she never looked a happy teenager. She always looked haunted. All through school I never saw her smile once.

After she left school, with few prospects Carol drifted into sex work on the streets of Dundee. Three months before her death she gave birth to a son, Derek. No father's name was entered on the birth certificate. Managing a young son and her work was a real challenge for Carol in the final weeks of her life, as she tried to co-ordinate childcare alongside earning money on the streets of Dundee.

Carol was last seen at 7.50pm on 20 March 1979, when she was picked up by the driver of a red Ford Cortina on the corner of Exchange Street and Commercial Street in what was then Dundee's red light district. The following afternoon her naked body was found in Templeton Woods on the outskirts of the city, partially covered in snow. The deposit spot was close to the Clatto reservoir, a popular salmon and trout river. Carol had been strangled.

The sex workers in Dundee did all they could to look out for each other, and despite the difficulties of coming forward to the police at that time, workers who saw Carol get into the car described the driver as a thin man with a pale complexion, short dark hair, sideburns and a moustache.

It was not until eleven days after Carol was found that a young boy found her missing handbag and some of her clothing almost ninety miles away, on the banks of the River Don near Kintore in Aberdeenshire. Ernie Leith was preparing for a charity race with his parents and other family members and friends. They had just put their homemade raft through its paces on a training run on the River Don when they made the find. For the bag to be this far north strongly suggested that the person who threw it into the water would have known the area. This was a quiet spot, well off the beaten track. It is not a place that is likely to be stumbled on by chance. What was the connection between the person who disposed of Carol's items and Dundee, where she was murdered?

Detective Chief Inspector Ewen West, who was heading the manhunt, appealed for information, saying:

> Since I have been running this inquiry, I have been utterly amazed by the amount of new information that has come forward to us. How close we are to identifying who killed Carol is a really difficult question to answer. But I firmly believe that if we do all the work we need to do, and we get all the assistance we can from the public, then that gives us the best opportunity of getting to that point of identifying who killed Carol Lannen.

He told a news conference at Tayside Police Headquarters that the inquiry was now focused on gathering fresh information about three separate strands of the inquiry. The first was centred on the area around the Aberdeenshire town of Kintore, where Carol's handbag and clothing were found on the banks of the River Don. The second involved identifying a man known as 'Roger', who was thought to have been a friend of Carol's, and lived on Main Street, Dundee, and was thought to have been a bus driver aged between twenty-five and thirty. The third focus was on building up a more detailed picture of the bars Carol frequented in the months before her death.

As a result of the last strand, detectives discovered later in their investigation that Carol was a regular at the Highwayman pub in the Hilltown district, to the north of Dundee centre. Detective Chief Inspector West said:

> It is very often the details that people believe to be insignificant, or of no real interest, that can drive an inquiry forwards. Individuals who believe that what they know about Carol, or others potentially involved in the inquiry, is irrelevant may actually hold the very information that could help to complete the jigsaw puzzle.

Owners of red cars were interviewed, and a photofit of a suspect was released. This was the first time that detectives in Dundee had done this.

But despite numerous pleas for information and a large investigation that saw over seven thousand people interviewed, they couldn't find any leads that would lead them to the man who killed Carol. Inevitably, as other priorities arose, the hunt for Carol's killer was scaled down.

*

Eleven months later, as the rabbit hunters walked through the undergrowth in Templeton Woods on the morning of 26 February 1980, one of the dogs began showing signs of obvious interest. He raced to a nearby mound, followed by the two men. When they caught up with their dog the men saw to their horror what he had been so excited about. They were looking at the naked body of a young woman covered only by a blue jumper and some of the surrounding fauna from the woodland around her.

The corpse, which was lying less than one hundred and fifty yards from where Carol had been found under a year earlier, was identified as twenty-year-old nursery nurse Elizabeth McCabe, who had been missing since 11 February. The day that Elizabeth was found was the day before she should have been celebrating her twenty-first birthday. Like Carol, Elizabeth had been strangled. The rest of her clothing and handbag were later found in three different parts of Dundee.

Elizabeth was the eldest of four children born to Jim and Ann McCabe; they had three daughters and a son. She had only recently started at college and was having the time of her life. As well as enjoying the studying, Elizabeth had lost a lot of her shyness and flourished socially. She had also discovered a love for disco dancing, which she enjoyed at some of the venues in Dundee.

Before Elizabeth was found her parents suffered terribly. They would just sit at home constantly waiting for any news. In the end, Elizabeth's dad Jim walked around the city centre, visiting her favourite spots, in the hope of finding some clue to his daughter's whereabouts.

Elizabeth had been missing since the early hours of Sunday, 11 February, when she had been out with her best friend Sandra visiting a few pubs before ending up at Teazer's discotheque in Union Street, in the centre of Dundee. From there, she seemed to have disappeared without trace.

Detectives appealed for anyone to come forward who had seen Elizabeth walking the two-and-a-half-mile route to her home in Lyndhurst Avenue in Lochee.

The exact details of what had happened that night were patchy. Elizabeth had left Sandra in Teazer's without saying that she was leaving, and headed outside at about 12.30am. What happened next is not known. Had she started to walk home and then got into an unknown car? Her friends didn't think this was the case, as there had been an earlier incident which had made Elizabeth very aware of the dangers of getting into an unmarked taxi. If this was the case, it may have been that Elizabeth got into a car with someone she knew. Detectives felt this was unlikely, instead suspecting that a licensed taxi driver had picked up Elizabeth as a fare, but rather than taking her home had killed her.

Based on this theory, every single taxi driver in the city was questioned in the hope that a much-needed breakthrough in the case could be made. Detectives were also very aware of the inevitability that the murders of Elizabeth and Carol were linked, although they kept an open mind on whether the same person was responsible for both crimes. There were obvious similarities, although they expressed caution in assuming there was a man on the loose who had killed both young women. In private, they tended to believe that Carol had been killed by a client buying sex, and Elizabeth had been murdered by a taxi driver. In Dundee, the public were convinced. There was real fear the 'Disco Killer' had struck again and young women, in particular, stopped going out in the centre of Dundee.

During the course of the enquiry one particular taxi driver, Vincent Simpson, was questioned. Although he was of enough interest for both his house and car to be searched, there was no evidence tying the one-time petty criminal to either murder. He was released without charge.

As the months passed, with no concrete leads once again the police operation was scaled down as they focussed on other priorities.

But in 2004 Angus Sinclair was identified as a suspect in both murders as part of Operation Trinity, the joint investigation between the three Scottish police forces of Lothian and Borders, Strathclyde and Tayside. The senior police officer who headed the operation was Tom Wood, the Deputy Chief Constable of Lothian and Borders Police. Operation Trinity seriously considered the possibility that Sinclair was responsible for both murders, to the extent that Wood travelled to Dundee to work with the Tayside force, who were still investigating the Templeton Woods killings.

He said in the *Evening Telegraph*:

> There were strong reasons to link Sinclair with the two Dundee murders. There were several similarities to other murders committed by Sinclair. The year that the girls were killed was close to the years that other murders were committed. The way that the two Dundee girls were killed was also similar to the methods used by Sinclair in other murders.

In both these cases a young woman on her own was either picked up or abducted by motor vehicle in similar areas in the centre of

Dundee close to midnight. This method screamed of Angus Sinclair. The deposition sites were so close together, and there were no murders either side of these two murders. Was it really likely that there was another murderer killing young women in a similar way to Sinclair at about the same time as him?

Carol Lannen was found in Templeton Woods, which is close to Clatto Reservoir, a popular fishing venue which Sinclair would have known and visited. Carol's handbag and clothing were recovered some eighty miles away washed up on the riverbank of the River Don near Kintore, a popular salmon and trout river. Again, an area known to Sinclair, who had worked in that area before. When the items were found, Sinclair was actually working at a motel in Aberdeen.

Elizabeth had been chocked with her blue jumper – this is a method of murder which had strong similarities to another of the confirmed victims of Sinclair, Mary Gallagher, who at just seventeen was murdered in Glasgow.

It was reported by those close to the Sinclair investigation that when questioned by detectives about the murders of Carol and Elizabeth, Sinclair seemed particularly concerned about being charged with the murder of Carol Lannen. Perhaps he was worried how closely the police photofit resembled him – it really did look very similar to Angus Sinclair. Although information from fellow inmates is highly unreliable, it was widely reported that he told a prisoner at Peterhead that he was worried that he was going to be charged with the two murders, and was particularly concerned about the Carol Lannen case. Sinclair supposedly said that he hoped she wasn't closely linked with him, especially as he was doing a job in a motel in Aberdeen at the time. He went on to say, 'I couldn't have done the two of them.' That was a strange comment in itself, and made some insiders working on the investigation wonder if he had maybe killed just one of Carol and Elizabeth. Maybe he had killed Carol, and Elizabeth was killed by a taxi driver in a copycat killing?

All the circumstantial evidence pointed to Sinclair being a major suspect for both these murders. However, Sinclair couldn't have killed Elizabeth or Carol, as he was in prison at the time of their murders. He was on remand at Barlinnie Prison from 30 January to 14 June 1979, when he was bailed. He was convicted on firearms charges on

21 January 1980, and sent to prison for six months.

The re-opening of the investigation due to Operation Trinity, and advances in DNA technology, did lead to the re-arrest of local taxi driver Vincent Simpson, who was now living in Camberley, Surrey and working as a window cleaner. He was charged with two counts of murder and faced trial at the High Court in Edinburgh. Simpson pleaded Not Guilty to both murders and provided the court with details of an alibi. His legal team produced a list of thirteen names, with it being argued that any of those people could be the true killer. A number gave evidence highlighting their innocence.

Retired detective Lesley Liney told the court he interviewed Simpson, then aged thirty-three, because two witnesses had seen his car in Templeton Woods on the night Elizabeth McCabe went missing. In a police statement given in 1980, Simpson admitted he took his dog for a walk at Templeton Woods at about 10.00pm and returned just after midnight on his way to collect a fare in Dundee. He said he went back after this to look for a car he had spotted earlier so that he could try to steal from it. He also told the court that he was a voyeur, who regularly spied on couples in Templeton Woods whilst walking his dog. But he insisted he had nothing to do with the murder, and a search of his Ford Cortina taxi at the time had not revealed anything to link him to Elizabeth.

Simpson claimed he did not pick up passengers from Teazer's disco – where Elizabeth McCabe left her friends after their night out – and when shown a photograph of Elizabeth he said he did not recognise her, and hadn't seen her before. He didn't pretend that he was an angel. As well as being a voyeur he was open about his heavy gambling habit, and admitted he had a criminal record for petty theft dating back to when he was a child. Crucially, he had no criminal record for crimes of violence or sexual assault.

His QC Mark Stewart suggested that the investigation into Elizabeth's murder was obsessed with taxi drivers, as the investigation lacked any concrete leads. He explained to the court that questionnaires had been distributed to Dundee taxi drivers asking all drivers about the night Elizabeth had disappeared. Simpson had quickly returned his one, answering all the questions and volunteering the information that he had been in the Templeton Woods area. It wasn't something that he had been trying to hide.

DNA was the cornerstone of the prosecution case. A hair found on Elizabeth's jumper led the prosecution to argue that the chances of the hair coming from another man, not related to Simpson, was one in three hundred.

But the defence really disputed the credibility of the forensic evidence. 'Am I correct in understanding that not one fibre, not one hair, not one bloodstain, not one piece of evidence linking Elizabeth McCabe to Vincent Simpson's car was recovered?' asked Stewart. 'Not so far as I am aware, no,' Liney replied.

The way forensic evidence was gathered came under scrutiny. Police admitted protective clothing was not worn when officers removed Elizabeth's body from the woods, and that none of the good practices around forensic evidence used today were used to safeguard evidence or protect the scene of crime. One officer told the court how the pathologist at the mortuary did not wear gloves when he removed the ring from Elizabeth's body. It was even revealed that swabs taken from Elizabeth's body had been stored in a paper folder inside a filing cabinet. In court, it was apparent that these doubts about the forensic evidence really resonated with the jury. It was clearly apparent to any observer that cross-contamination of the forensic evidence must have occurred, and the case for the prosecution – if not exactly blown totally out of the water – was certainly severely weakened.

After a trial lasting seven weeks Vincent Simpson was found Not Guilty by a jury and discharged from the dock. In the end, the jury took just three hours to reach their verdict. With no more than a quiet 'Thank you very much,' Vincent Simpson, whose personal life had been splashed across the papers on a daily basis, left by the side door a free man.

Speaking on behalf of the McCabe family, Detective Inspector Ally Reid of Tayside Police said:

> Elizabeth's family are understandably disappointed at today's verdict. They have been in court every day, an experience which has been both distressing and upsetting for them. Their only motivation was to seek justice for Elizabeth. They understand and support the reasons behind the re-investigation of Elizabeth's death, and appreciate the efforts of those involved in bringing the matter to court.

Speaking after the trial, Vincent Simpson said:

> I am a very relieved man. This has hung over me for twenty-seven years. I thought it was all behind me but I was wrong. I feel as if an enormous weight has been lifted from my shoulders. Last night I had no sleep, and today I was physically sick in the witness room with the tension of it all, but there are hardly words to describe how I feel at the moment. I was especially delighted that it was a Not Guilty verdict. A Not Proven would have still left an element of doubt in some people's minds.

He added, 'I feel desperately sorry for the McCabe family.'

Vincent Simpson's wife Gilly was visibly shaken by all that the couple had gone through when she spoke about the case later, telling the *Daily Record*:

> I sat in the witness room because I was so worried something would go wrong. I was mentally preparing myself for the worst. The stress of the whole thing has been enormous. I think they set their sights on Vincent and did not want to pursue anybody else. It's left me a bit sceptical about the police and the way they behave.

It must have been a tough decision for Tayside police to push for the trial of Vincent Simpson. Even if they believed him to be guilty, they must have been very aware of the limitations of the case that would be presented in court. With hindsight, the judgement to proceed appears to be a poor decision. The amount of public money wasted on an unsuccessful prosecution like this is substantial. But more than this is that the hopes of the families were raised, and they had to go through the huge emotional effort of a court case.

Since the trial, nobody else has ever been charged with the murders of Carol and Elizabeth.

Chief Superintendent Jim Cameron, the man in charge of the original enquiry, spoke to the *Evening Telegraph* in 2019, over ten years after the trial, to explain that if at the time of the murders detectives had enjoyed access to the technology available to officers today, they might have had more success in finding out who killed Carol and Elizabeth. He said:

> We weren't as forensically aware in those days as we are now. We

also didn't have DNA testing to rely on that would undoubtedly have given us more resources to call on during the interviewing of the seven thousand people we spoke to during our inquiries. In 1979 DNA techniques were in the very early stages.

We didn't have the same level of expertise in it that we have now. There were also issues in how the bodies were handled and there was cross contamination which caused problems.

Because of this, crucial evidence could have been unwittingly lost. In cases like this mistakes are made and lessons are learned. Police will never close a case if it remains unsolved. At this time there doesn't appear to be anything new to find the killer. It looks like we would be relying on a confession from the killer, which after all this time is highly unlikely.

That, or we need dramatic new evidence to emerge so police can take a fresh look at all the evidence gathered.

*

Over the years, the high profile of these two murders has resulted in some interesting theories.

In 1996 the murders were included in an investigation by the West Yorkshire Police chief Keith Hellawell into possible Yorkshire Ripper attacks in Scotland, but Peter Sutcliffe was discounted as the murderer.

More recently, an American family contacted a Dundee local newspaper to inform them of a relative of theirs who they felt could be responsible for both murders. US and Scottish investigators are believed to have been alerted to suspicions regarding the man, who is now dead. A relative was quoted in the *Courier* as saying:

> The police here don't tell me much, but they said the DNA link is still being investigated to rule him out or in, as the case may be. He hasn't been cleared as a suspect yet. I've contacted Crimestoppers UK over my suspicions about him and his connections to Scotland. My relative visited Scotland several times during the late '60s, '70s and '80s. He had family connections there, and was also in the military. He was extremely self-righteous. He was brought up in a strict Catholic family, and would've disapproved of prostitutes and single mothers, like Carol Lannen. He wrote about his fascination of nurses, like

Elizabeth McCabe. My theory is he was an organised serial killer who planned out and stalked his victims. He also looked for coincidences in names and dates of victims with that of his own history/family, which he would get amusement from when those details would show up in the newspaper following the murder. Maybe he was overlooked by Scottish police because he was a tourist, or they didn't know about him? I've offered my DNA so they can do a familial link.

Nothing has come of this.

Then, in 2018, investigators ruled out a link to a man who was a suspect in the Zodiac murders in northern California between 1968 and 1974. A file sent to the CID in Tayside suggested an American man had fled to Scotland, and said the 'Zodiac's last act' was the murder of Carol, but that theory was not given any credibility by Californian investigators.

Perhaps a more compelling suspect was proposed by local reporter Sandy McGregor, who believes Carol was killed by Andrew Hunter, who was convicted of the murder of his pregnant wife Lynda in 1988 after the case was among the first Scottish cases featured on the BBC's *Crimewatch*.

Hunter moved to Dundee in 1977 to work for the Salvation Army and as an unqualified social worker working in a variety of children's homes. But he had a secret life, one in which he used the services of sex workers. There is a strong chance he may have met Carol Lannen in a children's home in the city when she was in care and bought sex from her, and this could have led to him killing her. He was certainly capable of murder, being described in his trial as 'an evil man of exceptional depravity' after he strangled his wife with her dog's lead before burying the body in Ladybank, Fife, around forty miles north-east of Edinburgh. This case was astonishing for the range of tactics deployed by Hunter to cover up his crime. After the murder he drove his car over three hundred miles to Manchester and left it at a train station, to give the impression that his wife had moved away to start a new life. Hunter made his way back to Scotland, but all his elaborate planning counted for nothing where when his wife's body was found in its shallow grave in Fife.

McGregor said in a television interview:

Carol Lannen was a young prostitute and I think it's perfectly possible he met her in the course of his duties. It is certainly true that a police photofit of the murder suspect in Carol's case looks like Hunter. Even if he was seen as a genuine suspect, Hunter can no longer answer any of the questions as he died of a heart attack in Perth Prison, just six years after he murdered his wife.

Just who did kill Carol and Elizabeth? Could it potentially have been Gordon Hamilton, Sinclair's partner-in-crime? Was it a local man, as was always the view of detectives working on the original investigation? With the discovery of Carol's purse in Kintore, was it someone from Aberdeenshire, or even further north in Scotland? Or were both killings unconnected, and it is purely a coincidence the bodies were left so close together, unlikely as this sounds?

Unfortunately, with the passing of the years it seems as though the families of Carol Lannen and Elizabeth McCabe will never find out who murdered their daughters.

16

Margaret McLaughlin and George Beattie

Carluke is a pretty place, in an elevated position overlooking the River Clyde in the heart of Lanarkshire's fruit growing area. It was the home of Major General William Roy, who is widely acknowledged as the founding father of the Ordnance Survey. Three recipients of the Victoria Cross also lived here: Lance Corporal William Angus, Sergeant Thomas Caldwell and Commander Donald Cameron.

In 1973, 23-year-old Margaret McLaughlin lived in Carluke with her parents and two sisters, Jane, aged twenty-seven and Rosemary, twenty, at 30 Glenburn Terrace. Her thirty-one-year-old brother Edward had already left home. Life was good for Margaret, who was shortly to be married to Bob Alexander, who although young was making a real name for himself as the manager of a pump-making firm.

Margaret and Rosemary both worked at the post office in nearby Motherwell as shorthand typists, and they usually took the train to work and back together.

On Friday, 5 July 1973 they followed their normal routine. It wasn't much fun on this rainy evening on their way home, as it was a pretty rough path alongside the area known locally as Colonel's Glen, with nettles and other foliage up to around three feet high surrounding the narrow path. This sloped down the embankment with a fence on the right side, and you could sometimes hear the water in the shallow stream which ran through the Glen about sixty yards below at the bottom of the railway embankment. The sisters soon reached the clearer, flatter ground of the playing fields at the bottom of the slope, which they then crossed to reach the housing estate where they lived. This shortcut to and from the station meant the walk only took around eight minutes.

It was a Friday night, and the sisters were excited about their plans for the evening. Rosemary was out to see friends, and as Margaret's fiancé was away on business in South Africa she was off to stay with his sister in Partick that night, on the other side of Glasgow. They got on well, and Margaret was looking forward to going into Glasgow the following day to go shopping for the wedding. Margaret, who loved fashion and the latest trends, also needed to return a pair of trousers to a shop in the city she had bought from a department store there and had already placed them in a carrier bag inside her suitcase when packing for her trip.

Margaret and Rosemary got home at around 6.30pm and both their parents were home waiting for them. Their dad Hugh had been unwell of late and was resting, but as always their mum Jean was on hand to make dinner and help her two daughters get ready for their nights out.

Rosemary ate dinner with Margaret, then left the family home to catch a train to visit her friends as planned. Not too long afterwards Jean McLaughlin gave Margaret some money for her weekend away, before she too left the house, to catch the 8.03pm train. It was still raining at 7.52pm when Margaret opened the front door, picked up her tartan suitcase containing her clothes and the carrier bag with the trousers she planned to return, slung her bag across her shoulder, put her umbrella up and waved goodbye to her father. Margaret retraced her route from earlier as she headed to the train station, walking along the road to the snicket, across the playing field and into the woodland of Colonel's Glen.

But Margaret never arrived at her sister-in-law's house.

By Saturday morning concern was spreading, as she had not been seen since she left home on the Friday night. The police were called and Margaret was reported as missing. No witnesses had come forward to say they had seen her on the train from Carluke to Glasgow and her family were beside themselves with worry. This was completely out of character.

Police immediately feared the worst, and later on Saturday began the search for Margaret on the route she would have taken, but found nothing. It was not until 3.00pm on Sunday that Margaret's body was found at the bottom of Colonel's Glen, around thirty yards from the path leading to the railway embankment. She had been dragged away from the path through the nettles and undergrowth towards the stream.

The pathologist examined Margaret's body just after 6.00pm on the Sunday evening, and concluded that she had been dead for approximately 20-24 hours. Her death had been caused by some nineteen stab wounds inflicted upon her.

In addition, she had been punched in the right eye and on the mouth. Margaret must have been terrified throughout the brutal attack. The pathologist suggested that she could have stayed alive for a full five minutes before she lost consciousness due to her injuries. Those five minutes would have seemed like hours.

Police found Margaret's umbrella just five yards or so off the path, and just below this point was a broken cement post surrounded by flattened undergrowth. It was here that a knife was found stuck in the ground which was thought to be the murder weapon. Despite the rain, there was still evidence of blood soaked into the ground just to the left of the cement post. Further down the slope, towards the stream, was an area of newly-flattened vegetation, and closer to the stream was yet more blood on the ground.

Even further down the slope, towards the glen, was a bloodstained blue plastic bag containing a brand new pair of trousers, and it was just beyond this that Margaret's bruised and bloodied body was discovered.

A more detailed search the next day in daylight revealed one of Margaret's rings, and in a concealed part of the stream was her suitcase and other belongings.

The murder of this young, intelligent and pretty young woman with everything to live for caused shockwaves locally. On Monday, 9 July 1973, one of the most famous senior policemen in Scottish history, Detective Chief Superintendent William Muncie – himself from Carluke – lead the investigation to find Margaret's killer. Muncie was a maverick detective who believed his success was down to his special powers. He was well-known in Scotland and had personally solved more than fifty murders, including some very high-profile killings.

This was to be his last active investigation before he was promoted to Assistant Chief Constable. Muncie and his team were under significant pressure to get an arrest, and quickly.

Just a few days later, on Thursday, 12 July − nearly a week after Margaret's disappearance − detectives had a witness who appeared to know all about the murder, local nineteen-year-old George Beattie, who lived minutes from Margaret and had been questioned as part of routine door-to-door enquiries.

The next day George was taken to the murder scene, and he indicated where he said some men with top hats had put the murder knife into the ground. He knew it had been cleaned, and pointed to the exact spot it had been located. George also seemed to know the contents of Margaret's suitcase. The police had their man.

After sustained questioning, he told detectives that he was at the scene as Margaret was murdered by a group of six men, with two of those men wearing top hats with mirrors. Detectives didn't believe this apparently far-fetched story, and were convinced that he was the real killer. Later that day George Beattie was charged with murder.

But was George Beattie the murderer? We don't think so, and this view is shared by many who have looked at this case. But we can go further and say that it is our belief that Margaret was killed by Angus Sinclair.

Sinclair lived less than twenty miles from the scene, and the murder took place on a Friday evening, when Sinclair often headed off fishing for the weekend. The Burn which flows past where Margaret was killed runs into a very popular fishing venue. There was every chance Sinclair could have been in the area, and Margaret fits Sinclair's victimology which we have outlined in previous chapters. We believe Sinclair killed Margaret in a spontaneous attack.

But George Beattie was found guilty of the murder, and spent over twenty years of his life in prison for a crime he didn't commit. Now in his late sixties, in March 2020 he told STV News:

> Things were done the way they shouldn't have been done. The modern-day detective wouldn't have done what he [Muncie] did. To me the whole thing was a sham. The way he conducted the case from start to finish was outrageous. I think it's been set in concrete and there's nobody interested. I'd like it to be cleared before I pass on, but

that is something that is beyond my expectations. I feel that there's not much time left now. My mother died and I would have liked her to have seen me cleared, but that wasn't to be.

Let's look more closely at George Beattie, and why he was convicted of Margaret's murder. George was one of eight children who lived with his parents at 48 Unitas Crescent in Carluke. This was the third block of houses beyond the shortcut to the playing fields, where Margaret would have passed on the shortcut to the railway station on the night she died.

School had not gone well for George as he wasn't considered intellectual, and he had missed a lot of lessons due to illness. He also struggled with poor interpersonal skills, so had made few friends and was often the target of bullies. His nickname was 'Big Softie'. George left Carluke High School at just fourteen, and took a number of short-term jobs before securing work in the railway yards at the Lanarkshire Steelworks in Craigneuk.

He was already known to police over a minor incident when George had found a small boy crawling under his father's car and he had kicked the boy on the bottom. Although a complaint was made, the police felt George had done the right thing under the circumstances. He was also known to them for supplying information he knew about the theft of copper wire from the railway.

Because that was George's passion – railways. All his money went on a model railway he was building at his house. A member of the Scottish Railway Society, he owned twenty coaches and ten engines, and had even bought shares in a Highlands railway company. It was clearly his pride and joy; so much so that he had a share certificate which hung proudly on his wall. Trains were what George was known for locally, and he could often be seen at the railway station in Carluke.

George lived an insular life, with few friends and no girlfriends. As can often be the case in these circumstances, George developed a world for himself in which his life had more excitement and meaning. At the steel works George was known for making up stories, and the man who shared his locker, Colin McClair, spoke openly of him as part of the compelling campaign by the BBC's much-missed *Rough Justice* programme, saying how he would tell tales that none of the workers believed. Another colleague, William Campbell, said that in the macho culture in which they worked, this extended to stories about his drinking, adding 'But we know they are all lies'. His family saw this side of him too. His eldest brother William said:

> He fantasised a lot. He could go for a walk and lose himself just going down into the woods, looking at the stars, the trees.

He thought this was due to having to keep up with his older brothers, continuing:

> We did shooting, fishing and the like, where he was the odd man out. He'd never really done anything like that. He always had to try to live up to our image. So he was inclined to fantasise a wee bit, all younger brothers have a tendency to do that.

His sister Ena thought the same, saying:

> He liked to dream a bit. I think he liked to make himself out to be just a bit more important. But let's face it, sometimes we all do that, just to make ourselves look more important.

On the evening of the murder, George had slept for most of the day before watching *Top of the Pops* and eating dinner before heading to work. Interestingly, appearing on that episode were Slade with their number one hit, *'Skweeze me, Pleeze me'*. Singer Noddy Holder wore a top hat with mirrors on it, just like the murderers that George later claimed to see.

Margaret's mother told police that her daughter had left the family home at 7.52pm, so would have reached the glen within two to three minutes, around 7.55pm. This was the time George left his home for work, and his route was the same as Margaret's, towards the railway station. He would then continue through a residential area to where he caught his bus. That evening he was seen just after the railway station by a friend, Ian Freel, and they said hello. He then met another acquaintance, Tam Bryce, and they too chatted. Neither saw nothing unusual with George, who continued to pick up tomatoes for his co-workers at a local shop, as he always did, before clocking in at work at 10.00pm.

In early interviews with detectives George mentioned nothing about seeing Margaret or her murderers. But after further interviews and reconstructing his route to work that evening, George confessed.

Sergeant Dougie Mortimer from Lanark, who was conducting the interview, asked George again if he was 'quite sure' he hadn't seen Margaret the night she died. In hysterical tears George broke down, saying,

> I saw her. She had her umbrella in her left hand and her suitcase in her right hand. They told me they were going to cut me up into sardines if I told the police. There were six of them. Three came down from the banking, three from the wood side. Two of them were wearing tall hats with mirrors or glass in them. The tallest man held her. I felt sick. They poked me with umbrellas and made me watch.

He told detectives how they stabbed Margaret 'time and time again', and how he was restrained and forced to watch the murder. By this time, George was in such a state the detectives noted he seemed to be suffering a mild epileptic fit. The detectives left the room, leaving George with a towel and a cup of coffee so he could recover himself. No doctor was called. When George was cautioned and charged with murder at 1.30am he replied: 'I cannae say no more. I didn't do it. It was they six.'

He was taken again to the scene of the murder early that morning, where George pointed out what he had seen. But through all this time he didn't have access to a solicitor, and wasn't given the opportunity for any family member to support him. Psychiatric evidence suggested that George had low intelligence and was emotionally immature, and due to this his responsibility may have been 'somewhat', but not 'substantially', diminished.

The detectives, led by Scottish police superstar William Muncie, made so many mistakes that are painfully obvious. The detectives involved in the investigation came from a variety of stations, and subsequently communication and liaison was poor. Muncie himself let the *Daily Record* fly him around the area where the murder had taken place, and one of the pictures they published showed where the body was found. This is such a fundamental error it is hard to believe, as is the fact that two officers gave what was for all intents and purposes a guided tour of the scene of the crime to George Beattie. And at one stage in the investigation George was left waiting in a room where Margaret's clothing was laid out, so it isn't unsurprising that he was able to describe it so well. In fact, the murderer probably wouldn't have seen Margaret's clothing in such detail.

After George was charged at 1.30am, he was taken to see Muncie at 5.30am the same morning. Muncie asked him for details, yet didn't react to the clear mistakes that George made in his account. For example, George told him that the knife in the glen was the murder weapon – this was believed to be the case by most of the police officers who had shown him around the murder scene. But Muncie knew it wasn't, even at this stage. Forensics later showed there was no blood on the knife. How did Muncie let this go? George should have been pushed to reveal facts or 'special knowledge' not in the public domain, such as the fact that the murderer left Margaret's expensive engagement ring on her finger. George did not know this. When Muncie asked George where Margaret's body had been found he didn't know, even though Muncie had himself pointed it out on the photograph in the *Daily Record*.

There was also crucial evidence from the meal Margaret had eaten before she had left home that evening. That food was no longer in her stomach, so she can't have died as early as 8.00pm as police thought – it must have been much later. This alone rules out George, as he was seen by witnesses just after 8.00pm and at work later that evening.

The other main evidence used against him was blood found on tissues in a jacket that was owned by him. Two were bloodstained of a type different to George's and which matched Margaret's. But this blood type also matched 43% of the general population, and many animals. George was a keen hunter of rabbits, and the blood could easily have come from these or other animals. Blood was key to the enquiry. Margaret had blood under her fingernails, where she had bravely fought for her life, and yet there were no scratches on George. There was blood on the stones under Margaret's head which was shown to be hers, but when tested the sub-grouping did not match the blood found on George's tissue handkerchief in his jacket.

Despite the lack of meaningful evidence, George Beattie was convicted of murder by the jury on an eight to seven majority, reached after just thirty-five minutes' deliberation.

His conviction was outrageous. It is quite clear that he could not have killed Margaret. Unfortunately, this is another example of terrible police work where justice was just an afterthought. We would suggest that this conviction was all about Muncie, who wanted to complete a 100% murder conviction rate before being promoted.

In his recent book *Signs of Murder*, Professor David Wilson – a criminologist who lived in Carluke – agrees, saying:

> Muncie believed he had psychic powers when it came to solving murders. He would decide which suspect was guilty and then search for the proof to make his case.
>
> Today we would call this 'confirmation bias', but his methods worked back then, when he solved more than 50 murders, including some very high-profile killings.
>
> Muncie was a maverick. He was ambitious, and the Beattie case would become his last before he was promoted to assistant chief constable.
>
> To secure a conviction, police have to show evidence that, without a shadow of a doubt, proves they have the right man.
>
> Muncie was held back, he was engaged in a process where he has to demonstrate this psychic power, and he ignored all the evidence that would cast doubt Beattie was the killer.

The conviction was bad enough, but even worse than this is that despite a number of campaigns that clearly showed this was a terrible miscarriage of justice, George was not released on appeal, and even now the conviction still stands. We have to question other senior figures in the police force and legal system who, it appears, have closed ranks to protect the reputation of Muncie and other involved in the conviction.

The events of this evening in the summer of 1973 ruined the lives George Beattie and his family.

Former detective Peter MacLeod, who served with Nottinghamshire Police for twenty years, believes Sinclair should be the prime suspect of the killing of Margaret, stating to STV:

> The facts speak for themselves. There's no doubt about it. George Beattie could never have committed that murder.

In 2020, STV News asked Police Scotland about George Beattie and concerns over his conviction. In response, they said this was investigated by legacy force Strathclyde Police, resulting in a conviction. They also invited anyone with new information to contact them.

We believe that Angus Sinclair got away with it again. But even if we aren't correct, and Sinclair didn't kill Margaret, it certainly wasn't George Beattie who committed the crime.

Margaret's family were never given the opportunity to see the person who murdered her convicted. They haven't commented publicly on the case, but Margaret's fiancée Bob Alexander believes Beattie is innocent. He told STV News in 2020:

> I have absolutely no doubt now that George Beattie did not commit that murder. I don't know George Beattie, have never met him. There's no incentive for me to say anything, do anything, but this is wrong. George Beattie is innocent. At that time you just fully accept the police have done their job and he must be the guilty party. We were told there was quite compelling evidence so you accept that.

Bob was not impressed with Muncie, commenting:

> After a brief discussion, which was less than a minute with him, I came away with the impression that William Muncie was such an arrogant, pompous individual. He was actually saying to myself he would actually have this case resolved in a very short time. And he actually did, but he got the wrong man.

He is convinced the case should be re-opened, saying:

> I think this is the last opportunity for this to be investigated. It's really difficult for the police to reopen this case but it's the correct thing to do because it's compelling the evidence that this trial was wrong and that George Beattie couldn't have done this. My family are fully supportive of what I'm doing here and they believe it's the right thing to do.

Today, with there being seemingly no appetite to re-investigate the case, the families of Margaret McLaughlin and George Beattie, continue to suffer. What will it take for the authorities to finally take action?

See Appendix II for the 1993 *Hansard* entry discussing the conviction of George Beattie.

17

Mary Gallagher Murder Trial

In 1982, after Angus Sinclair had been found guilty of sexual assaults on children, trial judge Lord Cameron recommended that he should remain in jail for the rest of his natural life. But fifteen years later, in the spring of 1997, Sinclair was being considered for release. He had been a model prisoner, and was showing all the signs of a man who had come to terms with his past and now wanted to start a new chapter in his life.

It was at this time that Sinclair voluntarily gave a DNA sample to police to help them build the national database. As a prisoner keen to be released on parole, he was willing to do whatever it took to be helpful. It was the mid 1990s, and at that time DNA wasn't anywhere near as significant in helping to solve crimes as it is today. He could never have imagined it would lead to the dashing of all his hopes of ever being released, and instead lead to convictions for the murders of three women two decades earlier. With the potential impact for DNA relatively unknown at this time, Sinclair wouldn't even have considered that this sample would be used against him for crimes he had committed twenty years earlier.

Gaining parole is a long process for offenders like Sinclair, but as the reports began to be generated by various experts to assess the viability of release, he realised he needed to play his part too. This meant he had to be much more open with the authorities about the motives for his offending, in order to show he understood why he had committed crime. He also needed to be convincing in showing that if he was released he wouldn't be a danger to society.

He told how after being released for killing Catherine Reehill his life was all about working long hours to provide for his family. The time he had off work, he said, he devoted to his family. Having few friends and rarely going out. When he did, it was sometimes with his wife's brother Gordon Hamilton, and the two occasionally went to the pub or on a fishing trip.

Peterhead prison, where Sinclair was housed at the time, ran a very well-respected programme for sex offenders, where they were encouraged to confront their crimes and the effects on victims. Sinclair enrolled on this programme, knowing that it would be vital if he was to have any success with the Parole Board who could authorise his release. Sinclair would have known that he would be very unlikely to be approved on the first occasion; it was a process that would almost certainly take a number of attempts to be successful, but the key was to show progress each time. As expected, in 1999 Sinclair's first application for parole was declined.

But, due to the advances in forensic science, parole would never come for Sinclair. If he had not been charged with further offences it is possible he would have been released eventually. In reality, many of the decisions made around parole are surprising. It has been widely reported that Sinclair could have been released at the next Parole Board hearing. If this had happened, it is troubling to imagine how he would have spent his time as a free man. Would he have continued to offend? We will never know, as before he could get to the next Parole Board Sinclair was charged with the murder of Mary Gallagher.

The investigation into the murder of Mary Gallagher in November 1978 had never been closed, although with none of the leads progressing the investigation was wound down. But like most investigations, when new information was received it was looked at. In the spring of 2000 detectives were given the name of a prime suspect from a very credible source. Detectives began to investigate, and the standard process by now was to send original forensic evidence for further DNA testing. Astonishingly, the DNA came back as match to a man on the database – not to the initial suspect named by the source, who could now be eliminated from the investigation, but to Angus Sinclair. Forensic scientists had matched semen on a pubic hair taken from Mary's body to him, which strongly indicated that he was the man they had been searching for.

Once again Sinclair had not been a suspect in the original inquiry, but the DNA evidence showed that the chances of the semen not being his was a billion to one. Despite this, when the evidence was put to him Sinclair denied any involvement in killing Mary.

Sinclair was charged with the murder and the trial at the High Court in Glasgow last twelve days. A full twenty-three years had passed for the main witness in the case, the eleven year old boy who had been walking with Mary on the night she was killed. During that time, he had played back in his mind thousands of times what he had seen that evening, and he now came face to face with that same man again at the High Court. Sinclair was now much different to look at, older, with grey hair and glasses. But the witness, now in his mid 30s, immediately knew it was the same person and confidently identified Sinclair as the man he had seen that fateful night − the man he had described as having 'eyes like dark holes.' This evidence was so compelling in court that not a single member of the jury could have doubted that Sinclair was the man seen across the wasteland. Combined with the powerful DNA evidence, the jury took five hours to return a majority verdict, finding that Angus Sinclair was guilty of murdering Mary Gallagher. The jurors were unaware of his previous history of violence and abuse. Sinclair showed no emotion as the verdict was delivered, and didn't react as Mary's family and friends screamed abuse at him.

Judge Lord Carloway, who sentenced him to life in prison, described the attack as 'a callous, brutal and depraved act on a young girl.'

Mary's mother sat in the courtroom every day of the trial, supported by friends and relatives. Dignified as ever, she didn't comment to the press following the verdict but left quietly via a side entrance to take a taxi home. Finally, twenty-seven years on from the horrendous day that her daughter was killed, she knew for certain who had murdered her, and had seen him face justice in a court room. Her brother-in-law James Brown, who had identified his niece's body, said outside court after the verdict had been delivered:

> The family have never got over the tragedy. We are happy that this evil man has finally been brought to justice, but our pain and suffering is so deep it will never go away.

Speaking after the trial, Detective Chief Inspector Brian Murphy of Strathclyde police, who led the reopened investigation, said outside court:

> Even as part of our inquiry we interviewed three hundred and fifty people. The effort was immense, and it was a tireless task for the officers involved as they sifted through all the original evidence. It was the decision to look at the sample of pubic hair which gave us a breakthrough. That kind of evidence is not usually looked at in this way, but we thought we would give it a try. It proved crucial, and it gave us the vital link with Sinclair.

He continued by lamenting that Sinclair had shown no remorse for what he had done, concluding:

> He's one of the most evil people I've certainly interviewed in my life. There were things going on in his head which clearly I couldn't reach.

Whilst this was finally a form of closure for Mary's family and friends, for detectives working on the case who were acutely aware of the other unsolved murders in Glasgow and Edinburgh at a similar time, this moment felt like just the beginning. They knew that their task now was to try to establish which other unsolved murders might have been carried out by Angus Sinclair.

18

Re-investigation and Arrest of Angus Robertson Sinclair

The World's End murders were never forgotten. Like another Edinburgh murder, that of five-year-old Caroline Hogg, who was taken from the Portobello Beach area of the city by serial killer Robert Black in the summer of 1983, and later found murdered over 300 miles away, the story of the World's End murders made a lasting impact on the city. Black was caught seven years after murdering Caroline Hogg, and after twenty years detectives were still regularly reviewing the World's End case for any new information that could finally help solve the crime. But they were realistic, and understood that classic police work could only take them so far with a cold case. It was likely to be advances in forensic science that would provide the breakthrough needed to find the killers of Helen Scott and Christine Eadie, and in 1996 Lothian and Borders Police cold case unit instructed further work to be carried out on evidence retained from the investigation. In particular, it was DNA profiling that detectives hoped could provide the key.

In 1977 vaginal and anal swabs were taken from Christine and Helen, and semen was found. Two stains found on the inner lining of the back of the coat Helen Scott was wearing at the time of her murder were also able to be tested, and these were found to be a combination of semen and vaginal secretions.

Neighbouring force Strathclyde had made particular progress in their forensic capability, and they were able to make a DNA match between the samples taken from Christine and Helen, which showed that both women had sexual contact with the same person. It was now just a question of finding the man this DNA belonged to, which sounds simple, but of course in practice was a huge undertaking.

The starting point was taking a swab from five hundred potential suspects: the men who had been in the World's End pub on the night of the murders and others who had been of interest to detectives. These were compared to the new sample, but there was no match. Although disappointing, at least detectives knew that one of those men hadn't escaped justice twenty years earlier. The new sample also meant that if a new suspect came to their attention, they could say for certain whether or not the man had carried out the murders.

Detectives had always felt that two men had been responsible, for a number of reasons: two men had been seen with Helen and Christine leaving the World's End pub; there were two different knots used to bind the two women, and there was the practical problem of one man keeping both victims under control as they were assaulted.

As the science progressed, detectives became aware of a new development in forensics – ancestral, or 'familial' DNA. This exciting development established that the Y-chromosome in men would be the exact same for fathers and brothers. It had been used in London in the case of a young boy who had been ritually slaughtered, and this technique allowed the boy's relatives to be traced. They were later found guilty of the murder.

The cut-out section of Helen's coat was sent to the scientists behind the familial DNA. This wasn't a quick process, and the team waited anxiously for results. But eventually when the call came, it was a key moment in the investigation as it revealed two Y-chromosomes were found, which confirmed that two men were responsible for the murders. The sample they had found earlier was masking a second sample.

Even with this news, solving the case still seemed frustratingly out of their grasp as the more dominant profile was put through the database with no match, and the less dominant profile was still not clear enough to be run through the database. They now had both sets of DNA, but still didn't know the names of the men who had murdered Christine and Helen.

On 8 October 2003 the police team aired a reconstruction on the BBC's *Crimewatch* programme, hosted at the time by Nick Ross and Sue Cook, which sought help from the viewing public in solving crimes. It was a huge success, attracting up to 14 million viewers at the height of its popularity. It was successful in helping to solve serious crimes, such as the murder of toddler James Bulger in Liverpool, where, after video footage was shown on the programme, the two boys responsible were identified by viewers and convicted of James's murder in November 1993.

The 2003 *Crimewatch* broadcast brought a strong response, with over one hundred and thirty calls being made from potential witnesses who had not previously made themselves known to the original investigation. One significant call was from a man who told police how he was walking near Gosford Bay on the night when the murders took place and saw what he took to be a works vehicle driving erratically, which he noted as suspicious.

A week later, the headlines in the Scottish newspapers were that Lothian and Borders Police had asked for the help of the Forensic Science Service (FSS) in Birmingham to determine the identity of the key suspect whom the unknown DNA sample belonged to. This was indeed the case, and scientists at the FSS had been working on a DNA sample taken from Helen's coat.

In spring 2004 came the big breakthrough. There were further advances in low-copy number DNA testing being made by the scientists based at the FSS. This technique held great hope to detectives as it is a more sensitive technique, involving a greater amount of copying via polymerase chain reaction (PCR) from a smaller amount of starting material. In practice, this meant that a profile could be obtained from only a few cells, which could be a few cells of skin or sweat left from a fingerprint, for example. In this case, detectives wanted to see if any small DNA matches could be retrieved from the knots on the items used to bind Helen and Christine. The knots were carefully untied, and the results were startling.

The masked DNA that had only recently been extracted now matched a man on the national DNA register. It was a match to Angus Sinclair, whose sample had now been added to the database. Detectives were certain that if they investigated Angus Sinclair's movements in October 1977 they would quickly discover the identity of the other man.

Now detectives had the DNA of a man responsible for the World's

End murders they began to look for any connections with other murders of women in the area at the time, especially those that appeared to be similar to those killings. This initiative was named Operation Trinity, and was supervised by experienced detective Tom Wood, the Deputy Chief Constable of Lothian and Borders Police. The team concluded that five murders looked very similar to the World's End killings: the Glasgow murders of Anna Kenny, Hilda McAuley and Agnes Cooney, and the Dundee murders of Carol Lannen and Elizabeth McCabe.

The two Dundee murders were swiftly eliminated, as we have already heard, but by the summer of 2004 the team believed they had circumstantial evidence to prosecute Sinclair for the murders of Anna Kenny, Hilda McAuley and Agnes Cooney. They had identified the following key similarities in the murders of the five women who were killed within a six month period:

All were abducted within an hour either side of midnight on either a Friday or Saturday night.

Each victim had been out that night and, arguably, had drunk enough alcohol so that they were not aware of potential danger in the same way as if they had not consumed alcohol.

No witnesses saw them being abducted.

The victims were tied up and bound using their own clothing.

The bodies were taken to similar types of places to be discarded, which were quiet and off the beaten track.

Of course, copycat killings couldn't be completely ruled out, but with such similarities in these Glasgow and Edinburgh murders which took place within a six month period, it was hard to believe that there was more than one killer operating in these areas at the time using the same methods.

Tom Wood's team felt that it was not only necessary to show how similar in their distinctiveness these murders were, but their context in all murders carried out in the same period. This required setting up a database to look at details of every woman murdered in Scotland, which became known as Operation Scothom. Even the detectives involved were startled to find that between 1968 and 2004, excluding those who died via the terrorist attack in Lockerbie in 1988, one thousand and thirty eight women were murdered in Scotland. It is a staggering number in a country of around five million people.

From this work emerged another murder which seemed to be very closely linked to the others, that of Frances Barker. A major issue here, of course, was that Thomas Young was serving life in prison for Frances's murder.

Along with detectives, scientists from the University of Glasgow and a former FBI profiler by the name of Mark Safarik, who had been an FBI special agent for twenty-two years and who was an expert in behavioural analysis, examined the murders covered under Operation Scothom. They concluded that the six crimes identified bore a unique signature, and that 'Angus Sinclair and the person he had worked with on the World's End murders were responsible for all the linked crimes.'

Detectives building the case against Sinclair tried to find the caravanette bought by him just weeks after Frances had gone missing, a white Toyota Hiace caravanette, which they suspected he had used in many of his crimes including the World's End murders. This is the caravan which he would use for his weekend fishing trips with Hamilton – the trips where they never seemed to catch any fish. It emerged they were out of luck again, as it had been scrapped just the year before.

Tom Wood later said:

> We missed it by six months. It lay in the back of the last owner's house in Musselburgh until 2003. It was a sort of restoration project, and his wife persuaded him to get rid of it. He scrapped it only six months before we started looking. What is more galling was the fact the interior fabric, carpets and seats of the van were original and had not been replaced. Often we thought and wondered what kind of forensic treasure trove the inside of that campervan would have been. Would we have found traces of Anna, Agnes and Hilda there, as well as Helen and Christine?

However, after tracking down the manufacturer of the van and looking at similar vehicles, samples of the upholstery which would have been used in the caravan in its manufacture were obtained. These were examined by forensic scientists, who compared fibres from that upholstery with fibres taken from Helen Scott's coat. This analysis indicated that her coat had been in contact with fabric of the type that would have been used in the caravanette.

Helen had only bought her coat the week of her murder. The coat was of such material that fibres adhering to it would shed rapidly if the coat was being worn. It could therefore be strongly argued on this basis that the coat – and therefore Helen – had been in Sinclair's vehicle close to the time of her murder.

But after all the work that had been undertaken, and although the Operation Trinity team recommended that Sinclair should be prosecuted for the linked cases, the Scottish prosecuting authority, the Crown Office, disagreed. They didn't think that there was a strong enough case to prove Sinclair's guilt beyond reasonable doubt. This was a blow to the team, especially the officers from Strathclyde police, who were well aware of the mistakes made by their colleagues which they were desperate to rectify. But the big issue, as we have discussed numerous times, is that most of the evidence from those cases was either missing or destroyed. Without the DNA evidence maintained from the World's End murders, they too would not have been solved.

There has been lots of discussion about what happened to all the evidence, and much criticism of Strathclyde police. Was it ignorance of the potential benefits this evidence could provide in the future? Maybe, but as detectives investigating the World's End murders were so careful to preserve evidence, this is a difficult case to argue. Maybe the evidence was destroyed as it was not seen as valuable to the investigation, or maybe – just maybe – it is all still stored in some office in a police station somewhere and will one day be uncovered. Maybe.

With Operation Trinity establishing clear links between unsolved cases, it does beg the question why this was not done during the original investigations. Tom Wood questions why none of the cases were linked at the time, especially due to the heightened publicity caused by the horror at the attacks, both locally and across Scotland. There was the opportunity to do so in 1980, when representatives from all Scottish Police forces met in Perth to discuss whether any of their unsolved cases should be linked either internally or publicly, and resources and information shared. Unfortunately, and incorrectly, the forces decided against doing so.

Wood is interesting in his analysis of this, concluding that the main reason it wasn't done was due to the ever-present figure of the man known as 'Bible John', an unidentified serial killer who it is thought was responsible for the murder of three young women between 1968 and 1969 in Glasgow. The murdered women were all brunettes aged between twenty-five and thirty-two, who met their killer at the Barrowland Ballroom in Glasgow. The cases were linked, and the label 'Bible John' was applied by the press after a witness for one of the murders had spoken about a rather strange man who was in the ballroom that evening. He apparently quoted passages from the Bible in the course of normal conversation. He was never tracked down and eliminated from the investigation.

By publicly putting all the murders down to this one man, which many detectives think is unlikely to have been the case, the press created panic in the region. Wood believes that the decision not to link the cases was taken in Perth due to the fear of another 'Bible John' bogeyman being hyped across Scotland. The question does need to be asked that if the cases covered by Operation Trinity had been linked at the time, would they have been solved? It certainly seems that not linking the cases was a mistake, as greater sharing of information surely would have increased the chances of solving the murders. Maybe the presence of a white van could have been the key to unlock the investigations. We will never know.

*

Now detectives knew that Sinclair was responsible for the World's End murders, and they were clear of the other murders in which he was a prime suspect, they were ready to begin interviewing him at prison in Peterhead. Immediately, Sinclair had some advantages. Firstly, the press had named him as a suspect for the unsolved murders, a fact he would be fully aware of. Secondly, he was used to dealing with detectives and giving very little away. Thirdly, he knew that, with the passing of time, it was unlikely that detectives would have any 'silver bullet' to show that he was responsible for any of the murders they suspected he had carried out, however strong their suspicions.

Detectives had taken advice from psychologists on how to approach Sinclair, and they had a clear strategy in place. Essentially, in the past Sinclair had managed to dominate interviews with his controlling personality, and had intimidated some interviewing officers with his clear contempt for them and the process they were going through. In particular, his fixed stare combined with his silence could easily give Sinclair the upper hand over an inexperienced interviewer.

Detectives also knew that, for all the gruesome crimes he had committed, Angus Sinclair as the model prisoner was, on the surface, a very different man. He was looked on with some admiration by many of the prisoners, and was someone they would consult for advice and guidance. As the man who ran the kitchens in the prison with such a high level of precision, he had responsibility, autonomy and standing in that community.

The plan was to treat Sinclair with the utmost respect and politeness, believing that this would provide the greatest opportunity to get him to talk. This meant calling him 'Mr Sinclair' or 'Sir', and always being very clear about what was happening and what the next steps would be.

Detectives began by telling him that he was no longer a suspect for the Dundee killings, to again show Sinclair that he was being treated with respect and they were not just trying to pin their unsolved cases on him. Sinclair was told that he was a suspect in other crimes, and when asked whether he understood he replied very calmly and softly that he did. But in all the hours of interviews, that was about as much as Sinclair gave away. The one time that detectives sensed some real passion in his responses was when he spoke about the cars he had owned. It was clear that Sinclair had a real love for his vehicles.

In a way it was no surprise. As you have read, Sinclair had only previously confessed when he was just sixteen years old, to the murder of Catherine Reehill, and on the other occasion to the attacks on children, when he was under pressure from his wife. Detectives hoped that by hinting others had spoken to them, that some allegiances had changed over the years, they may have made him feel insecure after being away from people in his community for so long. They even hinted that his family had spoken to them. This wasn't untrue as his wife Sarah, in particular spent hours with detectives. This must have been incredibly painful for her as detectives went over every aspect of her life with Sinclair, but Sarah was very open and transparent and did everything she could to help the investigation. But none of these tactics appeared to work with Sinclair, and his response to all the questions put to him was 'nothing further to say', followed by silence.

The only time he did comment was when detectives touched on the murder of Helen Kane in 1970. Sinclair very clearly stated 'This one is nothing to do with me'. Was just this him being very clear that he was innocent of that crime? Or was it a rare moment when he dropped his guard? Could it be surmised from this response that the other crimes he was being asked about were something to do with him, or is that reading too much into one remark? Like so much with Sinclair, it is hard to say for sure.

There were odd moments when Sinclair briefly opened up on very small details with the interviewers. This was the case when the subject turned to ex-girlfriends – Sinclair seemed to like hearing that they spoke well of him. One time he was asked, "Did you enjoy sex?" to which he responded, "Yes, I did." On another occasion he told his interviewees that his first sexual relationship after being released for killing Catherine Reehill was with a woman in Edinburgh who passed him a sexually transmitted disease – that obsession that stayed with him all through his life. When asked about if he had ever been to the Hurdy Gurdy pub, where Anna Kenny had been the night she disappeared, Sinclair said no and emphasised that he wasn't much of a drinker. Then, without prompting, he added that he had once been on the roof of the building when it was a bookmakers, as he had been trying to break into the premises – yet another crime carried out by Sinclair which he got away with.

On 31 March 2005 Sinclair was arrested and charged by Lothian and Borders Police. The following day he appeared on petition in private at Edinburgh Sheriff Court charged with the murders and rapes of Helen Scott and Christine Eadie in October 1977. He made no plea or declaration at this time and was remanded in custody.

As Sinclair was facing detailed questioning about unsolved crimes, detectives and scientists had turned their attention to the weaker DNA sample, using principles used in the earlier familial DNA testing methods. They worked through all his known friends and acquaintances to track down who this DNA was from. In the end, this thorough journey of elimination led to Sinclair's brother-in-law, Gordon Hamilton. Previously, Hamilton's death in 1996 would have meant that he couldn't be tracked, but using the new techniques the living Hamilton brothers were tested. This matched the World's End sample, showing that the chances of the sample belonging to anyone other than Gordon Hamilton was thirty-eight million to one. They had finally found the second man responsible for killing Christine and Helen.

As detailed in the chapter on Gordon Hamilton, despite his death in 1996 a very small sample of his DNA was recovered from wires sealed behind a wall from a DIY job he carried out in a flat in Glasgow some years before he had died. Although a very small sample, it contained enough genetic material for his DNA to be matched to intimate swabs taken from Christine and Helen. Hamilton's profile was never stored on the database because he was never convicted of an offence.

The news that her brother had been involved in the murders was devastating for Sarah Sinclair and the rest of her family. She now worked even more closely with the investigation, going back through all her memories of Sinclair and doing all she possibly could to help the prosecution develop a strong case to convict him for his crimes.

With his conviction for murdering Mary Gallagher, there was no serious chance of Angus Sinclair being granted parole. He knew that he was going to die in prison. Because of this, occasionally detectives wondered if there was the possibility that he may plead guilty to killing Helen and Christine to save the families the emotional trauma of a trial. But then they snapped back in reality, and realised just who they were dealing with. Sinclair wasn't a man to confess or do anything to spare the feelings of others.

19

First Trial and Acquittal

Ahead of the trial, detectives were concerned. On the opening day, the advocate-depute assigned to the case made the decision that the trial was going to be shortened to just two weeks from the original six weeks estimated by the Crown Office. This would inevitably mean cutting the evidence presented to court. This was out of their control. This decision was taken for a number of reasons, but the primary one was that the prosecution wanted a very simple case so as not to confuse the jury, and this was all based around the strong primary DNA evidence.

Finally the day arrived, and on 27 August 2007 the trial of Angus Sinclair began in Court Three at the High Court of Justiciary in Edinburgh, with Lord Clarke the presiding judge. The prosecution was led by advocate depute Alan Mackay, and the defence by Edgar Prais QC. The indictment alleged that on the night of 15–16 October 1977 Angus Sinclair and Gordon Hamilton persuaded or forced Christine Eadie and Helen Scott into a motor vehicle and held them against their will in St Mary's Street, near the World's End pub. From there, it was alleged that Sinclair then drove Christine Eadie to Gosford Bay, Aberlady, and there or elsewhere attacked, stripped and gagged her with her underwear and tied her wrists before raping her and then killing her by restricting her breathing. He was further accused of raping and murdering Helen Scott in the same way, and driving her to a road near Haddington, and in a field there or elsewhere in Edinburgh and East Lothian attacked her.

Sinclair pleaded Not Guilty to rape and murder. He lodged two special defences, one of consent and one of incrimination, stating that any sexual activity between him and the two women had been consensual, and furthermore if they had come to any harm the person responsible was his brother-in-law, Gordon Hamilton. Of course, Hamilton was not present to dispute this.

On 28 August the jury of nine women and six men began hearing the evidence, which was wholly circumstantial. It was strange for the many members of the police who had been involved with the case over so many years as friends of Helen and Christine gave evidence. These witnesses were no longer teenagers but middle-aged women – with full lives and families like Helen and Christine should have had – and this added extra poignancy.

Helen's dad Morain, and Christine's mum Margaret, both talked about the days before their daughters were murdered, and it was impossible not to be moved to tears by their personal accounts of that one night almost thirty years ago that had affected their lives evermore.

On 3 September the advocate depute led evidence from Detective Constable Carol Craig, who confirmed that Angus Sinclair owned a Toyota Hiace caravanette at the time of the murders but the vehicle had now been destroyed. Because of this, she confirmed that police were unable to carry out forensic tests on any of the fabrics or seat upholstery inside the vehicle.

On 4 September forensic scientist Martin Fairley gave evidence that semen obtained from a vaginal swab from Christine and semen obtained from a vaginal swab from Helen shared the same DNA profile.

On 7 September another forensic scientist, Dr Jonathan Whitaker, gave evidence that semen matching swabs taken from Sinclair were found mixed with cells with the same DNA profile as Helen on her coat. He also confirmed to the court how siblings of Sinclair's dead brother-in-law Gordon Hamilton had provided samples for DNA testing, and that the results of these tests had been compared with the semen found in the bodies of the victims. He continued that the results obtained were what he would expect if semen found in the victims had come from a brother of the surviving Hamiltons.

Whitaker's information concluded the Crown case.

Later that day senior counsel for the defence, Edgar Prais QC, made a submission under section 97 of the Criminal Procedure

(Scotland) Act 1995 that Sinclair had no case to answer in respect of the charges libelled due to an insufficiency of evidence. In particular, he contended that the Crown had failed to lead evidence that Angus Sinclair had been involved in acting with force or violence against Christine and Helen, and that the advocate depute had not supplied evidence to prove that any sexual encounter between the panel and the women had not been consensual.

Sometimes in court there is a very strong feeling that momentum is strongly with the defence or prosecution. Here, it was felt that, on the conclusion of evidence from the prosecution, there was a sense of anti-climax around the courtroom. On the other hand, the defence case appeared to be a very clear and convincing one. They believed that the prosecution didn't have the evidence to show that Sinclair, rather than Hamilton, had harmed either victim. Nor did they prove that sex between Sinclair and Helen and Christine was not consensual. The law meant that Sinclair didn't have to explain or justify his claims that the sexual contact was consensual.

This was a strong line of defence from Sinclair's legal team, when combined with the fact that the prosecution had chosen not to present the low-copy number DNA evidence from the knots used to tie up the two women, along with expert witnesses able to explain the significance of these. In one particular knot a strand of DNA unique to Sinclair and not found in Christine, Helen or Hamilton was found. This would have strongly indicated that Sinclair had bound the women, which would have been a strong counter-argument to the claim of consensual sex. Another piece of evidence not used was from Allan Dixon, who had been Helen Scott's boyfriend for three years prior to her death. He would have given evidence that he had never had sexual intercourse with her, and that at the time of her death she had not ever had sexual intercourse with anyone. In front of a jury, this would have made Sinclair's claim that Helen had consensual sex with two strangers seem even more unlikely.

Then, much to the dismay of everyone connected to the prosecution, on 10 September 2007, following legal arguments on the matter, trial judge Lord Clarke upheld the defence submission of no case to answer and formally acquitted Sinclair. Lord Clarke said that although Sinclair could be shown to have had sex with at least one of the girls, the evidence was not strong enough to show that he had been involved with the murders. He said:

> I am of the view that the evidence... as a whole is neutral as to whether or not he [Sinclair] was involved in acting with force or violence against the girls, there having been some evidence of sexual contact between him and the girls in the 12 hours or so before they were killed. The question of timing seems to me to be critical. I'm not satisfied what the advocate-depute had to say overcame these difficulties in that respect.

Turning to the jury to explain the legal wrangling which had delayed the case, the judge said:

> I have reached the conclusion there was insufficient evidence in law to entitle you to reach a verdict, therefore you are not required to reach a verdict.

Sinclair showed no emotion as he left the court to return to prison.

It was only following the conclusion of the trial that it was revealed to the court that Angus Sinclair was a convicted murderer and serial sex offender who was currently serving two life sentences at HMP Peterhead.

The reaction from those in court soon turned from acute disappointment to exasperation and anger. Helen's dad, 77-year-old Morain Scott, who was in court to hear the judgement, had said during the trial that his wife had never recovered from learning of their daughter's death. Speaking outside the High Court in Edinburgh he said:

> I am absolutely shattered – words can't explain how I feel. Thirty years of trying to get a conclusion... I promised I would stick by this and get justice which, honestly, I don't think I got today. At least had it gone to a jury you can accept their decision, but for the case to be thrown out after all the hard work that was put in just astounds me completely.

He thought that the two weeks of evidence the prosecution had presented would be enough to prove their case, commenting:

> The girls had to get to East Lothian somehow. Both had their hands tied and to think that any one person did that is unbelievable.

He also spoke about the DNA evidence which was so important to the prosecution case:

> It was proved in court that DNA from Helen's coat was Sinclair's. I am just gutted. Absolutely gutted.

When reporters asked if he felt that Sinclair was responsible for the murders of both Christine and Helen, he continued:

> Yes, I do. He was involved, whether he was an accessory or not, he was involved. I couldn't see one person doing that. There must have been a vehicle to take them to East Lothian. It had to be someone who knew the area, which he knew. I am absolutely shattered. I just want to be left in peace now to see the rest of my days out. I just want to think about Helen and Christine, who had their lives taken away from them just when they were starting out. Helen would only have been 17 in July 1977 and she never got the chance for any ambition she had in life, and we as a family never got the chance to see where she would have gone.

He said it would be 'terrible' if it later emerged that there was evidence about the case which wasn't heard in court, but was full of praise for all the work carried out by the police, adding,

> The police, for thirty years, right from the word go – some have now even departed this Earth and others who have worked on this case – they've never given up. They've kept re-looking at it. I can't praise the police more for the work they've done. They must be gutted as well. They must feel terrible.

His son Kevin echoed his disappointment, talking of the emptiness and disappointment felt by both families:

> Having given so much support over the past two years, since the charges were brought, it obviously comes as a bitter pill to swallow. Having said that, we cannot thank enough Lothian and Borders Police for the tenacity and time that they have spent to try to bring a conclusion that would be acceptable to us as a family. I would finish off just by finally asking that once my father has spoken to you, that you will please give my father, and Christine Eadie's family, the time and space to come to terms with this disappointing decision.

After all the hours of work they had put in over three long decades to collect the evidence they believed would convict Sinclair, shattered detectives left the court in disbelief. Officers had been cautiously confident of securing a conviction. It was a body-blow for them personally, as they knew that Sinclair was guilty but hadn't been able to prove it. But, more than this, they felt that they had let down the families of Helen and Christine, and hearing their disappointment on the steps of the court having failed to see justice for the deaths of their daughters was a terrible moment.

A Lothian and Borders Police spokesman said:

> We are very disappointed at the decision. There have been numerous reviews of the brutal murders of Christine Eadie and Helen Scott over the past thirty years, and we have always taken very careful steps to review all the evidence. We put together a thorough and detailed case for the Crown Office to take to trial, and today's announcement is disappointing. Our primary concerns at the moment are for the families of Christine Eadie and Helen Scott. No-one can imagine the torment they have been put through. We have no plans to reopen the investigation.

Once again, Angus Sinclair had got lucky and escaped justice. Detectives knew he was guilty, and Sinclair knew that they knew he was guilty, but he returned to his prison cell that evening reassured that he would never again face a court about the murders of Helen Scott and Christine Eadie.

20

Reaction and Double Jeopardy Law in Scotland

As discussed earlier, the World's End murders had great significance with many people across Scotland. Because of this, the verdict was received badly, with the Scottish press appalled at how the case had not even been put to a jury. It just seemed unfair, and that justice hadn't been done.

On 13 September 2007, in a highly unusual measure, due to the level of public and media interest in the outcome of the case, the Presiding Officer of the Scottish Parliament allowed the then Lord Advocate, Elish Angiolini, to address Parliament on the case. The Lord Advocate read from a detailed prepared statement to the chamber, setting out the Crown case and explaining the reasoning for deciding to prosecute Sinclair. She is recorded in the official transcript of her address concluding that she was 'disappointed' with the result in court, and stating that she 'was of the clear opinion that the evidence that was made available to the court was sufficient to put before the jury to allow it the opportunity to decide on the case against Sinclair'.

Although this was received positively in some quarters, others were appalled that the Lord Advocate could show such a lack of public support for the judicial process, and feared this could have long-term negative effects.

One such person was the Lord Justice General, who on 26 September 2007 took the completely unprecedented move of publicly criticising the Lord Advocate's decision to address Parliament about this case. In an open letter to the Lord Advocate, Lord Hamilton wrote:

> The plain implication from your statements is that you were publicly asserting that the decision of the trial judge was wrong... her actions were incredibly serious as they could be seen to 'undermine public confidence in the judiciary.

The debate raged over the following days, with some of the most senior people in the Scottish justice system taking a public stance. On 28 September 2007 former Solicitor General and retired Senator of the College of Justice Lord McCluskey gave an interview to the *Herald* in which he expressed his strong view that Lord Hamilton had no grounds to accuse Elish Angiolini of threatening the independence of the judiciary. He said:

> He's quite wrong. What he fails to see is that it is sometimes essential for a minister to comment upon a case. It happens all the time in parliament.

This was backed by another senior figure, the retired Senator of the College of Justice, Lord Coulsfield, who told the BBC:

> The real issue here is whether a decision of the magnitude that Lord Clarke had to take should always be taken by a single judge.

The strength of feeling about Sinclair's acquittal didn't recede, and the debate around the outcome of the case led to a far-reaching and systematic review of the Scottish criminal justice system. On 20 November 2007 the Scottish Parliament Cabinet Secretary for Justice, Kenny MacAskill MSP, referred several issues arising out of HMA v Sinclair to the Scottish Law Commission for investigation, and to make recommendations for reform. One of these issues was the principle of double jeopardy, which prevents an accused person from being tried again in the same jurisdiction on the same charge following an acquittal.

On 31 July 2008 the Scottish Law Commission responded by publishing its first report, on the issue of Crown appeals. This lead, on 30 June 2010, to the Scottish Parliament passing the Criminal Justice and Licensing (Scotland) Act 2010. Following on from the recommendations of the Scottish Law Commission, sections 73-76 of the act make provisions for Crown rights of appeal against certain decisions taken by a trial judge sitting in solemn cases. Amongst other things, it provides a mechanism for Crown appeals against rulings on no case to answer submissions. On 28 March 2011 sections 73-76 of the Criminal Justice and Licensing (Scotland) Act 2010 came into force. Essentially, this meant that if this law had been in place at the time of Sinclair's trial, the Crown would have had a mechanism to appeal the decision made by the single judge.

In December 2009 the Scottish Law Commission published its report on the principle of double jeopardy. The commission recommended that the principle be retained in Scottish Law, but should be reformed and restated in statute. The commission further recommended that exceptions to the rule be created in three circumstances:

- Where the acquittal is tainted by offences against the course of justice such as (but not limited to) bribery, perverting the course of justice and subornation of perjury. The commission concluded that perjury in itself should not be suitable grounds to order a retrial.

- Where the previously acquitted has made a credible admission of guilt.

- Where new evidence which was not and could not with ordinary diligence have been available at the trial has been found. The commission recommended that this only be permitted where the new evidence 'substantially strengthens the case against the accused' and that if a reasonable jury had heard the evidence at the trial that this would have made it highly likely that the accused be convicted.

The commission addressed the issue of retrospectivity, recommending that any exceptions to the rule of double jeopardy only apply to cases heard after any legislation created to create the exceptions is passed.

This recommendation was not followed by the Scottish Government, and the Double Jeopardy (Scotland) Bill introduced on 7 October 2010 included provisions to apply the proposed legislation retrospectively.

This law came into force on 28 November 2011.

As the Scottish Act was passed, Justice Secretary Kenny MacAskill said it would mean prosecutors would no longer have their hands tied, as it ensured that nobody would be able to evade justice in Scotland. He said:

> The principle of double jeopardy dates back over 800 years, but we now live in a very different world. The law needed to be modernised to ensure that it is fit for the 21st century, and I am delighted that MSPs from all sides have voted in favour of these important changes.

Of course, this meant that after what so many people had thought was an absolute travesty of justice, if the Crown chose Sinclair could be tried again for the World's End murders. Retired detective Allan Jones was very clear in his view about what should happen next.

> In 2007 justice wasn't done. Double jeopardy gave us the opportunity to revisit the case using new evidence and again do what should have been done at the time, and find these people guilty of that horrific crime back in 1977.

21

Second Trial and Conviction

On 14 March 2012 the Crown Office issued a press statement saying that the Procurator Fiscal had instructed Lothian and Borders Police to re-open the investigation into the deaths of Helen and Christine following the introduction of the Double Jeopardy (Scotland) Act 2011.

To proceed to a new re-trial detectives had to show new evidence, and once more, it was advances in forensic science on which they pinned their hopes. The key advance, which wasn't available during Sinclair's first trial, was a piece of equipment resembling a torch. Crime-Lite uses LED to produce high-intensity light of varying wavelengths. When this is shone on the piece of evidence requiring analysis, potential DNA present becomes clear and directs the forensic scientists to areas to check which previously they would not have spotted. It sounds so incredibly simple, but this technology had only been introduced to forensic casework in 2009 and accredited in 2011. Could this really be the piece of equipment which held the key to finally solving the murders?

Helen's coat offered forensic scientists many possible DNA samples, and now, using Crime-Lite, they had a completely accurate guide as to where to take their samples from. The glow of the torch clearly showed specks of DNA that had been preserved within the twists of the knotted ligatures used to restrain and strangle the young women. Scientists discovered Sinclair's DNA within a fold of Helen's tights – proof, thought detectives, that it was deposited there whilst the clothing had been ripped and torn to bind and then strangle her.

They prepared their case for the court that was to decide whether Sinclair could be tried again for the crime. They would argue that the chances of the DNA found inside Helen's coat belonging to anyone other than Sinclair, and on the ligature formed of a bra and tights around her neck, and a belt used on Helen, were more than one billion to one. Sinclair had always asserted that someone else must have killed Helen and Christine, so the fact that there was no DNA belonging to anyone else was highly significant as it could show this claim to be untrue. The detectives believed this was the compelling evidence required to bring Sinclair once more in front of a jury.

In October 2013, three judges set aside eight days of court time for prosecutors to make their case that Angus Sinclair should stand trial again for the World's End murders. This was a nerve-wracking time for all involved with the case.

On 15 April 2014, Lady Dorrian delivered the opinion of the court.

The judges had decided that the new evidence provided met the standards required as part of the new double jeopardy legislation. Given the seriousness of the case, they had authorised a second trial. It was a legal first for Scotland, and the detectives were delighted and even more determined that Sinclair would not again escape justice for the deaths of Helen and Christine.

The trial commenced on 13 October 2014 at the High Court of Justiciary, sitting this time in Livingston, West Lothian. Livingston was the location for two main reasons: firstly, it was a modern court building with all the technology needed for a high-profile case, and the prosecution, led by Lord Advocate Frank Mulholland, intended to use this technology to build the case against Sinclair. Secondly, although close to Edinburgh, it was far enough away to hopefully counter the defence objection they were almost certain to face about prejudice due to pre-trial publicity. It was difficult given the preceding years had presented so much speculation of Sinclair being responsible for the murders, but the judge, Lord Matthews, would be directing the jury to disregard all information about the case other than presented to the court during the trial.

When Sinclair was brought to the dock from custody, though not yet seventy he looked much older. He had grown a long beard and put on weight, and certainly seemed a very different character to the imposing and intimidating figure he had cut for so many years. He made his plea of Not Guilty to both murders and lodged special defences of incrimination, consent and alibi. Once again, he claimed that Hamilton had been responsible for both deaths.

The case started with the Lord Advocate proving that a crime had been committed. This involved the awful, graphic black-and-white photographs of Helen and Christine at the crime scenes being shown to the jury, along with the clothing that had been used to kill them.

The next day was an emotional one, as family members of the dead women spoke about them. After all they had been through, and having gone through the same experience at the first trial in 2007, detectives hoped that this would be the last time they would have to face this ordeal. Throughout, Sinclair listened carefully, his face and body portraying no emotion.

A stream of police witnesses gave evidence, but this was increasingly difficult. Many of these officers were older than Sinclair and had retired. Being asked to recall all the details from almost forty years ago wasn't easy, and some observers felt that not all of the evidence came over as wholly convincing. But the Lord Advocate was absolutely thorough in presenting the evidence, and in this trial every detail was shared. They had learnt their lessons from the previous trial.

The second week began with evidence from pathologists, followed by a forensic odontologist who gave his opinion on a bite mark that was found on Christine's arm which, he stated, was clearly not the sort of bite that might have been given during consensual sex, but was an attacking move with a clear aim to subdue, scare and hurt her.

Next up was an expert on knots, aiming to show that two men were responsible for the knots. This was another that wasn't called during the 2007 trial, and this witness was compelling. Christine had been tied with reef knots by someone who knew what they were doing. This matched the police suspicion that Christine had fought back and needed to be restrained with someone who really knew what they were doing with knots, whilst Helen had resisted less – probably due to shock – and the knots used on her were much less accomplished. This directly contradicted Sinclair's claim that he was not involved. Hearing the evidence reminded detectives again of the violent reality of what happened that night and how, as Helen had lived longer than Christine – as was shown from their blood alcohol levels – she was likely to have witnessed the dreadful murder of her friend.

There followed the key part of the trial focussing on DNA, where expert witnesses took the stand. It was a very different trial to 2007, which this time saw all the evidence put before the jury. By the end of week two, the jury had even visited the scene of where the bodies were found near the East Lothian coast. They were told not to carry out their own investigations outside the trial, so jury members asked Judge Lord Matthews to see the locations. They were taken to East Lothian where they walked along Gosford Bay in Aberlady where Christine's body was dumped. They were then taken to the field where Helen's remains were discovered 37 years earlier. Lord Advocate Frank Mulholland QC and defence lawyer Ian Duguid were also present. Looking at the pictures of that trip to the deposition sites is difficult; the smartly-dressed legal teams and people serving on the jury look wildly out of place in the beautiful, rural places were Helen and Christine were dumped. We have stood looking out to sea at the spot Helen was found, and it is hard to believe that an act so horrendous happened in such a beautiful spot.

Detectives are used to gauging the mood of the court during the trial. Although of course an inexact science, they were cautiously optimistic that the case against Sinclair was building and that the jury of six men and nine women were being persuaded. But there was a long way still to go.

By the end of four weeks, the prosecution case was complete.

As the defence opened their case, they produced a forty-seven page document calling into question all the forensic evidence produced by the prosecution. And after all these years of silence, for the first time Sinclair provided an account of what had happened that night. In reality, he had little choice, as there had been no technicality that had led to the collapse of the trial so he had to give an account of the evening for his special defences to work.

Sinclair claimed that he and Hamilton had met Christine and Helen on the night in question and had taken them to nearby Holyrood Park where they had had consensual sex. From there, Hamilton had driven the four of them to the East Lothian coast, dropping off Sinclair so that he could go fishing on the coast nearby. Although there are people who love night fishing, this explanation of what happened in the early hours would, we suggest, be seen as wildly implausible to most observers. Sinclair claimed the last time he saw Christine and Helen they were still with Hamilton. He had elected to give evidence on his own behalf, which was a shock to the prosecution team. Perhaps, after finding his silence hadn't prevent him from being found guilty of killing Mary Gallagher contributed to this, or maybe he just felt at this time that he had nothing else to lose.

Frankly, Sinclair wasn't a credible witness, mainly as the lie he was trying to tell was one that any QC could pull apart and the Lord Advocate was very skilled in his craft. He failed to give any plausible explanation when asked how the post-mortem reports showed injuries on Christine and Helen were entirely consistent with rape as opposed to consensual sex. By the end of the cross-examination Sinclair made it clear he had no empathy for Helen and Christine, seeing them merely as sexual objects to be used. This cast doubt on whether consent for sexual contact was ever given. Overall, Sinclair came across very poorly. In the end, even he admitted that his story didn't sound plausible. Throughout his evidence Sinclair was cold, uncaring and callous. Maybe, for the first time, the public saw the real Angus Sinclair.

Finally, the evidence had all been heard except for the closing speeches, where Lord Advocate Mulholland spoke very powerfully to conclude the case for the prosecution:

> It has been thirty-seven years since Christine and Helen were murdered. But Christine's mother and family are still here to see justice. Helen's father and family are also all still here to see justice. Despite the passing of so many years, the case has not been allowed to sit on a shelf and gather dust. The file has never been closed.
>
> Instead, the items in the case, the girls' clothes, the ligatures, samples taken from their bodies, even the soil from the field have all been carefully preserved, returned to with each step forward in technology and science, until now, when using forensic tools such as Crime-lite, we can see the hidden evidential remains of that night in 1977.
>
> What we see is Angus Sinclair and Gordon Hamilton all over the ligatures. Angus Sinclair, all over Helen's coat. We also see Sinclair in all the areas we see Hamilton, bar one. And that is what this case is all about. Sinclair and Hamilton together beating, raping and then murdering the girls.

This new forensic evidence is added to all the other evidence I have discussed. The totality of this evidence is considerable, powerful and quite frankly overwhelming.

It exposes as a lie the incredible story put forward by the accused as to what he says happened that night, a story which on numerous occasions even he agreed sounded ridiculous.

The body of Prosecution evidence has not come from forensics alone. It has come from numerous sources – from the families of the girls, from friends of the girls, from police officers at the time, from acquaintances of the accused, from witnesses long since dead but whose statements remain for you to consider, from a knot expert, a dental expert, a soil expert and medical experts.

It is on the basis of all this evidence that I invite you to find Angus Sinclair Guilty of both charges.

It was a powerful speech, based on fact but also using emotion to play to the jury.

In contrast, the defence closing speech was all about doubts. Was the forensic science evidence correct? With the passage of time, could the DNA really be relied on? Were the witnesses all reliable after all these years? The aim was just to place that element of doubt in the minds of the jury.

After the judge had summed up the case, the jury retired to reach of one of three verdicts: Guilty, Not Guilty and Not Proven. And just two hours later, on 14 November 2014 the jury delivered their unanimous verdict – Guilty on both counts.

Sinclair had been found guilty of the murders of Helen Scott and Christine Eadie on 15 October 1977. Following the conviction Lord Matthews sentenced Sinclair to life imprisonment, with a minimum term of thirty-seven years. This would mean he would be 106 years old before being eligible for parole.

Lord Matthews said the following in his sentencing statement to the court:

Angus Robertson Sinclair, there was no reason for Christine Eadie or Helen Anne Scott to think that 15 October 1977 was going to be particularly eventful. To all intents and purposes they would have a pleasant Saturday night out, the sort of occasion they would look forward to enjoying for many years to come with friends and family, including perhaps children and grandchildren.

Helen, shy and retiring, and Christine, more outgoing, had not long left school and started work, no doubt harbouring ambitions of moving on to greater things. It was not made clear in the evidence how Christine saw her future but we know that Helen wanted to be a children's nurse.

Whatever dreams they had, they turned into nightmares shortly after they left the World's End pub, the name of which has become synonymous with these notorious murders. Little were they to know that they had the misfortune to be in the company of two men for whom the words 'evil' and 'monster' seem inadequate.

Unless one day your conscience, if you have one, motivates you to tell the truth, no-one other than you will ever know precisely what part you and Gordon Hamilton played in these awful events. Perhaps it does not matter. What does matter is that the girls were subjected to an ordeal beyond comprehension and then left like carrion, exposed for all to see, with no dignity, even in death. For them at least the nightmare is over and if they were not resting in peace before today I hope that they are now.

The nightmare for their families and friends, on the other hand, has gone on from those first awful moments when they heard the news no-one should hear until even now, thirty-seven years later and counting. It will never end. No-one who saw the evidence of Helen's father, sisters and boyfriend and Christine's mother could fail to have been moved by it. They are an example to us all, waiting patiently for justice while the authorities have worked tirelessly to achieve it.

As for you, you have displayed not one ounce of remorse for these terrible deeds. The evidence in this case as well as your record, details of which have now been revealed, shows that you are a dangerous predator, who is capable of sinking to the depths of depravity.

I do not intend to waste many words on you. You are well aware that the only sentence I can pass is one of life imprisonment.

Merely sentencing you to life imprisonment is not the limit of my duties. The concept of parole does not sit easily with your crimes, and indeed seems like an insult to the girls' memories, but nonetheless I have to designate a period which must pass before you can apply to be released on licence. The purpose of that period, known as the punishment part of the sentence, is to satisfy the requirements of retribution and deterrence. Whether you are ever released thereafter will not be a matter for me but for the Parole Board, although I intend to make matters easier for them.

On both charges one and two in cumulo I sentence you to life imprisonment to run from today and I fix the punishment part at thirty-seven years.

Lord Matthews also thanked the jury for their diligence, saying:

Ladies and gentleman, as you now know you have participated in legal history, the first trial to be conducted in this country after the abolition of the principle of double jeopardy. It has been obvious to me and to all of us in court that you have been paying particular attention to the evidence and addresses in this case. That was exemplified by your request to see the various places of importance referred to in the evidence.

The families and friends of Christine Eadie and Helen Scott have had a long wait for justice. I don't think any of you will easily forget the photographs which we saw, showing the terrible contrast between two young girls with everything to live for and their two corpses left to rot in East Lothian.

At this time of year and particularly on Monday we heard the famous words of Laurence Binyon in his poem 'For the Fallen'. That was written for the young people who gave their lives in the Great War but may have some resonance for the families of Christine and Helen:

'They shall grow not old as we that are left grow old.
Age shall not weary them nor the years condemn.
At the going down of the sun and in the
morning we will remember them.'

I say that because, while all of their loved ones would have wished to see them live on to a ripe old age, the memories they will have of them will always be of two happy home-loving innocent girls unbesmirched by the ravages of time.

That is, indeed, how I think the whole of the country will remember them, thanks to the iconic photograph of the two of them which the media have published many times over the years. It looks like it was taken in a photo booth, it has all the appearances of a 'selfie', and it sums up in more than mere words what a dreadful loss was caused by Angus Sinclair and Gordon Hamilton.

I doubt if you have enjoyed this experience, but I hope that it has given you a good insight into how our system of justice works.

> We are all grateful to you. Lawyers and judges have important roles
> to play, but the ultimate decision in any trial is committed to jurors,
> without whom there would be no justice. Your labours are now at an
> end and I can now discharge you. Thank you.

Helen's dad, Morain Scott, who was then age eighty-four, said he
had promised his wife Margaret on her deathbed in a hospice in 1989
that he would secure justice for his daughter. Finally that day had
now come, and his thoughts were similar to those he had struggled
with every day since her death when he said:

> I wonder where she would have been today. Would she be married?
> Would she have children? Would I have grandchildren? They've
> stolen life from two youngsters who had their whole lives ahead of
> them.

Speaking outside the court, Helen's family said, 'We finally have
justice for Helen and Christine.' Her brother Kevin said he felt
the thirty-seven year minimum sentence was appropriate, as it had
been thirty-seven years since the murders had been committed. He
described his sister as a 'country girl with beautiful blue eyes and a
beautiful smile, never to forget.' He also spoke about the positive that
came from such a terrible act saying:

> Decades after their deaths, Helen and Christine's legacy is to have
> changed Scotland's justice system for the better. The introduction of
> the double jeopardy amendment will prevent other families suffering
> the way we have.

Angus Sinclair was already serving a life sentence in prison until
he died, so the sentence didn't affect him. Nonetheless, for so many
others it meant absolutely everything.

Sinclair had now been found guilty of four murders: Christine
Eadie, Helen Scott, Mary Gallagher and Catherine Reehill. He had
voluntarily given a DNA sample to police in the mid-1990s, and that
had led to convictions for the murders of three women two decades
earlier.

Although Sinclair was now convicted of the crimes, his unwillingness
to confess combined with Hamilton's early death meant that many
questions still remained about what happened on that night in

October 1977.

Retired detective superintendent Allan Jones, the lead investigator responsible for bringing Sinclair to trial the first time, gave his considered view on what really happened, and his interpretation of some of the gaps in what is known. Few know the details of the case, or have studied Sinclair, as much as him. He believes that Helen and Christine would have endured an ordeal lasting up to four hours, with Sinclair using two separate dump sites purely just to 'prolong his enjoyment' of their agony.

In his long police career, he has no doubt that he was the worst criminal he ever dealt with, and in the killings of Helen and Christine he saw the very worst of Sinclair. He told the *Edinburgh News* what he believed truly happened that night, and why he believes it was all planned:

> He's choreographed it in his mind before he's actually done it. That sets him apart from someone acting on the spur of the moment or out of anger... Hamilton was twenty-two, Sinclair was thirty-three. He looked upon Sinclair with admiration. He would see the criminality Sinclair was involved in – robberies, violent crime. Sinclair was a hard man, and a lot of the things that Gordon probably wasn't. I think Sinclair manipulated him like he did with many people, and got him involved. At the same time, Hamilton committed these monstrous acts. You can't force someone to do these horrific things. He's been complicit. But he's been taken there and manipulated by Sinclair.

> Two girls or one girl. I think that's been his plan. He's so fastidious in his planning. He would watch people, he would stake places out and then target them at a time that suited him. In the World's End, it's been an opportune moment for him. There's been two really young girls. He's in a strange town so nobody knows him. It's almost like he's operating in anonymity. Helen and Christine had the misfortune of being there at the same time and place as these two individuals. I think it would've changed pretty soon after the girls got in Sinclair's Toyota Hiace. There would be a lot of physical violence to subdue them. The minute they got in that car, that would be it for them. It's a fourteen mile drive to Gosford Bay, and Sinclair knows one of the few places you can park up – not a recognised parking area but flattened grass – and Christine is deposited on the beachline. Then they've managed to make their way up into the Huntington/Coates

field, in close proximity to the old A1. Once they've did what they've did with Helen, they've literally been one hundred yards on to the A1 and on their way back home to Glasgow. So it's textbook stuff. This is not just chance and happenstance. He's planned it, prepared it.

He's used their clothing as ligatures. He's got ingenuity about him that he doesn't even need to take along weapons. That's not to say that he didn't have a knife to threaten the girls with, but he's not used it.

We were never able to establish where Christine was killed. There was not enough movement on the sand to suggest she was killed on the beach. I think it more likely to have happened in the open air rather than the vehicle, or in a disused building or somewhere we've never been able to find. I think Christine was the initial attack and Helen was still alive when her friend's body was dumped. It's another indication of what an audacious individual Sinclair is. He had the conceit to murder a girl then have time to take Helen away and do things there.

We always speculated about why they did that. It may be he was prolonging the whole event for his enjoyment. This is a personal opinion, but I think it was 3am or 4am before they've left. It's been protracted. You can see from the amount of violence used. The girls were both really badly beaten.

He spoke about the caravanette saying:

Two people can travel in it and control a person or two people. It's better than a normal saloon car, especially if you have to bundle someone into it.

Jones also gave his view on why not all of the girls' clothes were found, saying that in his view they were taken as trophies. In a number of the cases covered in this book we have seen items taken by Sinclair following the murder. If he did take trophies, is there somewhere he stored them, somewhere that is yet to be discovered? Or did he destroy them?

Morain Scott died in October 2015, aged eighty-five, a year after seeing justice for his daughter Helen. There were lots of public tributes paid to him, including the following from Lord Advocate Frank Mulholland QC:

'I am saddened to hear of Morain's death. Morain was a lovely man who bore his daughter's murder with great dignity and forbearance. He never gave up hope that one day Helen's murderer would be brought to justice. I was pleased to play a part in this and that this happened during Morain's lifetime. I know that he promised his late wife that he would do everything in his power to achieve this. He made good on his promise. May he rest in peace.'

22

2016 Appeal Against Sentence

APPEAL COURT, HIGH COURT OF JUSTICIARY

[2016] HCJAC 24

HCA/2014/004974/XC

Lady Paton

Lady Clark of Calton

Lord Malcolm

OPINION OF THE COURT

delivered by LADY PATON

in

APPEAL AGAINST SENTENCE

by

ANGUS SINCLAIR

Appellant;

Against

HER MAJESTY'S ADVOCATE

Respondent:

Appellant: Duguid QC, McCall QC;

(Faculty Services Limited for AFJ Solicitors)

Respondent: F Mulholland QC, Lord Advocate; Crown Agent

24 March 2016

PUNISHMENT PART OF 37 YEARS

[1] On 14 November 2014, after trial at Livingston High Court, the appellant (then aged 69) was convicted of the following offences:

"(001) on 15 and 16 October 1977 between the World's End Public House, High Street, Edinburgh and Gosford Bay, Aberlady, East Lothian and elsewhere in Scotland you ANGUS ROBERTSON SINCLAIR did, whilst acting along with Gordon Hamilton, born 1 March 1955, your brother in law, now deceased … assault Christine Eadie, born 21 February 1960, aged 17 years … repeatedly punch and kick her on the head and body or otherwise inflict blunt force injuries on her, bite her on the body, remove her clothing, force her legs apart, insert your penis in her anus and vagina and rape her, force her pants into her mouth, tie a ligature around her head thereby holding said pants in her mouth, bind her wrists, tie a ligature around her neck, compress her neck and asphyxiate and strangle her and did murder her, and further did steal her clothing and footwear, her handbag and contents, jewellery and personal effects, with intent to prevent law enforcement from recovering these items and did thereby attempt to pervert the course of justice;

and

(002) on 15 and 16 October 1977, between the World's End Public House, High Street, Edinburgh and a field at Huntington to Coates Road, near Haddington, East Lothian and elsewhere in Scotland you ANGUS ROBERTSON SINCLAIR did, whilst acting along with Gordon Hamilton, born 1 March 1955, your brother in law, now deceased … assault Helen Anne Scott, born 5 July 1960, aged 17 years … force her to walk barefooted into said field, forcibly remove the strap from her handbag, repeatedly punch and kick her on the head and body or otherwise inflict blunt force injuries on her, stamp on her head, remove her trousers, tights and pants, insert your penis in her vagina, rape her, force her pants into her mouth, bind her wrists, place a ligature around her neck, compress her neck and asphyxiate and strangle her and did murder her, and further did steal items of her clothing and footwear, her handbag and contents and personal effects, with intent to prevent law enforcement from recovering these items and did thereby attempt to pervert the course of justice."

[2] The trial judge, Lord Matthews, imposed a life sentence with a punishment part of 37 years.

EVENTS IN THE APPELLANT'S LIFE

[3] The following events occurred during appellant's life:

7 June 1945: The appellant was born.

25 August 1961: The appellant (then aged 16) was convicted in

Edinburgh High Court of culpable homicide. The victim was a young girl aged seven. Lord Matthews in his report at page 2 notes: "I was told that the conviction on 25 August 1961 for culpable homicide involved his interfering with the private parts of his victim, aged seven, tying her with a ligature and strangling her." The appellant was sentenced to 10 years detention.

1968-69: The appellant (then aged 23-24) was released from custody.

15-16 October 1977: The appellant (then aged 32) murdered 17-year-old Christine Eadie and 17-year-old Helen Scott, in what became known as the "World's End murders". As detailed in the charges (paragraph [1] above) the modus operandi included punching, kicking, biting, raping (vaginally and, in the case of one victim, anally), and strangling with a ligature. The murders remained unsolved for about 30 years.

1978 (i.e. within a year of the 1977 murders):The appellant (then aged 33) murdered 17-year-old Mary Gallagher, using a similar modus operandi to that adopted in the World's End murders, although also using a knife. The murder remained unsolved for over 20 years.

31 August 1982:The appellant (then aged 37) was convicted in Edinburgh High Court of three charges of rape, seven charges of lewd and libidinous practices, and breach of the peace. He was sentenced to life imprisonment. He has been in prison ever since.

4 June 2001: The appellant (a life prisoner aged 56) was convicted in Glasgow High Court of the 1978 murder of Mary Gallagher. A further life sentence was imposed, with a punishment part of 15 years.

2007: The appellant was tried for the 1977 World's End murders. The trial court sustained a "no case to answer" submission, and the appellant was acquitted.

2011: The Double Jeopardy (Scotland) Act 2011 was enacted by the Scottish Parliament, and came into force in November 2011.

27 March 2014: The High Court granted an application by the Crown under the 2011 Act (based on advances in DNA techniques) for authority to bring a fresh prosecution against the appellant in respect of the World's End murders.

INDICTMENT AND TRIAL FOR WORLD'S END MURDERS

[4] An indictment for the World's End murders was served on the appellant. The productions listed in the indictment included the following:

Production 47: the extract conviction (1961) of culpable homicide of the seven-year-old girl

Production 48: the extract conviction (1982) of rape and lewd practices

Production 49: the extract conviction (2001) of the murder of 17-year-old Mary Gallagher

Production 50: a certified extract of the indictment for the 1961 culpable homicide conviction

Production 51: a certified extract of the indictment for the 1982 rape and lewd practices conviction

Production 52: a certified extract of the indictment for the 2001 murder of Mary Gallagher.

[5] The trial began on 13 October 2014 and lasted about five weeks. Each day, the appellant appeared from custody. On 14 November 2014 the appellant, then a serving life prisoner aged 69, was convicted unanimously of charges 1 and 2, namely the World's End murders.

[6] The Lord Advocate moved for sentence. It was not necessary to lay before the court a social enquiry report or a criminal justice social work report, as the appellant had previously served (and was obviously serving) a prison sentence. In the course of his address, the Lord Advocate advised the court of the appellant's history, and made reference to productions 47 to 52, described in paragraph [4] above. The trial judge records this part of the proceedings in his report at pages 2 to 4 as follows:

"In moving for sentence the Lord Advocate not only tendered a schedule of previous convictions but advised me of the detail of the most significant of those in terms of the case of Riley v HM Advocate 1999 SCCR 644. A copy of the convictions will doubtless be with the papers. I was told that the conviction on 25 August 1961 for culpable homicide involved his interfering with the private parts of his victim, Catherine Reehill, aged 7, tying her with a ligature and strangling her. He was convicted of firearms charges on 21 January 1980 and then on 31 August 1982 was convicted of three charges of rape, seven charges of lewd and libidinous practices and behaviour and one charge of breach of the peace. He was imprisoned for life on charges 1 to 3. The sexual charges involved young children. On 4 June 2001 at the High Court of Justiciary sitting in Glasgow he was convicted of murder. The victim was a 17 year old girl and the crime was committed on waste ground. He presented a knife at her, forced her onto the ground, raped her, compressed her neck, repeatedly struck her on the neck with the knife, tied a ligature around her neck and compressed her neck with it.

He had received a determinate sentence of 10 years for the culpable homicide charge and was released in 1968 or 1969 but was now serving two life sentences. I understand that the punishment part in respect of the conviction on 4 June 2001 was 15 years imprisonment.

He had never spent any time in custody on remand in connection with the current case. He appeared on petition on 31 March 2005 and the case duly proceeded to trial but he was acquitted on 10 September 2007 when a submission of no case to answer was upheld. The Double Jeopardy (Scotland) Act came into force in November 2011. The Crown obtained authority for a new prosecution on 27 March 2014, largely based on new evidence as a result of DNA work which had been carried out at Cellmark. He was reindicted in May 2014.

For the appellant, Mr Duguid QC reminded me that many of the convictions were not previous ones but he accepted that it was appropriate that they be brought to the attention of the court. He had nothing to say about the appellant's personal circumstances."

[7] On 14 November 2014 Lord Matthews imposed a life sentence (a third life sentence for the appellant) with a punishment part of 37 years. In his sentencing statement, the judge said:

"There was no reason for Christine Eadie or Helen Anne Scott to think that 15 October 1977 was going to be particularly eventful. To all intents and purposes they would have a pleasant Saturday night out, the sort of occasion they would look forward to enjoying for many years to come with friends and family, including perhaps children and grandchildren.

Helen, shy and retiring and Christine more outgoing, had not long left school and started work, no doubt harbouring ambitions of moving on to greater things. It was not made clear in the evidence how Christine saw her future but we know that Helen wanted to be a children's nurse.

Whatever dreams they had, they turned into nightmares shortly after they left the World's End Pub, the name of which has become synonymous with these notorious murders.

Little were they to know that they had the misfortune to be in the company of two men for whom the words evil and monster seem inadequate.

Unless one day your conscience, if you have one, motivates you to tell the truth, no one other than you will ever know precisely what part you and Gordon Hamilton played in these awful events. Perhaps it does not matter. What does matter is that the girls were subjected to an ordeal beyond comprehension and then left like carrion, exposed for all to see, with no dignity, even in death.

For them at least the nightmare is over and if they were not resting in peace before today I hope that they are now.

The nightmare for their families and friends, on the other hand, has gone on from those first awful moments when they heard the news no one should hear until even now, 37 years later and counting. It will never end. No one who saw the evidence of Helen's father and sisters and Christine's mother, as well as Helen's boyfriend, could fail to have been moved by it. They are an example to us all, waiting patiently for justice while the authorities have worked tirelessly to achieve it.

As for you, you have displayed not one ounce of remorse for these terrible deeds. The evidence in this case as well as your record, details of which have now been revealed, show that you are a dangerous predator who is capable of sinking to the depths of depravity.

I do not intend to waste many words on you. You are well aware that the only sentence I can pass is one of life imprisonment.

Before I turn to the details of that I must deal with two matters which are frankly academic.

I certify that the offences of which you have been convicted attract the notification provisions of the Sexual Offences Act 2003. In other words you are on the so-called Sex Offenders Register but the chances of your ever having to notify the police of anything in the future are remote in the extreme.

Secondly I direct the clerk to notify the Scottish Ministers of your conviction in terms of the Protection of Vulnerable Groups (Scotland) Act 2007.

Merely sentencing you to life imprisonment is not the limit of my duties. The concept of parole does not sit easily with your crimes and indeed seems like an insult to the girls' memories but nonetheless I have to designate a period which must pass before you can apply to be released on licence. The purpose of that period, known as the punishment part of the sentence, is to satisfy the requirements of retribution and deterrence. Whether you are ever released thereafter will not be a matter for me but for the Parole Board but I intend to make matters easy for them.

On both charges 1 and 2 in cumulo I sentence you to life imprisonment to run from today and I fix the punishment part at 37 years."

APPEAL AGAINST SENTENCE

[8] The appellant appeals against the punishment part of 37 years. His ground of appeal is in the following terms:

"5. The punishment part of 37 years was excessive. The selection of the punishment part reflected the length of time between the date of the murders and the conviction of the accused. It appears that was the principal basis for its selection. The passage of time prior to conviction should not have been a relevant factor in determining the length of the punishment part in circumstances where the accused was not actively evading arrest and had previously been tried and acquitted (in 2007) for the current offences. The trial judge failed to take sufficient account of comparable sentences. He failed to take sufficient account of what period a judge might have recommended be served had the appellant been convicted in 1977. Having regard to the appellant's criminal record (in terms of section 101 and 101A of the 1995 Act), the punishment part of 37 years was excessive."

RELEVANT LEGISLATION

[9] The Criminal Procedure (Scotland) Act 1995

"Section 101: Previous convictions: solemn proceedings

(3) Previous convictions shall not … be laid before the presiding judge until the prosecutor moves

(a) for sentence …

and in that event the prosecutor shall lay before the judge a copy of the notice referred to in subsection (2) or (4) of section 69 of this Act.

(7) Where a person is convicted of an offence, the court may have regard to any previous conviction in respect of that person in deciding on the disposal of the case …

Section 101A: Post-offence convictions etc

(1) This section applies where an accused person is convicted of an offence ('offence O') on indictment.

(2) The court may, in deciding on the disposal of the case, have regard to —

(a) any conviction in respect of the accused which occurred on or after the date of offence O but before the date of conviction in respect of that offence ...

(4) The court may have regard to any such conviction ... only if it is

(a) specified in a notice laid before the court by the prosecutor and

(b) admitted by the accused or proved by the prosecutor (on evidence adduced then or at another diet ...)"

[10] Section 101A was inserted in the Criminal Procedure (Scotland) Act 1995 by section 70 of the Criminal Justice and Licensing (Scotland) Act 2010. The commencement date for section 101A was 28 March 2011: see paragraph 2(1) and Schedule 1 of the Criminal Justice and Licensing (Scotland) Act 2010 (Commencement No 8, Transitional and Savings Provisions) Order 2011 (SSI 2011/178), where the date of commencement for section 70 ("Disclosure of convictions and non-court disposals") was defined, "[f]or all purposes in respect of offences committed on or after [28th March 2011]", as 28 March 2011.

THE SENTENCING JUDGE'S REPORT
TO THE APPEAL COURT

[11] The sentencing judge reported to the appeal court inter alia as follows:

"It is said that the punishment part of 37 years was excessive. It is said that the principal basis for the selection of that period was that it reflected the length of time between the date of the murders and the conviction of the appellant. That is not a relevant factor in determining the length of the punishment part. The appellant was not actively evading arrest and had previously been tried and acquitted for the offences. It is said that I failed to take sufficient account of comparable sentences and failed to take sufficient account of what period the judge might have recommended he serve had the appellant been convicted in 1977.

I had regard to the nature of these offences and the appellant's dreadful criminal record. That included the convictions which post-dated the offences, in terms of section 101A of the Criminal Procedure (Scotland) Act 1995, as amended. I concluded that a punishment part of a period of years in the high 30s was appropriate. I could have chosen a longer period than 37 years but it did seem to me that coincidentally there was an element of real justice in the period I selected which reflected the length of time the families had had to live with the consequences of these dreadful crimes. There was in my opinion no comparable case. I am aware that periods of 30 and 33 years imprisonment was not overturned on appeal in the case of Wade and Coats v HM Advocate [2014] HCJAC 88 and periods of 29 and 33 years imprisonment were not challenged in Snowden and Jennings, for what it is worth. As it happens the appellant is already serving two life sentences and by my calculation the period of 37 years is effectively one of just over 35 years when account is taken of the expiry date of the sentence imposed in 2001. There is no reason of which I am aware why I should take account of the period a judge might have recommended he serve had he been convicted in 1977. There are far too many imponderables to take account of that and given the later offences as well as the effect of cases such as HMA v Boyle and others [2009] HCJAC 89, it would have been unrealistic."

SUBMISSIONS FOR THE APPELLANT

[12] Senior counsel for the appellant submitted that the punishment part was the longest in Scotland to date. While the case concerned the brutal and merciless murders of two young girls, the question was whether 37 years was necessary, appropriate, and fell within the judge's discretion.

[13] The sentencing judge's reasoning could be criticised in several respects.

Length of time since commission of offence

[14] The judge's report seemed to indicate that 37 years had been selected because 37 years had passed since the murders. If adopting that approach, the judge should have taken into account the first abortive trial in 2007, and the passage of time between 2007 and the trial in 2014 (seven years, not attributable to the appellant), and should have deducted seven years. But in any event, the passage of time since the crimes was an inappropriate consideration to take into account.

COMPARABLE CASES

[15] It was for the High Court of Justiciary to set the parameters for punishment parts in life sentences to reflect contemporary Scotland (Boyle v HM Advocate 2010 JC 66 paragraph [18]). There should be a degree of consistency. Each case turned on its facts, but if the appellant was to receive the longest punishment part to date, there

had to be some reason to distinguish his case from other cases.

[16] A punishment part of 32 (discounted from 35 for a plea of guilty) was imposed in Smith v HM Advocate 2011 SCCR 134. That case involved the murder of a mother and her 10-year-old daughter with several aggravating features of the kind referred to in Walker v HM Advocate 2002 SCCR 1036, namely (i) a child victim; (ii) a sexual assault on the child; (iii) injuries to the private parts of the mother; (iv) concealment of the bodies; (v) a previous conviction for indecent assault resulting in a custodial sentence. If such a case attracted a starting point of 35 years, it was difficult to justify 37 years in the present case which had none of those aggravating features.

[17] The case of Wade and Coats v HM Advocate [2014] HCJAC 88 concerned the loss of one life (not two, as here), but there had been illegal detention, torture, the cutting off of parts of a live victim's body, and disposal of the dead body such that it was never recovered. Arguably that case involved a higher level of depravity. The punishment parts imposed were respectively 30 years and 33 years.

[18] In his sentencing statement in HM Advocate v Snowden and Jennings in October 2015 (murder by fire of three quarters of a family) Lord Matthews had observed that the case was "without doubt the most appalling crime I have ever been involved with in my professional career". The two accused had masterminded a fire in which three people (one a child) lost their lives. Another person was attacked with ammonia. The punishment parts were respectively 33 years and 29 years.

[19] In HM Advocate v Tobin 2008 GWD 40-607, the accused received a punishment part of 21 years for the murder of Angelika Kluk, and subsequently a punishment part of 30 years for a murder which had taken place prior to the Kluk murder.

[20] Further punishment parts included Beggs, petitioner 2005 SCCR 47, a sexual murder in 1999 (20 years); Campbell v HM Advocate 2004 SCCR 220, a murder with six victims (20 years); Chalmers v HM Advocate 2014 JC 229, murder and dismemberment (23 years); Coubrough v HM Advocate 2008 SCCR 317, a murder in 1971 (12 years); Currie v HM Advocate 2003 SCCR 676, the murder of a 76 year old woman in 1985 (18 years); McPhee v HM Advocate [2005] HCJAC 137, a murder in 1984 (a recommendation of 25 years); Walker v HM Advocate 2002 SCCR 1036, the shooting in 1985 of

two soldiers, with aggravating factors (30 years reduced on appeal to 27).

[21] The cases cited were all examples of terrible crimes. Each turned on its particular circumstances, but if the punishment part imposed on the appellant was the longest of all, there had to be some justification, such as the nature of the crime, or the particular circumstances of the appellant. No appropriate justification on a comparative basis had been given.

THE APPELLANT'S CRIMINAL RECORD

[22] The sentencing judge had also fallen into error by taking into consideration offences which took place after the 1977 murders. The only relevant previous conviction was the one dated 25 August 1961 for culpable homicide. However the judge, in his sentencing address, referred to the appellant as "a dangerous predator". Thus it appeared that the judge had taken into account a murder committed by the appellant in 1978 (for which he was eventually tried and convicted in 2001, and received a punishment part of 15 years); and 11 sex-related offences committed during 1978-1982. But the judge had not been entitled to do so. Although in his report the judge referred to section 101A(2) of the Criminal Procedure (Scotland) Act 1995, that provision applied only to offences committed after 28 March 2011. Accordingly the judge had erred by taking into account the offences which post-dated the 1977 murders.

The expiry date of the punishment part imposed in 2001

[23] The sentencing judge in his report suggested that the punishment part which he had imposed was "effectively one of just over 35 years" when account was taken of the expiry date of the 2001 sentence (i.e. the punishment part then imposed of 15 years, expiring in 2016). However that approach was erroneous, as the sentence imposed in 2001 was not a determinate sentence, but a life sentence.

What a judge might have recommended in 1977

[24] Finally, the trial judge failed to take sufficient account of what period a judge might have recommended to be served had the appellant been convicted in 1977.

CONCLUSION

[25] For all these reasons, the appeal court must look anew at the question of a punishment part. The appeal should be allowed, the punishment part of 37 years quashed, and a lower punishment part

imposed.

SUBMISSIONS FOR THE CROWN

[26] As issues of law had been raised, we called upon the Lord Advocate to offer submissions.

[27] In relation to section 101A, the Lord Advocate submitted that the common law was wider than that section, and that section 101A did not extinguish any part of the common law. Reference was made to Penman v HM Advocate 1999 SCCR 740; HM Advocate v Tobin 2008 GWD 40-607; and to an illustrative example, namely an offender who committed two offences; the second offence was discovered prior to the first offence; when being sentenced for the second offence, the offender would be treated as a first offender; but when the first offence came to light, it would be an injustice if the offender were to be sentenced without having regard to the whole circumstances of his case. For the same reason, the extract convictions and indictments/ complaints had been lodged in the present case, giving fair notice to the appellant that they might ultimately be referred to if he were found guilty. They were highly relevant to the sentencing process.

[28] Section 101A would allow the Crown to libel a conviction (whether previous or post-dated) in a case involving similar criminal conduct. But the present case was a different situation: it was simply necessary for the sentencing judge to be aware of all the circumstances, including the appellant's current status (a lifer twice over) and the fact that he had in the past been convicted of similar offences. The 1982 conviction and the 2001 conviction demonstrated a pattern of offending. It was important for the court to take that pattern into account in the context of deterrence.

[29] Lord Emslie had taken that approach in Tobin. Vicky Hamilton disappeared on 16 February 1991. Angelika Kluk was murdered on 24 September 2006. Tobin was taken into custody, tried, and convicted of the Kluk murder on 4 May 2007. He was given a life sentence with a punishment part of 21 years. Subsequently in 2008 he was tried, and on 2 December 2008, convicted of the murder of Vicky Hamilton. It was clear from Lord Emslie's sentencing statement that he had taken into account all the circumstances, including the Kluk case and the punishment part of 21 years. Section 101A simply offered a means whereby (after 28 March 2011) that information could be communicated to the court. The necessary information could be placed before the court as outlined in section 101A(4). But following

previous procedure, the means of communication could also be a social enquiry report, oral submissions, or the Riley procedure (which had the advantage of advance notice to the accused).

[30] Reference was made to page 3 (at the foot) of the sentencing judge's report in the present case (see the end of paragraph [6] above). It was logical for such information to be drawn to the attention of the court, in order that it be taken into account when sentencing. The media reporting the appellant's trial were well aware of his offending history. Judges should not be blind to information which was publicly available: such information must form part of the sentencing process. It would defy logic and common sense to have the appellant sentenced as a first offender in relation for the World's End murders. When selecting a sentence with deterrence in mind, the sentencing judge had to be aware of all the circumstances.

[31] The Crown's approach in the trial had been based on Riley v HM Advocate 1999 SCCR 644, at pages 648A-C, and 650A-B, F-G (Lord Sutherland). The Crown had followed that procedure in the present case. It was accepted that the issue in Riley was whether the sentencing court could go behind the bare terms of a schedule of previous convictions, and that the decision did not directly raise the point which arose in the present case. It was also accepted that the established sentencing practice was to treat previous convictions as an aggravation of the offence for which the judge was imposing a sentence, and accordingly later crimes were irrelevant for that purpose. However Riley was in effect an expansion or development of modern sentencing practice. As was explained at page 650F, what was sought to be achieved was an "appropriate disposal … in the circumstances of the case".

[32] In the present case, the relevant dates were as set out in paragraph [3] above. It was highly relevant for the judge in November 2014, when addressing the question of sentence in respect of the World's End murders, to be aware of the pattern and sequence of events, including the fact that the appellant had, in the year directly following 1977, carried out such a similar attack on and murder of a 17-year-old girl (Mary Gallagher). Thus the Crown had made all the relevant information available with fair notice to the appellant by lodging the certified copy indictments and the extract convictions. The court was then aware of all the circumstances when carrying out the sentencing exercise. Senior counsel for the appellant appeared to have accepted that approach at the trial (page 3 of the judge's report, the end of

paragraph [6] above).

FINAL RESPONSE FOR THE APPELLANT

[33] Senior counsel for the appellant submitted that a perceived injustice, namely the possibility that an accused might be treated as a first offender twice over, had been corrected by section 101A. However section 101A only affected offences committed after 28 March 2011, and there was no provision for back-dating. That did not sit comfortably with the Lord Advocate's position.

[34] Riley dealt with the particular question of a previous conviction, and whether the court should have more detail about that previous conviction.

[35] Penman concerned a determinate sentence, not a punishment part. The court was therefore entitled to take into account not only retribution and deterrence, but also the protection of the public. By contrast, when dealing with a punishment part, the court was expressly directed by section 2(2) of the Prisoners and Criminal Proceedings (Scotland) Act 1993 not to have regard to the protection of the public: that was a matter exclusively for the parole board. While therefore it was accepted that if subsequent offences were referred to in, say, a social enquiry report, it would be appropriate for the court to take that information into account (for example, if the accused was in prison, probation was not possible), whether such information could be used in other ways was another matter. The commission of subsequent offences should not impact on the offence for which the court was sentencing. It was not clear why post-dated offences could be taken into account for the purposes of retribution and deterrence. Lord Emslie's approach in Tobin had never been tested in the appeal court. The law prior to the 2011 Act had not been clear. Matters had only been clarified by section 101A of the 2011 Act.

DISCUSSION

[36] The appellant was found guilty of assaulting, raping, and murdering two young women in 1977. Those appalling crimes demonstrated an immeasurable capacity for evil, depravity, and sadism. The suffering of the victims and their bereaved families is, in our view, incalculable.

[37] On 14 November 2014, the appellant was sentenced to life imprisonment with a punishment part of 37 years.

Length of time since commission of offence

[38] We do not accept that the sentencing judge selected 37 years because that represented the length of time which had passed since the commission of the murders. As the sentencing judge explains, he had concluded at the outset that a punishment part "in the high 30s" should be imposed. That was his assessment of the gravity of the case. As he puts it, it was only "coincidentally" that the period selected mirrored the passage of time since the murders. In the result we are not persuaded that there is any merit in this argument.

COMPARABLE CASES

[39] We accept that comparisons with other cases may, in some circumstances, be of assistance. Nevertheless each case must be decided on its facts. There is no mandatory upper or lower limit set by either statute or case-law (cf paragraph [7] of Boyle v HM Advocate 2010 JC 66; paragraphs [12] to [15] of Smith v HM Advocate 2011 SCCR 134). As was further noted in Boyle at paragraph [7]:

"… [Section 2(3A)(b) of the Prisoners and Criminal Proceedings (Scotland) Act 1993] makes it plain that the specified period may exceed the likely extent of the remainder of the prisoner's natural life. Thus, while the statute does not empower the judge to specify a 'whole life' period, in an appropriate case a prisoner in Scotland may be sentenced to a period which in practical terms will extend until his or her death."

[40] It seems to us that an experienced sentencing judge who has presided over the trial, heard the witnesses, and seen the labels and productions, is in the best position to decide, in his discretion, the punishment part appropriate to the circumstances of the case. An appeal court should be slow to alter such an assessment, a fortiori as other punishment parts may have been imposed in different circumstances and in a different sentencing era: cf the observations of Lord Carloway (now Lord Justice General Carloway) in Smith at paragraph [15]. What may be regarded as an appropriate punishment part may vary from era to era.

[41] Against that background, it is our view that the present case, one of a sadistic double murder and rape of two young girls in the circumstances outlined in the judge's report, was truly horrific. In addition, the previous conviction for culpable homicide of a young girl was a major aggravating factor. In all the circumstances, we consider that the sentencing judge was entitled, exercising his discretion in the context of retribution and deterrence, to select a punishment part at

the very top of the range. We note the cases cited by senior counsel for the appellant, but bearing in mind the observations we have made in this paragraph and the two preceding paragraphs, we are not persuaded that the discretion of the sentencing judge was restricted in his selection by either statute or other cases, nor are we persuaded that the sentencing judge erred in his selection.

THE APPELLANT'S CRIMINAL RECORD

[42] We agree with the Lord Advocate that the common law, as it has developed over the years, is at least as wide as (if not wider than) section 101A of the 1995 Act. A judge is, at common law, entitled to have regard to all the relevant circumstances for the purposes of sentencing: it would be wholly unrealistic to suggest otherwise. Thus at common law, if an accused appears from custody throughout a trial, a sentencing judge would need to know what had given rise to such circumstances. Again at common law, if a judge is considering a non-custodial disposal such as a community payback order, information concerning convictions and disposals subsequent to the current offence might demonstrate that the accused (a) cannot be relied upon to co-operate with a non-custodial sentence, and (b) is, in any event, the subject of a substantial custodial sentence.

[43] Thus the common law, as developed in the context of modern sentencing practice, clearly envisages that a sentencing judge should have an overall view of the accused's life in order to be able to sentence him or her appropriately. Such an overall view may properly be obtained from oral submissions, medical reports, reports from psychologists or psychiatrists, social enquiry reports/criminal justice social work reports, and/or the production of extract convictions with certified extracts of the indictments, following the procedure suggested by Lord Sutherland in Riley v HM Advocate 1999 SCCR 644 at pages 648A-C and 650A-B, F-G (and being the procedure adopted by the Crown in the present case).

[44] At least two authorities cited by the Lord Advocate illustrate such common law sentencing powers, namely Penman v HM Advocate 1999 SCCR 740; and HM Advocate v Tobin 2008 GWD 40-607.

[45] In Penman, the criminal appeal court approved the taking into account of a conviction dated 1996 (relating to criminal conduct between 1982 and 1987) when sentencing an accused in 1999 (in relation to criminal conduct between 1966 and 1976). We accept that the sentencing judge in that case had regard to retribution, deterrence,

and risk to the public, whereas the judge in the present case was concerned with deterrence and retribution but not risk to the public (section 2(2) of the Prisoners and Criminal Proceedings (Scotland) Act 1993). Nevertheless we consider that the court's observations, particularly at page 745, give guidance. Thus in the present case, the convictions of 1982 and 2001 were proper and relevant matters for the sentencing judge to take into account at common law.

[46] In Tobin, the sequence of events was as follows:

16 February 1991: Tobin murdered Vicki Hamilton

24 September 2006: Tobin murdered Angelika Kluk

4 May 2007: Tobin was convicted of the murder of Angelika Kluk and given a punishment part of 21 years

2 December 2008: Tobin was convicted of the murder of Vicky Hamilton and given a punishment part of 30 years.

When sentencing Tobin in 2008 for the murder of Vicky Hamilton, the sentencing judge (Lord Emslie) was, at common law, entitled to take into account the whole circumstances of the case, including Tobin's current status as a prisoner serving a life sentence; the reason for that status; and the details of his offending history including the punishment part of 21 years for the murder of Angelika Kluk (which occurred chronologically after the murder of Vicki Hamilton). Had a social enquiry report been necessary (which it was not), that report would have revealed those details. While in terms of section 2(2) of the 1993 Act, the sentencing judge was not to take into account risk to the public, nevertheless the judge was entitled to have regard to the whole circumstances of the case.

[47] It is our opinion therefore that section 101A merely reflects the current common law position, as it has developed, and does not detract from or limit existing common law sentencing powers. Section 101A also provides a procedural route for giving appropriate notice to the court and to the accused (cf Renton & Brown Criminal Procedure Legislation paragraph A4-228.6).

[48] Against that background, the judge's reference to section 101A was unnecessary, as the murders for which he was sentencing the appellant occurred before 2011. However the approach which he adopted did not demonstrate any error or departure from common law sentencing powers as they have developed. As we have already indicated, the judge was faced with the double murder of young women on the threshold of life, in a brutal and sadistic attack. The

circumstances of the offence justified a punishment part at the top of the range. In addition, there was the previous conviction of the appellant (then aged 16 years) for an offence of culpable homicide only eight years previously, the victim being a young girl aged seven who had been sexually interfered with, for which offence the appellant had been sentenced to 10 years detention – all justifying the judge's description of him as a "dangerous predator". Those matters, set within the pattern of the appellant's life to the date of the current sentencing, were entirely relevant and to be taken into account by the sentencing judge.

[49] We therefore reject the arguments relating to the appellant's criminal record.

THE EXPIRY DATE OF THE PUNISHMENT PART IMPOSED IN 2001

[50] As for the judge's reference at page 25 of his report to "the expiry date of the sentence imposed in 2001" (i.e. a previous life sentence with a punishment part of 15 years imposed for the rape and murder of another young woman), we note that the reference is prefaced by the words "As it happens". Properly construed, the judge was, in our view, indicating that he had selected the period of 37 years, and following upon that selection, made the observation concerning the 2001 sentence. We do not accept that the reference to the expiry date of the 2001 punishment part made any significant contribution to the judge's selection of 37 years.

WHAT A JUDGE MIGHT HAVE RECOMMENDED IN 1977

[51] We do not accept that the sentencing judge was obliged to carry out some sort of retrospective assessment of what a sentencing judge in 1977 might have recommended, had the appellant been convicted at that time. The sentencing of the appellant should not be based on such a hypothetical, theoretical or speculative exercise: rather it is a matter to be assessed at the time of his conviction, when all the relevant circumstances can be taken into account. Accordingly we reject this argument.

CONCLUSION

[52] In the result we are not persuaded that the judge erred.

Decision

[53] For the reasons given above, we refuse the appeal against sentence.

23

Similar FACT Evidence in Scotland

In 2007, after the unsuccessful first prosecution of Angus Sinclair for the World's End murders, in the legal debate that followed – as we have already discussed – the Scottish Government asked the Scottish Law Commission (SLC) to consider a number of points that arose from the Sinclair trial. Specifically, they asked them:

> To consider the law relating to:
>
> * Judicial rulings that can bring a solemn case to an end without the verdict of a jury, and rights of appeal against such;
>
> * The principle of double jeopardy, and whether there should be exceptions to it;
>
> * Admissibility of evidence of bad character or of previous convictions, and of similar fact evidence; and
>
> * The Moorov doctrine.

We have already seen how the first two points were considered and the law changed. But what about the next two points?

Firstly, let's consider similar fact evidence. Across the globe, similar fact evidence (or the similar fact principle) establishes the conditions under which factual evidence can be used at trial for the purpose of inferring that the accused committed the offence for which they are being tried.

A good example of similar fact evidence used in practice is the high-profile trial of Rose West, which began on 3 October 1995 at Winchester Crown Court. Although her husband Fred had admitted the part he played in murders, after he took his own life in prison Rose West faced ten counts of murder alone. She pleaded Not Guilty. The difficulty for the prosecution was that there was no specific evidence connecting Rose West to the murders.

Similar fact evidence was given by the women who bravely faced the court to tell of the unbelievably cruel sexual assaults in which Rose took part along with with her husband. The prosecution argued that this showed that based on the way she had behaved previously, Rose West was also involved in the attacks on the victims who had been murdered. Her legal team tried to argue that the evidence was inadmissible. According to her solicitor Leo Goatley, 'Similar fact evidence is circumstantial evidence... it's the smoke rather than the fire.'

Rose West was found guilty of ten counts of murder.

But at her appeal, similar fact evidence was again central in the legal arguments of her solicitors. They argued that as such a long period of time had passed since the deaths of the victims it was not known how they had died. They continued by arguing that Rose West had never admitted being involved in the murders, and there was some evidence that Fred West had carried out two murders and other attacks on his own, and the fact that one of the victims – Ann McFall from Glasgow, who disappeared before Rose and Fred even met – was found dismembered and bound with cord. The defence said this showed that Rose West had not been involved in killing the seven Cromwell Street victims discovered in similar circumstances. The appeal was dismissed, and Rose West is still in prison.

Similar fact evidence is clearly relevant for the trials of Angus Sinclair. After the first trial collapsed, there was considerable comment about how a change in the law in this area could have resulted in Sinclair being convicted. For example, the method of binding and killing Mary Gallagher could have made a huge difference to the jury if it had been used in Sinclair's first trial, as it clearly showed his method for a crime where he had been convicted. It is understandable why the Scottish Government asked the SLC to look at this area and make recommendations.

Before we consider the proposals made by the SLC in response to this request, let's touch briefly on the final point that the Scottish Government asked to be reviewed in 2007, which was the Moorov Doctrine, which is closely linked to similar fact evidence. It comes from a decision in Moorov (Samuel) v HM Advocate (1930) and is, to quote the SLC,

> A mechanism which applies where a person is accused of two or
> more separate offences, connected in time and circumstances. In such
> a case, where each of the offences charged is spoken to by a single
> credible witness, that evidence may corroborate, and be corroborated
> by, the other single witnesses, so as to enable the conviction of the
> accused on all the charges. In order for the doctrine to operate, each
> of the offences must be competently charged. It is not possible to rely
> for corroboration of a charge upon evidence of conduct, however
> similar, in respect of which the accused has previously been convicted
> or acquitted. The operation of the doctrine involves similar issues
> to cases of similar fact evidence, since it permits evidence relating
> to one alleged crime to be used in support of a charge relating to a
> separate incident. We have considered the origins and present state
> of the doctrine, and whether any reform is required. In particular, we
> have considered whether it would be appropriate, as part of a wider
> reform of the law of similar fact evidence, to allow corroboration to
> be found in evidence of similar offences which cannot be tried on the
> same indictment, such as, for example, offences in relation to which
> the accused has already been tried and acquitted or convicted.

In 2010, the SLC published a Discussion Paper on Similar Fact
Evidence and the Moorov Doctrine before producing their final
report in 2012. In their brief summary of their findings, they said
the following:

> As the law stands, the prosecution in Scotland cannot rely upon
> previous convictions to help prove their case against an accused
> person. If an accused, charged with murder, has been convicted
> of a number of other murders, the jury will not know this when
> considering their verdict. Other jurisdictions – most notably England
> and Wales – have rules which allow such evidence. Should Scots law
> be changed?

> According to the Scottish Law Commission in their Report on
> Similar Fact Evidence and the Moorov Doctrine, which is published
> today, the answer is 'Yes'. The Commission concludes that the present
> rules restricting the use of evidence that the accused has acted in a
> similar way on other occasions – including evidence that he or she
> has committed similar crimes – lack both logic and coherence. The
> Commission recommends that the law recognise that such evidence

can be highly relevant to the question of guilt or innocence. The Report argues that all relevant evidence – including evidence of similar previous convictions – should, in principle, be admissible. Included with the Report is a draft Bill which would give effect to the Commission's recommendations by replacing the present law with a clear and coherent statutory framework for the admission of all relevant evidence in criminal proceedings.

But as of today, in early 2021, nothing has changed and leading legal figures in Scotland are still debating whether or not changes should be made, with it seems, the majority arguing that it needs to change. We agree.

The fact is that the law on Similar Fact Evidence in Scotland is completely different to that currently in force in England and Wales and urgently needs to be updated so that unsolved cases where there is an offender like Sinclair can be proceeded to a jury and with a satisfactory conclusion. It feels wrong that this law as it stands prevents closure for relatives of victims and justice for those victims who are now unable to speak for themselves.

The discrepancy between the law in England/Wales and Scotland was highlighted in the trial of R v Robert Black in 1994. Serial killer Black had been arrested in Scotland for abduction of a six-year-old girl, and in the following re-investigation charges were brought for the murders of three other girls, dating from 1982 (Susan Maxwell), 1983 (Caroline Hogg) and 1986 (Sarah Harper). The first two offences were committed in Scotland, and were heavily reliant on similar fact evidence. Because of this, the prosecution decided to hold the trial at Newcastle Crown Court in England, which led to a successful prosecution and conviction.

When will these necessary changes finally be implemented?

Aftermath

The census of 1981 revealed that Scotland had a population of five million and thirty-five thousand. This makes it even more astonishing that at the time of the World's End murders there were three serial killers operating in Scotland. As well as Sinclair, Scotland was a hunting ground for Peter Tobin and Robert Black.

Black killed at least four girls, almost certainly more, and was only caught after a member of the public in the village of Stow, around thirty miles south-east of Edinburgh, by chance witnessed an abduction. David Herkes had been on the other side of the road as a young girl heading home after visiting a friend who wasn't home walked along the pavement past a parked transit van. Mr Herkes watched as she briefly paused at the passenger door and then was gone, as Black pushed her into the footwell and headed off. David had noted the number plate and informed police, who quickly set up a road block. Luckily for them, Black decided to turn round and drive back through Stow on his way south to Galashiels, running straight into the roadblock and was captured, He told officers, 'What a day it's been. It was a rush of blood. I've always liked young girls since I was a young kid.' Unfortunately, the girl had been sexually assaulted, but this vigilance from a member of the public certainly saved her life – and potentially the lives of other young girls.

Tobin killed at least three young women, and sexually assaulted others. He was only captured when the body of one of his victims, Angelika Kluk, was found in the church where he was employed as a handyman under the false name of 'Pat McLaughlin'.

All three men had sexual motives for their crimes. But they all managed to avoid being caught through traditional policing methods for long periods of time. Would all have avoided capture for so long today, in a world so different with increasing CCTV surveillance, mobile phone records, automatic number plate recording (ANPR), advances in forensic science and widespread sharing of information via social media? It is hard to say for certain, but it is unlikely.

Victims

We suggest that Sinclair was a more prolific killer than either Robert Black or Peter Tobin.

Sinclair was found guilty of four murders: Catherine Reehill, Christine Eadie, Helen Scott and Mary Gallagher. We believe he also killed Helen Kane, Patricia Black, Frances Barker, Anna Kenny, Hilda McAuley, Agnes Cooney, Eddie Cotogno and Margaret McLaughlin. That is a total of twelve murders. There is also a strong possibility that he was responsible for the deaths of Lesley Perrie and Sandy Davidson, which would bring the total to fourteen.

These are just those we know about. How many other missing persons lost their life at the hands of Sinclair? We have seen how he had an uncanny knack of spotting vulnerable people who he could exploit for his own gratification. How many sex workers or other vulnerable people at the edges of society, without a family or support network to report them missing, could he have killed?

It is unfortunate, to say the very least, that so much of the forensic evidence and other documentation related to unsolved crimes in the period when Sinclair was active was destroyed, especially by Strathclyde police.

We believe that there should be a public enquiry into the unsolved murders covered in this book, and the lost evidence. This should be accompanied with a public apology from Police Scotland. It is just absolutely unacceptable that so many families have been unable to find out what happened to their loved ones, and to be told that the files have been lost with no other explanation is outrageous. It is a national embarrassment, and a scandal. Politicians should rectify this today, and establish a public enquiry to close the chapter on this unsatisfactory period.

There are two other major victims who have been treated appallingly by the police and legal system in Scotland, Thomas Young and George Beattie. It is too late for Thomas Young, who has now died, but while George Beattie is still alive every effort must be made to clear his name. He didn't kill Margaret McLaughlin, and he should not go to his grave with this terrible miscarriage of justice still hanging over him. We urge the authorities to take action to correct this before it is too late.

Hamilton

Before we focus on Sinclair, let's reflect on the forgotten man, Gordon Hamilton. It is known beyond doubt that he committed the World's End murders with Sinclair, where he certainly raped both Christine and Helen, and was involved to some extent in their murder – just how much so is unclear. How many of the other crimes carried out by Sinclair also included Hamilton? It is known that he was involved in a number of robberies with Sinclair, so having been used to the level of violence used, it is difficult to believe that he wasn't responsible for more crimes. It is hard to believe that, however much he was manipulated by Sinclair, his only serious crime was a double abduction, double rape and double murder – and after this nothing.

Sinclair was taken into custody for the final time in 1981 and Hamilton didn't die until 1996. Did he commit more crimes on his own during this time, on his own or with someone else? His DNA hasn't matched any other unsolved crimes – yet – so maybe, as the alcoholism really took hold of Hamilton, and without the guiding figure of Sinclair, his criminal activity proceeded no further.

Families

Of course, our sympathies lie with all the families and friends of the people who had the misfortune to be a victim of Angus Sinclair. The other victims, usually the forgotten victims, are often the family of the murderer, and the actions of Sinclair certainly had a large effect on his own family.

If you recall, his son Gary was only aged ten when Sinclair was arrested for the rape of three young girls and the sexual assaults of a further nine in 1982. Just like Sinclair's mum had to leave the neighbourhood after her son had killed Catherine Reehill, so his wife Sarah felt that it would be best if she and Gary left the area.

They moved to the south of England, a long way from the terrible memories of Scotland.

Sarah and Gary had no contact at all with Sinclair from 1982, until she gave evidence against him at the World's End murder trial. Sarah wanted to completely forget Angus Sinclair, and wanted her son to be kept well away from him. When, not long after his conviction in 1982, Sinclair wrote Sarah a letter apologising for all that had happened and expressing his remorse, she told detectives that she ignored it. As Sinclair's wife, Sarah has suffered terribly. But detectives preparing for the World's End murder trials have spoken openly about how helpful, open and honest she was at all times. This must have been incredibly difficult, as Sarah was asked to dissect so much of her life with Sinclair. She and her son — and in fact all of his family — were also victims of Angus Sinclair.

We mentioned earlier that Gary had problems making friends and controlling his temper when he was at school. After leaving he joined the armed forces, in the hope of gaining some stability and discipline. He wasn't noted as a great talent, and after five years in the army hadn't progressed beyond the rank of private. In 1994, aged twenty-two, he was a soldier in the Highlanders Regiment, which was a new grouping formed by the amalgamation of the Queen's Own Highlanders (Seaforth and Camerons) and The Gordon Highlanders.

Gary was based in Edinburgh, but ahead of a forthcoming tour in Northern Ireland the group were training at an army camp in Wretham, Norfolk. Unlike his dad — who rarely drank alcohol — Gary was very fond of a few drinks, and one night when away training he left the camp without permission to go drinking with two of his colleagues in nearby Thetford. That night was just a normal one for him in terms of his drinking, and he consumed around seven pints of lager and four rums as his group spent some time in the pubs before heading off to a nightclub.

There were other members of the armed forces in the club, and outside, as the different groups got increasingly drunk, Gary Sinclair got into an argument with two welsh Guardsman over a wallet. He still had major issues with his temper, and in a rage violently assaulted both men before running off, climbing over a wall and trying to hide in someone's garden, next door to a Chinese restaurant. 25-year-old Wayne Garwood, an amateur footballer, had also been drinking heavily that evening, and he was in the wrong place at the wrong time. He almost literally stumbled across Sinclair in his hiding place and the two began to fight. Gary was a powerfully-built man, and during the altercation Wayne was badly hurt, so much so that he would later die of his injuries in the garden. Sinclair stripped an unconscious Wayne of his clothes before leaving the scene and heading back to the training camp. Wayne's body was not found for two days.

Gary Sinclair was arrested and charged with the murder of Wayne Garwood. It is hard to imagine quite how Sarah Sinclair must have reacted when she heard the news that her son had been charged with murder. Later, at his trial, Sinclair claimed that Wayne had attacked him, and he head-butted him in self-defence as he feared he was going to get hurt. He told how he felt Wayne's arms go limp after he struck him, but Sinclair was used to fighting and just thought that, like any other fight, Wayne would quickly get up and go home with nothing more serious than a few bruises.

Wayne's mum Mary was unaware of who Sinclair's dad was when she commented outside court that she felt so sorry for the parents of the man who killed her son, saying: 'I know what his mum and dad will be going through. It must be terrible for them, like it is for us.'

Gary Sinclair was sentenced to life in prison for murder. He spent his first four months in Wormwood Scrubs before being transferred to a jail closer to his mother's home in the south of England. Gary was released after thirteen years, and moved in with his mum Sarah at her house in Dorset. In 2010, he moved to Gloucestershire, where he married. Sarah now lives with her son. For a long time Sarah was criticised by the media as she remained married to Sinclair, saying that the wedding certificate was just a piece of paper. After Sinclair's conviction for the murders of Helen and Christine she finally divorced him.

Gary's only contact with his father was to write him a letter in 2007, as he faced the first trial for the World's End murders, begging him to plead guilty and save his family going through the ordeal of a trial, just as his mum had urged Sinclair to plead guilty to the assaults in children in 1982. In 2007, as we have read, Sinclair took no notice of the pleadings of his son.

What happened to other members of Sinclair's family? We have heard how his brother John never spoke with him again from way back in 1961, after Sinclair murdered Catherine Reehill. His sister Connie and her daughter Heather stayed close to Sinclair for a long time. Now Connie is widowed and living on the outskirts Glasgow, and her daughter Heather is still living in the house in Maryhill. Both stopped visiting Sinclair in jail in 2001 following his conviction for the murder of Mary Gallagher.

Sinclair's mum Maimie Sinclair never fully accepted the truth about her son. She died of a heart attack in 1987 aged eighty-one, enjoying a long life and a quiet death in the privacy of her own home. The same cannot be said of those who lost their lives at the hands of her son, Angus.

*

Summing up Angus Sinclair isn't easy.

This man, who kept all parts of his life in neat compartments separate from each other, and was able to act almost as a completely different person depending on the situation, is remarkable. We can also reflect on his cruelty, capacity for violence, ability to exploit vulnerability and desire to control every situation.

One trait that stands out more than any other, it can be argued, is his complete lack of empathy for any of his victims. Sinclair didn't care who he hurt, and after he had done so he showed no remorse for what he had done. This lack of empathy meant that he was a danger to those he met throughout his life.

At the beginning of this book we asked if Sinclair was Scotland's luckiest serial killer. We believe that the answer is almost certainly yes. From incompetent police work through to managing to slip away from almost every crime scene, Sinclair was certainly lucky. But he was also cunning and calculated, and this gave him the opportunity to remain lucky.

It is a sad fact that serial killers like Sinclair are remembered more than their victims. Not just those they have killed, but their families too. In this book we have tried to redress the balance and turn the attention to those who deserve to be heard – these victims.

For many, the death of Sinclair gave them some sort of closure.

Helen Scott's brother Kevin, on hearing of Sinclair's death, told the *Daily Record*:

> He was a monster. To treat innocent people the way he did was just evil. You would need to be a beast to commit those crimes. I would have wanted him to live longer, to serve more of the thirty-seven-year sentence, as opposed to getting the easy way out. I do feel for the families of the other victims that he may have had. They'll never be afforded the kind of justice that we received.

Every Christmas there are empty spaces at many dining tables, and at every school sports day they are missing parents and grandparents, due to the actions of Sinclair.

For all the reasons covered in this book, many will feel cheated that they will never know for sure whether Angus Robertson Sinclair was responsible for the deaths of their loved ones. We must give these people the public enquiry they deserve.

More than that, we must never forget them.

Angus Robertson Sinclair Timeline

1945   Angus Sinclair born 7 June in Glasgow

1959   Stole an offertory box from a Glasgow church, aged 13

1959   Housebreaking charge

1961   Committed lewd and libidinous practices on a seven-year-old girl. Sentenced to three years' probation

1961   Convicted of killing Catherine Reehill, aged seven. Sentenced to ten years in prison

1968   Serves six years and released

1970   Marries trainee nurse Sarah Hamilton (Gordon Hamilton's sister) and has a son two years later

1970   Suspected of the murder of Helen Kane in Edinburgh

1973   Suspected of the murder of Margaret McLaughlin in Carluke

1976   Suspected of the murder of Patricia Black

1977   Suspected of having murdered six Glasgow women within seven months: Frances Barker, 37, Hilda McAuley, 36, Agnes Cooney, 23, and Anna Kenny, 20, all from Glasgow, as well as Christine Eadie and Helen Scott from Edinburgh

1978   Murdered seventeen year-old Mary Gallagher in Glasgow

1979   On remand at Barlinnie Prison from 30 January 1979 to 14 June 1979, when he was bailed. Offence not known

1979   30 July: Suspected of the murder of Eddie Cotogno

1980   Illegal possession of a .22 calibre revolver: imprisoned

1982   Pleaded guilty to rape and sexual assault of eleven children aged between six and fourteen. Sentenced to life in prison

2000   Cold case review of 1978 Mary Gallagher murder

2001   Convicted of the murder of Mary Gallagher

2004 Sinclair's DNA is identified from semen taken from Christine Eadie and Helen Scott

2007 Trial for murders of Christine Eadie and Helen Scott collapses

2014 Following double jeopardy law change in Scotland retrial finds Sinclair guilty of World's End murders

2019 Sinclair dies aged 73 in Abercrombie wing of Glenochil Prison, Clackmannanshire on 11 March

2019 His death was the subject of a fatal accident inquiry at Stirling Sheriff Court because he died in jail

2020 The inquiry was told that Sinclair had suffered from deteriorating health for about 18 months prior to his death. Cause of death was certified as bronchopneumonia, ischaemic heart disease and cerebrovascular disease

Hansard Record of Debate into the Conviction of George Beattie

HC Deb 03 March 1993 vol 220 cc426-34426

Motion made, and Question proposed, That this House do now adjourn.—[Mr. Andrew Mitchell.]

11.55pm

Mr. Jimmy Hood (Clydesdale):

Tonight's Adjournment debate is about a 19-year-old Carluke boy who was convicted of murder in 1973. A simple lad − not very well educated − he was known in Carluke as a big softie. My speech will be confined to George Beattie's conviction, and I seek to prove to the House that it was a great miscarriage of justice. George Beattie did not and could not have murdered Margaret McCloughan. George Beattie is innocent.

A major problem with miscarriages of justice is getting the case reconsidered by the authorities. The only way to make Ministers or civil servants sit up and take notice is to get the message through to the public, through the newspapers or television. Miscarriages of justice − particularly those involving murder − are generally so complicated that newspapers and television present only a simplified version of the case, and then from one particular angle. In reality, such cases have many aspects and involve many intricate pieces of evidence.

George Beattie was convicted of murder in 1973. BBC Television broadcast two *Rough Justice* programmes about him in 1983 and 1985, and produced persuasive evidence that he was innocent of the crime for which he is in gaol today.

Those programmes concentrated solely on the evidence put before the court, and there is now evidence concerning police conduct in the case that points to George Beattie being a victim of a miscarriage of justice on several levels.

The aspect of Beattie's case to which I refer concerns personalities, professional reputation, police bureaucracy and—yes—politics. To understand fully what happened to Beattie, one must understand what was happening during the police investigation. The leading figure in the police work was Scotland's finest detective, William Muncie. Coincidentally, Muncie was born in Carluke, where the murder took place.

Success in the case against Beattie meant that Chief Superintendent Muncie would bring his career in Lanarkshire CID to a triumphant end, in the town of his birth. After the case, he went on to be Lanark assistant chief constable—then, even better, assistant chief constable of Strathclyde. Muncie's promotion meant that he left behind him an investigative disaster, with an innocent man gaoled and a murderer gone free.

Muncie had an impressive reputation. He had investigated 53 cases of murder, and the McCloughan case was to be his 54th. He had found the murderer every time—not one failure in any of his cases. It was a remarkable record to live up to.

Among Muncie's big murder case successes was the serial killer Peter Manuel; Gordon Hay—the Biggar murder: and James Keenan, the Lanark case. They were all solved using Muncie's favourite method, which was outlined in his memoirs. He first decided who was guilty, then took months finding the proof. That method failed him in the case of the murder at Carluke, when George Beattie was convicted.

To understand what happened, we must imagine being present at some of the investigations. Perhaps the key moment was 6 am on 11 July 1973. In the dawn light, Chief Superintendent Muncie questioned George Beattie in the Carluke glen, where the body of a young woman, Margaret McCloughan, had been found four days earlier. The superintendent had already been up half the night dealing with this, his last case. Perhaps it is not surprising in the circumstances that he forgot all his own golden rules, and allowed his men to charge Beattie. No doubt in other circumstances he would have shown better judgment.

In fact, Mr. Muncie was trusting to luck: he had been very lucky during his career, but his luck ran out that morning. No doubt he thought that the evidence against Beattie would turn up, but it did not. Nothing seems to have gone right in the case from the start.

When Beattie was charged, Muncie was already four days into a botch-up of an investigation over which he had lost control. Uniformed police had trampled all over the scene of the crime before Muncie even got there; the photographer, acting without Muncie's direction, had missed a vital shot of the umbrella that the victim had used to defend herself. It would have told the court so much about what had happened—but there was no photographic evidence of where that umbrella had been found, and in what condition. One of the key points is whether the umbrella was up or down at the time; but, because Mr. Muncie was not on top form, we cannot say with any certainty which was the case.

Most important of all, Muncie's men had found a knife on the ground near the victim. They were all convinced that it was the murder weapon, but they were wrong. The chief superintendent himself soon realised that the rust on its blade ruled it out. What happened to his opinion shows the lack of organisation on the team: it did not reach all its members. That may not be surprising. The team of detectives came from half a dozen different stations, and examination of the police work reveals that liaison was poor.

Mr. Muncie, however, added to the problems himself, perhaps because of his robust personality. He let a Scottish newspaper fly him around the area in a helicopter; he said that it helped him to see the hidden paths around the glen. We may wonder why he did not know all those hidden paths, having spent his boyhood in the village when all the children played in the glen. The important point, however, is that the *Daily Record* picture taken from the helicopter was an investigative mistake of the first order. The picture that the newspaper published gave away one of the key police secrets—where the body had been found.

But there was worse to come. Two of Mr. Muncie's officers gave a guided tour of the scene of the crime to the man on whom Muncie eventually fixed as the murderer. That suspect—my constituent George Beattie—told officers John Adam and George Waddell that he had walked through the glen at the time when they believed that the murder had taken place. The officers decided to take him to the scene—through the police cordon, past Muncie's caravan headquarters, right to where the murder had happened. It started to rain.

Hon. Members may think that what happened next was highly irregular. There the men were, standing right by the scene of the murder—on the very spot where the attack on the victim had begun. When it began to rain, they did not walk the few yards to the police caravan headquarters for shelter; instead, Detective Constable Waddell ran past the caravan, nearly a mile to the car. The other officer—Adam—was left alone with Beattie at the scene of the crime. Apparently, he took no notes of what he did or said to Beattie while they were there.

The police would claim that Beattie was not a suspect at the time; he only became that when he told them details about the scene of the crime. But Beattie was the only man whom the police found who had been in the glen at about the time when they thought that the victim had been killed, so he must have been some kind of suspect. Why take him to the scene of the crime, leave him alone with an officer and then claim that he could not have known details of the scene unless he had committed the murder?

The story told by the two police officers had changed by the time it got to court. Adam, the man who stayed with Beattie in the glen, later claimed that he, not Waddell, had gone to the car. Waddell did not corroborate the second version. What was the head of a police investigation doing allowing such behaviour? Muncie knew that detectives should never show a suspect the scene of a crime. Perhaps it is no coincidence that Adam and Waddell were immediately sent back to base in Motherwell and took no further part in the inquiry after that incident.

We might wonder why none of the other detectives heard of the "guided tour" of the scene of the crime. Of course, the officers involved were no longer on the case, because they had been sent back home, but no one told the other detectives on the investigation what had happened. Later, when another two detectives questioned Beattie, they were surprised to learn that he knew so much about the scene of the crime.

The handling of Beattie got worse. He was left waiting in a room where the girl's clothing was laid out. His interrogators were doubly surprised when he described clothing that had been locked in her suitcase. The most astonished was Sergeant Dougie Mortimer from Lanark. He knew little about the case, because he had been on holiday and had only just joined the inquiry. When Beattie came out with the details about the victim's clothing, Mortimer persisted until the young lad was having something like an epileptic fit.

There followed an aspect of the case that the police completely failed to investigate. Beattie concocted a hare-brained story that men in top hats with mirrors had committed the crime. One can imagine that such a strange story would have mystified the police, but if they had carried out any sort of investigation, they would have found where the tale came from, and realised that Beattie was saying the first thing that came into his head at the time.

The officer questioning Beattie, Detective Sergeant Mortimer, was not a pop fan. He did not know that, just before Beattie had gone out on the Friday, the night of the murder, men in top hats with mirrors—a pop group called Slade—had been on television. Beattie had seen them, and it had been one of the few visually memorable images that he had seen that evening. I have here a picture of the men in the top hats with mirrors—Slade, a top of the pops British pop group. Such a simple answer to an important question in the case against Beattie was an answer that any teenager could have given, but it completely foxed the officers on the case.

At 1.30 am, after about six hours of interrogation, Mortimer charged him with murder. Personalities now came into the case. Muncie liked to charge suspects himself, but a mere sergeant, who had been on the case for only a day, was stealing his thunder. At 5.30 am, having had no sleep, the lad was brought before the chief superintendent at the scene of the crime. Muncie was making sure—in fact, the stage was set for Muncie's biggest mistake.

Muncie was proud of his investigative technique, and often talked about it. His motto was "always alert". He had a golden rule that all his men were supposed to follow: if a suspect was apparently admitting to facts which could incriminate him, they should be repeated to an officer who was not in any way connected with the inquiry. That is a good and fair way of conducting an investigation—it is a pity that Chief Superintendent Muncie totally forgot about it when it came to nailing the murder on George Beattie.

What is more Beattie was ill when Muncie saw him, yet Muncie denied him a doctor for a further 16 hours. By then, Beattie had been awake for about 20 hours. He had already been charged, but here he was, at the scene of the crime, tired and poorly and being made to postulate what must have happened when the murder took place, to policemen who avidly took down his every word as gospel—except, of course, those sections which did not fit their theory. Of course, Beattie, although charged, had no solicitor present. What a botch-up of an investigation.

It got worse. Muncie asked the accused to retell his tale. Beattie tried to repeat his "guided tour", but he made several mistakes, on which Muncie should have pounced.

Beattie said that the knife found in the glen was the murder weapon. We must remember that most of the detectives on the case were of that opinion, but their boss knew that it was not correct. The forensic department later proved him right—there was no blood on that knife, so it was not the murder weapon. Muncie said nothing about Beattie's mistake.

Muncie should have probed for special knowledge. He did not. One fact which the police knew but which was still secret was the fact that the murderer had not taken Margaret's expensive engagement ring. Beattie did not know that. Indeed, he had no special knowledge. He knew nothing of the one item of Margaret's that was never found— her charm bracelet.

What about the fact that Beattie had described details of the clothes in the victim's suitcase? Muncie should certainly have spotted the mistakes that Beattie made about the clothing. He himself noticed that the clothes had not been exposed during the murder—so even the murderer could not have known the details that Beattie had blurted out under interrogation. When Muncie asked where the body had lain, Beattie did not know, even though Muncie had marked the spot on the *Daily Record* photograph.

Any reasonable person would have known that there was something wrong with the arrest, yet here was a police team that lacked simple liaison procedures, and operated without proper briefings. The men were working almost 24 hours a day. In such circumstances, people do not think straight, and officers can become desperate to write cases off.

No one heard of those circumstances during the trial, of course. In court, it seemed that police procedures were perfect, working hours magnificent, and venerable chief superintendents infallible. But no one is infallible. Although Chief Superintendent Muncie was the famous detective who had spotted the teeth marks that convicted

Hay in the Biggar murder case, that sharpness was missing when he dealt with the forensic evidence in the Carluke case—because that evidence showed that Beattie was innocent.

Normally, Muncie would have spotted that, in the Carluke murder, the meal that the victim had eaten before leaving home was not in her stomach. That was vital evidence, because it meant that she must have died at about 11 pm, not 8 pm. But the police missed the significance—just one mistake among many.

There is a lurking doubt that the police had smelt that there was something wrong with their case. In Scotland solicitors have the right to question prosecution witnesses such as police before the trial—but Muncie was "too busy" to give a precognition. Perhaps that was because he could not afford to be questioned before the trial.

Picture him in his office as he prepared the case for trial. He knew that at least he had one "ace"—a blood spot on a tissue handkerchief found in Beattie's pocket. The blood grouping was not Beattie's and matched the victim's in two main—though common—groups. Unfortunately, that evidence had been handled in a nonchalant manner. There were no proper notes of its discovery, and no protective measures were taken—poor police work again.

Some of the other scientific evidence was worrying. There was blood under the victim's fingernails—she had scratched her attacker. Although the scratches would have shown on the murderer for days after the murder, Beattie had no scratches. And they could not match the blood under the victim's nails to Beattie.

A greater problem was the blood on the stones under the victim's head. It was clearly hers, but the sub-grouping in the blood did not match the blood found on Beattie's tissue handkerchief. How can Chief Superintendent Muncie have felt when that news came through? His "ace" was gone. There was only one solution. It would have to be claimed that that blood had no relevance to the guilt of the accused. The snag with that argument was that it was a lie—because the blood actually proved that Beattie's guilt did not exist.

So what could be done to lessen the damage that that evidence did to the police case? Quite simply, the evidence was suppressed. We can only guess who suppressed it—but the fact is that it never appeared in the documents presented either to the defence or to the court.

I can tell the House about that evidence now only because the information was let slip after the trial in a letter to Beattie's lawyer from the deputy Crown agent in the Crown Office: Mr. Eynon did not examine stones found under the body of the deceased. Another forensic scientist did". I understand that Mr. Eynon was the forensic scientist during the case. We now know, after the trial, that a separate secret forensic test was taken on the blood.

He goes on: They were stained with human blood of group O MN. He also analysed a sample of the deceased's blood which was of group O MN. There was no O MN in the sample on the tissue, and that proved conclusively that Beattie was innocent.

The report was withheld from the court and from the defence, and it must be asked why. It is new evidence; it was not given to the court, so it should be examined closely now. The letter also said: I am not prepared to make a copy of his report available to you. As George Beattie's Member of Parliament, I am asking for a copy of the report, because I want to see what is in it.

As for the problem of the wrong knife that Beattie had chosen as the murder weapon, Muncie glossed it over in court with an adroit answer. He said that the most important thing was blood. Let me refresh the Minister's memory; it was the same knife that Muncie had eliminated because there was no blood on it.

What was the chief superintendent thinking? Of course he knew that defence lawyers tend to stick by their written questions. Beattie's lawyer had no questions about the blood on the knife as none had been found. The court did not take Muncie up on the matter. It let it lie, so that the jury was left with the impression that there had been blood on the knife and that it was the murder weapon.

The kindest thing we can say about Chief Superintendent Muncie and this incident is that he must have momentarily forgotten that the knife he was describing to the jury was the very weapon that he had eliminated at the start of the case because it had no blood on it at all. It would not be nice to say that an officer with such a high reputation deliberately lied to make sure that his last case ended in a conviction, ensuring him a 100 per cent. success record before he left for one of the highest-ranking police jobs in Scotland. However, we might excuse George Beattie in his cell in Saughton prison tonight for thinking that.

Those are not matters that Scottish Office Ministers would take seriously when reviewing Beattie's case, but they might well say that it was a matter for an internal inquiry into the police force concerned.

At the bottom of the case is the motive. The police totally failed to come up with any motive for George Beattie to commit the crime, but there is motive for the police to pursue Beattie. The whole case went wrong because of their botched investigation.

Beattie is not in Saughton prison because he committed a murder in Carluke in 1973. He is in gaol because, if the truth comes out, too many reputations will suffer in high places. That is the sad truth; it is something that the Scottish Office and its Ministers must stand up to and answer. They have hidden behind the many complications, twists and turns in the story of George Beattie. They must now realise that the guilty verdict was a miscarriage of justice.

As we sit in this place, proud of its history and its democratic processes, the conviction of George Beattie is a blight on us all. George Beattie is innocent, and the Minister must realise that everyone knows it. He seeks justice from Parliament and the Secretary of State for Scotland. In the name of justice and decency, I ask that George Beattie be given that justice.

12.17 am

The Parliamentary Under-Secretary of State for Scotland (Lord James Douglas-Hamilton): In the eight minutes which remain available to me I cannot cover all the points I should like to have raised if I had the full 15 minutes. However, I can tell the hon. Member for Clydesdale (Mr. Hood) that his remarks tonight will be closely examined and carefully studied. I appreciate that he has deeply held views about the conviction of George Beattie, and in responding I shall deal first with the conviction and then with the life sentence aspects.

George Beattie was convicted of murder on 4 October 1973 in the High Court in Glasgow. The victim was a 23-year-old woman from Carluke. She had been stabbed repeatedly on the body and robbed. Doubts have been raised subsequently about the safety of this conviction. I know that various submissions have been made to previous Secretaries of State about Mr. Beattie's case.

In particular, a former Member of Parliament, the late Dame Judith Hart, who was Mr. Beattie's constituency Member of Parliament at the time, wrote to the then Secretary of State in November 1983. She drew to his attention the findings of the BBC production team who had studied Mr. Beattie's case in preparing a programme in the *Rough Justice* television series, which had been shown earlier that month. Having examined these points carefully, the Secretary of State replied in April 1984 explaining that there were not sufficient grounds for him to intervene in the case.

Dame Judith wrote to the Secretary of State again in May 1984, enclosing a paper written by the BBC producer involved, seeking to challenge the Secretary of State's decision. It dealt with several forensic matters and, again, it was carefully examined. The forensic evidence in the case was re-examined by an independent expert with no previous involvement in the case—the director of the medico-legal department at Liege university, Belgium. His report confirmed the validity of the techniques that were used by the forensic scientists in the case and showed that the BBC material did not materially affect the consideration of the case.

The Secretary of State replied to Dame Judith in June 1985, explaining that there remained a lack of any grounds on which he could properly intervene in the case.

I know that there has been some renewed interest in the conviction recently, on the part of the hon. Gentleman and others. I realise that this may have been intensified by Mr. Beattie's recall to custody. Indeed, the hon. Gentleman met my right hon. and noble Friend the Minister of State, Scottish Office, to discuss the case on 4 November 1992. I can confirm that at present there is no petition before the Secretary of State on Mr. Beattie's behalf. However, if the hon. Gentleman, or anyone else, has new evidence or other considerations of substance in the case which have not previously been examined, he or she should submit a petition to the Secretary of State as soon as possible.

The hon. Gentleman has expressed concern that a forensic report on blood found at the scene of the murder has not been made available. The report was referred to in a letter of 25 June 1974 from the Solicitor-General of the time to the late Dame Judith Hart, who was Mr. Beattie's Member. The report classified the victim's blood and blood found on stones beneath her head as group O,MN, and accordingly did no more than suggest that the blood on the stones was that of the victim. The then Solicitor-General also confirmed to Dame Judith that no blood was found near the scene of the crime belonging to a group other than Beattie's or the victim's.

Indeed, both the blood on the stones and the blood on the tissues was found on testing to be similar to the victim's blood. The confusion arose because of a misconception that the victim's blood could not have been both group O,MN and group 0 rhesus D positive. In fact, it could be both. I stress that both tests were carried out on blood taken from the same sample of the victim's blood.

I have noted the hon. Gentleman's criticisms of the police conduct of the inquiry into the murder of Margaret McGlouchlan. As I have said, his words will be carefully considered and examined. If he has evidence in support of his allegations, and sources, he should arrange to submit them to my right hon. Friend the Secretary of State, who will ensure that they are closely examined.

It may be helpful if I explain the review procedures for life sentence prisoners in Scotland. The mandatory life sentence exists to protect the public from those who have committed the extremely serious crime of murder. Our system of law provides safeguards and hurdles so that the very greatest care and consideration precedes the release of any life prisoner. The hon. Gentleman said on 19 October: Prisons are there to contain people who threaten our community, but people should not be imprisoned unless they deserve it.".-[Official Report, 19 October 1992; Vol. 212, c. 272.] If, at any time, a life licensee's behaviour gives cause for concern, the Parole Board may recommend his recall to custody, whereupon my right hon. Friend the Secretary of State may revoke a life licence. A person recalled to custody is informed of the reasons for his return to prison and has the right to make written representations.

In Mr. Beattie's case, there were several reviews. He had regular local and home leaves, which with the exception of one, when he returned to the hostel late, passed without incident. He was released on life licence in August 1986. He was supervised in the community first in Scotland and later—

Mr. Hood rose—

Lord James Douglas-Hamilton: I have only two more minutes. I shall write to the hon. Gentleman. I have had only a brief—

Mr. Hood: I wish to be helpful to the Minister.

Lord James Douglas-Hamilton: I have only two more minutes.

Mr. Hood: Will the Minister make available to me the report to which he has referred that deals with the blood that was found under the victim's head, which was found to be O,MN? Will he provide that report, provision of which has so far been refused?

Lord James Douglas-Hamilton: I shall certainly make inquiries on that point in co-operation with the Lord Advocate, after which I shall write.

The key point about the blood is that the forensic report of 20 July 1973, which was a production at the trial, indicated that the blood stains on the paper tissues and the blood sample from the victim were group 0 rhesus D positive and that the blood sample from Mr. Beattie was group A rhesus D positive.

As I said, he was released on licence. He returned to Scotland in August 1990, when he took up residence with his mother and began working as a bus driver. The first incident related to his conviction for breach of the peace which gave rise to concern. He was alleged to have confronted and verbally abused the female driver of a car which was obstructing the bus he was driving. Following that, there was a breakdown in relations with his female supervising officer.

The final incident took place on 23 April 1992, when Mr. Beattie visited the office of his new male supervising officer. He was alleged to have kicked the officer on that occasion. He was subsequently convicted of breach of the peace and admonished. That incident was the culmination of what was considered to be a worrying pattern—

The motion having been made after Ten o'clock on Wednesday evening, and the debate having continued for half an hour, Mr. DEPUTY SPEAKER adjourned the House without Question put, pursuant to the Standing Order.

*

MP VISITS BEATTIE AFTER PAROLE BOARD REVIEW
Herald Scotland, 30th December 1993

A Scots MP is today visiting a prisoner who claims he is innocent of murder, just 24 hours after it was revealed that 39-year-old George Beattie has been before a parole board. Lanarkshire Labour MP Jimmy Hood and lawyer Joe Beltrami have been campaigning for Beattie's conviction to be quashed because they believe his sentence was a miscarriage of justice.

Beattie was jailed in 1973 for the murder of 23-year-old Margaret McLaughlin near Carluke. She was found with multiple stab wounds in a field not far from her home. Mr Hood and Mr Beltrami have already had Beattie's case referred to the Court of Appeal by Scottish Home Affairs Minister Lord Fraser.

A parole board assessment is due to be sent to Scots Secretary Ian Lang. But the board's current review is a separate one, and will not take into account the appeals referral. Beattie was just 19 when he was sentenced to life imprisonment for killing the young typist.

He was released on licence in 1986... but was recalled to jail to continue his life sentence last year after he was convicted of breach of the peace.

Clydesdale MP Mr Hood said last night:

'I hope to see George in good spirits. I'll be keeping him in touch with developments. A recommendation from the parole board is due in the next few weeks. But my main concern is that justice is done at the Court of Appeal, and the board's assessment is not connected with this.'

A Scottish Office spokesman said:

'We cannot discuss individual cases. The board will make a recommendation to the Secretary of State which will then be acted on. Each case is different.'

Beattie is serving his sentence at Saughton Prison, Edinburgh. His appeal − which will be heard early in the New Year − is based on claims that vital evidence was never heard at the trial.

Bibliography

Freedom of information request revealing prison/probation/psychiatric reports 1961-68. March 2021.

Green, R. (2018). *Sinclair: The World's End Murders Through the Eyes of a Killer*. CreateSpace Independent Publishing Platform.

HANSARD HC Deb 03 March 1993 vol 220 cc426-34426. Commons Sitting. George Beattie.

Wood, T. & Johnston, D. (2014). *The World's End Murders: A Thirty-Year Quest For Justice*. Birlinn

www.bbc.co.uk
www.thecourier.co.uk
www.dailyrecord.co.uk
www.edinburghnews.scotsman.com
www.eveningtelegraph.co.uk
www.theglasgowstory.com
www.theguardian.com
www.heraldscotland.com
www.judiciary.scot
www.legislation.gov.uk/asp/2011/16/contents
www.pressreader.com/uk/the-scottish-mail-on-sunday
www.roughjusticetv.com
www.scotcourts.gov.uk
www.scotland.police.uk
www.scotlawcom.gov.uk/law-reform/law-reform-projects
www.sps.gov.uk
www.thescottishsun.co.uk

www.sundaypost.com
www.takeabreak.co.uk
www.thetimes.co.uk

Index

Index

Index